Dimensions of Ageing

Dimensions of Ageing

Indian Studies

Editor

K.L. Sharma

Rawat Publications

Jaipur | New Delhi | Bangalore | Guwahati | Kolkata

ISBN 978-81-316-0258-4

Reprinted, 2016

Published by
Prem Rawat for **Rawat Publications**
Satyam Apts, Sector 3, Jawahar Nagar, Jaipur 302 004 (India)
Phone: 0141 265 1748 / 7006 Fax: 0141 265 1748
E-mail: info@rawatbooks.com
Website: www.rawatbooks.com

New Delhi Office
4858/24, Ansari Road, Daryaganj, New Delhi 110 002
Phone: 011 2326 3290

Also at *Bangalore, Guwahati* and *Kolkata*

Typeset by *d'lines* DTP SERVICES, Jaipur
Printed and bound in India

Contents

Section B
Personality and Adjustment

Section C
Attitude towards the Elderly

Section D
Problems of the Elderly

Section E
Social Status and Social Support

Preface

The Information Exchange System on Ageing was established in 1978 by the Social Development Branch, Centre for Social Development and Humanitarian Affairs and Department of Economic and Social Affairs of the United Nations. Its purpose was to monitor the present and prospective changes in the numbers and proportions of the aged and the underlying demographic factors, to maintain a system of collection and dissemination of information on ageing and to promote research at the international and national levels in the field of gerontology. On the basis of information gathered from different countries UN planned to organize First World Assembly on Ageing which later took place in Vienna at the Hapsburg Palace in 1982.

India, as the member country of United Nations, nominated Department of Social Welfare (now known as Social Justice and Empowerment) as the focal point for the purpose of communication with Information Exchange System on Ageing. In order to discharge its function as a disseminating centre for the United Nations, the Department of Social Welfare was assigned the task of collecting information on ageing in India. As a first step, the department prepared a bibliography of the books and articles on ageing, which had appeared in the various professional journals since 1950 to 1979. This annotated bibliography was named as "Ageing in India". This bibliography had papers under five broad categories relating to demographics, economics, health, social and psychological aspects. The purpose of this bibliography was to "acquaint potential users with the type of information that was available in the field of ageing in India". The editor of this bibliography, Mr Saran Singh (the then Secretary to the Government of India, Department of Social Welfare) further said that "it is hoped this bibliography will be of use to policy makers, planners, researchers, and social workers in the field of ageing and will help them obtain relevant information for improving the planning, delivery, integration and evaluation services as well as for developing new and improved methods to meet the human and environmental needs of ageing".

It is worth pointing out that twenty out of seventy-nine articles mentioned in this bibliography, were from the *Indian Journal of Gerontology*. In fact, *Indian Journal of Gerontology* (ISSN 0971-4189, Registration No. 17985/69) published by the Indian Gerontological Association has the honour of being the first-ever Indian journal on ageing from the first institution of its kind dedicated to ageing. It was first published in the year 1969 and was 19th journal on ageing in the world. In the sixties only three or four doctorates were awarded for work in gerontology (in social sciences) in India. After the First World Assembly on Aging in 1982, social scientists in India started taking interest in the field of gerontology. As a result, a number of NGOs or organizations in this field were registered and started working for the cause of the elderly.

This book, *Dimensions of Ageing* is a collection of thirty three empirical Indian studies published in the *Indian Journal of Gerontology* from. The six sections of this compilation are: Quality of Life, Personality and Adjustment, Attitudes towards the Elderly, Problems of the Elderly, Social Status and Social Support, and Successful Ageing.

Though most of the papers in this volume deal with individual ageing or the growth of an individual, some of the papers are related to population ageing or collective ageing in the Indian society. Population ageing is the result of demographic transition. The population or society ages when there is a quantitative increase in the elderly population along with a quantitative decrease in the rest of population. The studies on ageing, individual or collective, are significant for the understanding of problems related to elderly care, which is an urgent need in the 21st century. These studies will certainly provide theoretical background to understanding the problems related to elderly care, strengthening of intergenerational relations, elder abuse, elimination of poverty in elderly, elderly widows, social security and health issues.

I take this opportunity to express my gratitude to all the contributing authors. Special thanks are due to Prof R.S. Bhatnagar, Prof P.K. Dev, Dr Vivek Sharma and all the members of editorial board of *Indian Journal of Gerontology* for their participation in the growth of the journal.

I deeply appreciate the continued and keen interest and full cooperation of Rawat Publications, Jaipur, in the publication of this book.

Section A
Quality of Life

The word quality is derived from the Latin term *qualis,* i.e., what kind, sort, size, colour etc., therefore, *what is* this or that life and *what it may be*. But the adjective *qualis,* has its origin in the pronoun *qui*; hence, we might also formulate our question as: Who has what sort of life? Or else how does someone's life differ from that of others and let us add, how does it differ here and there, now and formerly. In implicit psychology, Western culture primarily equates the quality of life with good health, a well-functioning family and then with the possession of material goods or money. According to the political élite in advanced countries, the quality of life is mainly ensured by economy-height of the GDP, symbolized mainly by costs of the shopping basket. But what about the sick, handicapped and elderly? The non-quality of their life was first noticed by medical experts in the early 30s of the 20th century. They primarily underlined a relief from pain-discomfort, independence from medicaments, medical aids and the milieu. More or less in parallel with this, the psychologists also became interested in researches on the quality of life. Their principal criteria for it came to be experience of satisfaction, well-being and happiness. Gradually, the phenomenon of quality of life became a subject of scrutiny by sociologists, environmentalists and political scientists.

A wider concept of the quality of life in comparison to existing concepts, especially focuses the basal (universal) plane, from the individual-specific (civilizing) and meta (cultural-spiritual) level. It furthermore includes a definition of at least six components on the basal level which, along with other components, becomes transformed into higher levels. Nonetheless, decisive for the quality of life on any level is the meaning of life as a universal psychological regulator of human behaviour. It is a spirituality that most abundantly satiates the meaning of life.

It is not enough for people to live long they should also live well. But the quality of life is a difficult concept to define and measure. Although there are universal aspects of quality of life (QOL) recognized by all societies, there are also cultural nuances. Subjectivity and nuance are essential. Let us start with a question: What do most people want? The simple answer would be: they want love, meaningful work, safety and security, energy and health, power, fame and wealth to varying degrees, a long life of high quality and a society that provides support in achieving these goals. In the light of this fact that people are living longer quality of life becomes much more important. It is a valid goal of life.

Quality of life is an individual's satisfaction or happiness with life in domains he or she considers important. Historically known as 'life satisfaction' or 'subjective well-being', it is now sometimes referred to as 'overall quality of life' or 'global quality of life' to distinguish it from 'health-related quality of life'. It is the broadest of all concepts we are concerned with, being influenced by all of the dimensions of life that contribute to its richness and reward, pleasure and pain. These dimensions include health, but are not limited to it. A person's assessment of satisfaction with life involves two subjective considerations: how important a given domain is for that person, and how satisfied one is with that domain. One can be unsatisfied with a domain that one considers to be of relatively little importance, and thus maintain a satisfactory overall quality of life. Dissatisfaction with a domain of great importance to an individual, however, would clearly contribute to lower overall life quality.

How QOL is measured? Here, societal and scientific perspectives will necessarily lead to personal, cultural values and to philosophy. QOL is an open concept which is constantly changing. The definition of QOL varies in different historical periods, cultures and stages of life. People with many interests enjoy more of life's pleasures. But the supportive structure and attitudes of society also affect the individual's QOL in the perception of reality. The question is how quality of life is to be evaluated? It is exceedingly difficult one to answer in relation to life as a whole. The attempt may also be dangerous under certain circumstances. One's personal definition of QOL is and should be highly individualistic and subjective, and quantifying someone else's QOL should be done with great care.

The popular view is that no one wants to live long if he or she is no longer able to enjoy life? People are ambivalent. They want to do every thing possible to survive illness and trauma but often become upset over the means employed. Of course health is major constituent of QOL, but not the only one. Health and material status are relatively easier to measure. But neither fully encompasses or defines or equals QOL, for example people of limited means can enjoy a high QOL.

Quality of life means an overall sense of well-being. An older person's QOL improves when he or she is productive and feels that he/she is not treated a burden to society. Some of the aspects of QOL are obvious and basic: physical, personal and societal well-being. They also include possession of intellectual ability, the capacity to perform activities of daily living, freedom from pain or suffering, preservation of the senses and sensuality, a social support system, an adequate financial base, mastery over one's life (independence, autonomy and choice) a purpose outside of oneself that offers a sense of usefulness and some degree of happiness and morale. QOL also comprises freedom, legal protection and human rights. Far from being immutable even these basic elements are relative and their importance varies widely according to personality and circumstances.

Other aspects of QOL such as possession of a sense of purpose, moral well-being and spirituality are more complex, subjective and relative. QOL may mean very different thing to different individuals. The most complex areas of QOL are life satisfaction and coming to terms with one's QOL at the end of life. The classic simplest equivalent of QOL is happiness which is usually regarded as something under one's own control. The content and the indicators of quality of life may be summarized as follows:

Quality of Life Indicates

1. *Physical well-being:* Energy and function, sexuality, quality health, care, freedom from pain, preservation of senses – vision, hearing, smelling etc., adequate rest and sleep.
2. *Financial and material well-being:* Financial security and independence, income from variety of sources, having a job.
3. *Personal well-being:* Mental health and well-being, self esteem/dignity, identity, continuing growth, body image/appearance, memory, control over ones own life, independence, dignity, morale, freedom from excessive stress, adaptiveness, choice, opportunity, education, love.

4. *Social well-being:* Family, friendship, social network support system.
5. *Life satisfaction:* Reminiscences, life reviews, accomplishments, full life, creativity.
6. *Purposefull well-being:* Contributions to others/altruism, productive ageing, knowledge, truth.
7. *Aesthetic well-being:* Exposure to music, arts – aesthetics, leisure time.
8. *Joyfullness:* Pleasure – big or small, food, recreation, travel, adventure, excitement, merriment.
9. *Moral well-being:* Clear conscience or goodness.
10. *Enjoyment of ones life time:* Feeling that "it has been a good time to live alive".
11. *Living in the present:* Elementality, simplicity, freedom from pre-occupation with past and future.
12. *Spirituality:* Beyond self, spiritual beliefs.
13. *End of life:* Quality dying, sense of control, quality care – pain and suffering.

Numerous taxonomies of life domains have been proposed by social, psychological, gerontological, and health sciences researchers based on studies of general populations of both well and ill people. A typical taxonomy is that of Flanagan[2], which categorizes 15 dimensions of life quality into five domains, are shown as:

1. *Physical and material well-being:* (a) Material well-being and financial security and (b) health and personal safety.
2. *Relations with other people:* (a) Relations with spouse, (b) having and rearing children, (c) relations with parents, siblings or other relatives and (d) relations with friends.
3. *Social, community and civic activities:* (a) Helping and encouraging others and (b) participating in local and governmental affairs.
4. *Personal development and fulfillment:* (a) Intellectual development, (b) understanding and planning, (c) occupational role career and (d) creativity and personal expression.
5. *Recreation:* (a) Socializing with others, (b) passive and observational recreational activities and (c) participating in active recreation.

Health is one of many dimensions contributing to overall quality of life in Flanagan's taxonomy. The World Health Organization defines health as "not merely the absence of disease or infirmity" but as a concept that incorporates notions of well-being or wellness in all areas of life (physical, mental, emotional, social and spiritual). Health, according to this definition, is a broad concept that subsumes the related concepts of disease, illness, and wellness. When considered as a dimension or domain of quality of life, however, health is best thought of in the narrower sense of factors that are generally considered to fall under the purview of health care providers, or that are likely to be the target of a health care intervention.

Summary of Papers

In this section there are seven papers. In these papers the authors have presented the empirical studies which cover various aspects of quality of life.

According to Audrey Pinto and Indira Jai Prakash's findings life review plays a therapeutic role in enhancing the quality of life of elderly. They administered a fully structured Life Review and Experiencing Form (Haight and Bahr) to their experimental group (N=120) and found that LRFE enhanced QOL of elderly. They also found that home-based elderly had greater positive effect than the institutionalized subjects.

On the basis of his study "A Survey of the Happiness and Unhappiness in Old Age", K.L. Sharma is of the view that various patterns of life activities leading to social as well as personal adjustment are discernable in old age. The happiness in old age to a great extent depends on good health, feeling of paucity of funds, having spouse and social contacts.

Saroj Rathore in her paper "Subjective Well-being in Old Age" found significantly poor subjective well-being (measured by quality of life scale, well-being scale, PGI general well-being scale, self-esteem scale and positive effect and negative effect scale) in old men as compared to their middle-aged counterparts. She suggested that all aged may not be unhappy and happiness is determined by several factors such as personality and social support

In the study "Life Satisfaction in the Older Years", P.V. Ramamurti found a decline of life satisfaction around the age of 55th year and also beyond the 61st year and an improvement in between these. He suggested that the first decline may be due to retirement effects and the later decline was due to psychological and physical effects of old age as such.

P.V. Ramamurti and D. Jamuna are of the view that those persons who find life in old age satisfying are individuals who have a positive self-perception of health, positive acceptance of age changes, positive perception of functional ability, interfamilial and intergenerational amity, flexibility, belief in after life and 'Karma philosophy', those who engage in moderate activities, have marital satisfaction and positive perception of social support. The findings of this study have given us gleaning to some of the factors relevant in the Indian context that significantly contribute to life satisfaction.

The utilization of time after retirement in purposeful activities leads to increased well-being. This is the findings of the study "Time Structure and Well-being Among Retired Persons" conducted by S.P. Sinha and Richa Singh.

Narender K. Chadha et al. in their study "Hopelessness, Alienation and Life-Satisfaction Among Aged" (conducted on 109 married and widow/widower older subjects) have tried to assess the psychological health of the aged. The three psychological variables namely hopelessness, alienation and life satisfaction were measured with the help of objective psychological tests. They found that females scored more on helplessness. They were less satisfied from life as compared to males. Married aged were found to be low on helplessness and high on life satisfaction as compared to widows/widowers. Married females were high on alienation as compared to married males. The differences found on the basis of gender were quite prominent which could be explained by sociocultural differences and roles which are fixed for males and females separately in Indian context. Women's field is restricted to home and homely responsibilities. Women's have narrower circles as compared to males. It led to social alienation and hopelessness in turn to low life satisfaction.

References

Flanagan, J.C. 1978. "A Research Approach to Improving Our Quality of Life", *American Psychologist*. 33: 138–147. doi: 10.1037//0003-066X.33.2.138.

Flanagan, J.C. 1982. "Measurement of the Quality of Life: Current State of the Art", *Arch Phys Med Rehabil*. 3: 56–59.

CHAPTER 1

Role of Life Review in Enhancing the Quality of Life of the Elderly

Audrey Pinto and Indira Jai Prakash

Man's conception of his own self at any stage of his life is influenced by his individual past, his present and what he expects for himself in future. Even the well-balanced and integrated aged individuals make future plans for short duration of time. Moreover, as a person becomes old, this awareness of time running out also makes one think loss of the future. But his long past, punctuated with many pleasant events becomes more delectable than an uncomfortable future. Hence the process of aging obviously effects every type of social group and indeed every type of social relationship in all societies.

Quality of life is a major criterion to evaluate health intervention in general and medical intervention in particular. It stresses the importance of taking into account values and personal interpretation of life experience. Several studies conducted on elderly, reveal significant relationship among the related variables to the psychological well-being of the aged. Reich et al. (1987) reported influences of mood status, activity level and subjective well-being on quality of life of the elderly. Decline in life satisfaction were associated with higher initial levels of psychological distress by Markides and Lee (1991).

Loneliness is a feeling that is subjectively experienced by a fairly large majority of older people. Lee and Ishii (1987) reported that loneliness had a major negative effect on morale and transmitted large

Indian Journal of Gerontology, 1996, Vol. 10, Nos. 1–4, pp. 20–24.

proportion of the effects of social integration measures. All these investigations reveal that there are a number of factors that contribute to the quality of life. Though these variables are not necessarily present in a proportion, yet the happiness and satisfaction in the latter part of life are within the reach of the great majority of people.

From the perspective intervention, approaches play a crucial part in the alleviation of seemingly deficient behaviour. Wotzel (1980) reports that involving young people with elderly has an almost certain success. A particularly relevant programme is the life review. Life review potentially proceeds towards personality reorganization, including the achievement of such characteristics as wisdom and serenity in the aged; thus it is a potential force towards increased self-awareness (Butler, 1963). Clinicians have long observed the therapeutic value of life review (Hauseman, 1980; Lewis, 1971; Thumher, 1977). Haight's study (1988) indicated significant positive impact on life satisfaction and psychological well-being and also provided evidence for the therapeutic or intervention value of life review process for homebound elderly persons. In the light of these findings, this study examines the role of life review in enhancing the quality of life of both home-based and institutionalized elderly.

Method

Sample

For this study 180 elderly, living in the five institutions for the aged and 180 home-based elderly from in and around Mangalore city were selected. Male and female in equal numbers were included in the sample.

Procedure

The research was conducted in three phases – the pre-therapeutic, intervention and post-therapeutic. Apart from an information schedule, a number of scales were administered to measure the indicators of quality of life. Quality of life was conceptualized as high psychological well-being, measured in terms of higher life satisfaction (LSI), increased activities of daily living (ADL), higher cognitive ability, lower psychological distress, absence of loneliness, good morale and positive affect (ABS).

On completing the pre-therapeutic assessment of quality of life, the subjects were assigned to one of the two groups.

1. Experimental group which received fully structured Life Review and Experiencing Form (LREF) consisting of 6 one hour visits during which all stages of life in chronological order were discussed starting with childhood. Life Review and Experiencing Form (LREF) is a structured process which involves analysis and evaluation of all phases of life.
2. Control group or no treatment group which merely participated in the testing phase.

Results and Discussion

The baseline assessment showed no significant difference in quality of life between experimental and no treatment group before intervention. Whereas in the past assessment comparison the LREF has positively affected the quality of life of the experimental group. Except ADL all the other variables have significantly changed as shown in the Table 1.

LSI and cognitive ability has improved, loneliness has decreased and there is an improvement in psychological well-being.

The home-based and institutionalized elderly showed a significant difference (P < 0.01) in ADL, cognitive ability and loneliness before intervention as shown in Table 2. Hence the home-based and institutionalized elderly do differ significantly in the quality of life.

Table 1

Post-assessment of the experimental and no treatment groups

Variables	*Experimental N=120*		*No treatment N=120*		*'t' value*
	Mean	*SD*	*Mean*	*SD*	
LSI	12.0	3.2	8.7	4.0	7.1**
ADL	24.4	5.4	25.1	5.3	0.93
Cog. ability	2.3	2.0	3.0	2.4	2.67**
Psy. distress	1.9	1.4	3.5	1.9	7.61**
Morale	15.7	1.8	17.8	3.4	5.82**
Loneliness	8.1	1.3	9.6	1.7	4.05**
ABS	2.2	2.4	1.3	3.4	9.00**

**P < 0.01, N.S.= Not Significant.

The life review process has significantly changed all the variables of home-based elderly in comparison with no treatment group and some variables of institutionalized elderly, in the post-assessment phase.

Table 3 clearly shows a significant difference in LSI, ADL, cognitive ability, psychological distress, morale, loneliness and ABS of the home-based experimental group in comparison with no treatment group.

Table 2

Pre-intervention assessment of the home-based and institutionalized elderly

Variables	Home-based		Institutionalized		't'
	Mean	SD	Mean	SD	
LSI	8.8	3.76	9.54	3.83	1.79
ADL	25.9	3.47	23.98	5.33	4.1
Cog. ability	2.15	1.95	3.8	2.47	7.4
Psy. distress	2.9	2.04	3.0	1.98	0.5
Morale	17.13	3.24	17.46	2.7	1.1
Loneliness	8.97	1.56	9.6	1.53	6.3
ABS	0.42	3.33	–0.12	3.09	0.9

**P < 0.01, N.S.=Not Significant.

Table 3

Post-assessment of home-based experimental and no treatment group

Variables	Experimental		No treatment		't'
	Mean	SD	Mean	SD	
LSI	11.7	3.1	3.5	3.5	5.12
ADL	25.0	4.5	26.8	2.7	2.63**
Cog. ability	1.5	1.5	2.2	2.1	2.16*
Psy. distress	1.6	1.1	3.8	1.8	8.15**
Morale	15.8	2.2	17.4	3.3	3.12**
Loneliness	7.8	1.5	8.8	1.6	3.46**
ABS	2.7	2.4	1.4	3.2	7.74**

**P.01, *P.05

Table 4

Post-assessment of institutionalized experimental and no treatment group

Variables	*Experimental*		*No treatment*		't'
	Mean	*SD*	*Mean*	*SD*	
LSI	12.2	3.3	8.8	4.2	4.88**
ADL	23.8	6.1	23.3	6.5	0.43
Cog. Ability	3.0	2.2	3.8	2.5	1.91NS
Psy. distress	2.1	1.6	3.2	1.96	3.21**
Morale	15.7	1.5	18.2	3.4	5.19**
Loneliness	8.4	0.98	9.9	1.8	5.64**
ABS	1.8	2.4	1.1	3.6	5.22**

**$P < 0.01$, N.S.= Not significant.

In the case of institutionalized elderly (Table 4) there is a significant change in LSI, psychological distress, morale, loneliness and ABS. Whereas ADL and cognitive ability has not changed significantly.

LREF has positively affected the LSI, morale and ABS. It has significantly decreased the psychological distress and loneliness of the institutionalized elderly.

The correlation coefficients shows that LSI has a direct relationship with ADL and ABS. Whereas it has an inverse relationship with cognitive ability, psychological distress, loneliness and morale. Higher the score on these factors, greater is the disability. Hence as LSI increases, the presence of these four variables decrease significantly.

To conclude, LREF has enhanced the quality of life of the elderly. The home-based and institutionalized elderly significantly differ in ADL, cognitive ability and loneliness. LREF has enhanced the quality of life of the home-based and institutionalized elderly. However the LREF has greater positive influence on the home-based elderly than the institutionalized subjects.

References

Birren, J.E. and Schaie, K. (Eds.) (1977): *Handbook of the Psychology of Aging*. Litten Edn. Pub. Inc.

Butler, R.N. (1963): "The Life Review: An Interpretation of Reminiscence in the Aged". *Psychiatry* 256, 65–76.

Haight, B.K. (1988): "The Therapeutic Role of the Structured Life Review Process in Homebased Elderly Subjects". *Jr. of Gerontology : Psychological Science* 1988. Vol. 43 (2) 40–44.

Haug, M.R. and Folmar, S.J. (1986): "Longevity, Gender and Life Quality". *Jr. of Health and Social Behaviour*. Vol. 27 (4) 332–345.

Hauseman, C. (1980): "Life Review Therapy". *Jr. of Gerontological Social Work. 3* (2) 31–37.

Lee, B.R. and Ishii, K. (1987): "Social Intervention, Loneliness and Emotional Well-being among the Elderly". *Research on Aging* 1987. Vol. 9 (4) 459–482.

Lewis, C.N. (1977): "Reminiscing and Self Concept in Old Age". In *Psychology of Aging* (Eds.) J.E. Birren and K. Schaie.

Markides, K.S. and Lee, D.J. (1991): "Predictor of Well-being and Functioning in older Mexican Americans and Anglos: An Year Follow-up". *Jr. of Gerontology*. Vol. 45(2) 569–573.

Reich et al. (1987): "Activity, Event, Transactions and Quality of Life in Older Adults". *Psychology and Aging*. Vol. 2(2) 116–124.

Thurner, M. (1977): "Adaptability of Life History Interviews to the Study of Adult Development". In J.E. Birren and K. Schaie. *Hand Book of the Psychology of Aging,* Litten Edn. Pub. Ind.

Wotzel, J.W. (1980): "Intervention with the Depressed Elderly in Institution". *The Jr. of Contemporary Social Work,* 1980. Vol. 61 (4).

CHAPTER 2

A Survey of the Happiness and Unhappiness in Old Age

K.L. Sharma

It is generally assumed that a particular pattern of life activities, participation in a board range of activities, keeping up a variety of active social contacts with friends, relatives and children in family and generally positive outlook of life, characterizes the happy or well-adjusted older individual. But the assumption leaves out the possibility of there being a number of patterns of good adjustment. A life of guilt, non-participating solitude may be a good life, for a person who wants it. The empirical findings have shown that demographic variables play an important role in determining the pattern of life in terms of life-activities of the older individuals (Sharma, 1969). The purpose of the present study was to find out the patterns of happiness and unhappiness among retired persons and their life activities.

44 male retired persons residing in Tilak Nagar and Gandhi Nagar, Jaipur were interviewed to find out their life activities and resulting happiness and unhappiness from those activities. The following five questions were put to each individual: (1) Do these things (activities which the subject reported as occupying his daily time table) interest you? (2) Do you have any hobbies? (3) Generally speaking do you enjoy life now? (4) What do you think as the greatest comfort to you in your old age? (5) What has worried you most in your old age?

IJG, 1971, Vol. 3, No. 3 and 4, pp. 76–77.

Almost 83.73 per cent subjects feel themselves interested in the activities they pursue while 11.63 per cent do not feel zest in these activities. Regarding hobbies it can be stated that more than 50 per cent of the retired persons do feel interested in the various activities. Percentage of the people pursuing one kind of hobby or the other is 56 while 44 per cent of the subjects have no hobbies at all. Gardening occupies time of 20.93 per cent subjects. The other hobbies reported are: morning walk, radio listening. 'Poojapath' (worship of God) in the morning, carpentry, 'gosewa' (serving the cows), homeopathic treatment, reading of religious books and listening to religious discourses, reading horoscope by Indian method, self-study preaching morality and character formation, philanthropic work, teaching and poetry composing.

In response to the question whether they enjoy life now, 43 persons answered (one person did not answer), 31 were found to be fully happy, 10 fully unhappy, one revealed happiness to some extent and stated that he was just dragging on. In response to the fourth question, 43 persons answered (one person did not state any thing) that they need rest with no worries, that is, complete physical and mental relaxation; the same number (i.e., 8 persons) included meditation and peace of mind as the greatest comfort. The needed comforts by the rest are: religious discourses, increase in pension amount, 'Bhajan-Poojan-Kirtan and Satsang', eternal bliss, marriage of children, residence in Brindaban or Rishikesh, undertaking religious tours with wife, social-service, preaching on morality and character-building, respect and affection derived from children and grandchildren, morning walk and reading.

In answer to the last question about worries, 23 of the 43 subject who answered, reported as having no worries, whereas 67 had one sort of worry or the other. Thirty per cent were under the grip of financial stringency while 16 per cent were worried about the marriage of their children due to the unavailability of suitable matches. Death was the target of curse of 9.3 per cent people as it had snatched away from them spouses untimely and the same percentage of the subjects needed some suitable occupations for themselves. The other worries revealed were: second marriage, short-temperedness of wife, quarrels in home, governments' early retirement policy, death of children, debt, social evils, bad administration, feeling of loneliness as married children keep themselves away from the joint family and lastly biological decrements. On the basis of the present findings, it may be concluded that various patterns of life activities leading to social as well as personal adjustment are discernable in old age. The happiness in old age to a great extent, depends upon busy life, good health, feeling of paucity of funds, having spouse and social contacts etc.

Reference

Sharma, K.L. (1969): "Leisure Time Activities of Retired Persons". *Indian Journal of Gerontology,* Vol. 1, No. 1, 32–37.

CHAPTER 3

Subjective Well-Being in Old Age

Saroj Rathore

Subjective well-being in old age has not been systematically studied in our country. Old people are regarded to be among the most unhappy of all groups. They are believed to entertain low subjective well-being or poor emotional quality of life. More recently, the present investigator (Rathore, 1991), in her study on aged and middle-aged men found that the old men had scored significantly higher on somatic anxiety, psychic anxiety, muscular tension, suspicion, inhibition of aggression and psychasthenia as compared to their middle-aged male counterparts. Indian and Western observations on negative stereotypes of ageing have also been extensively reviewed in the same paper.

Several factors put old persons at high risk of depression, suicide, serious physical illness, feeling of hopelessness, social isolation, loss of loved ones and dire financial circumstances (Pfeiffer, 1977). That is why old age is characterized by a sense of hopelessness towards the world, a sense of loss shadowed by loneliness, lack of care, respect for self and others. Of course, the feeling of insecurity persists along with high expectations which are often childlike. Conflicts arise when the sick, tired in mind and body fail to cope with psychological, emotional and physical stresses. However, survey research from the West has recently shown that the old people are not particularly unhappy. Whether there is any evidence that life is better for the aged there than

IJG, 1992, Vol. 6, No. 1–2, pp. 37–43.

we thought of? Could their responses to measure of subjective well-being be meaningless, only rationalizations, a brave but false front intended to deny the inevitable? Or is happiness possibly determined by other factors that do not change with age? Costa and McCare (1984) held that these issues are of more than academic interest, but even as intellectual problems, they are fascinating. Their answers depend on an understanding of the relation between environment and cognition, cognition and affect on personality. As Badar and Hoffman (1966) have explained, "Older people are a very diverse group, more so than their younger counterparts, because of differences in social, cultural and economic experiences extending over long period of times and these differences tend to increase with age." None of these issues is fully understood, but some progress has been made in this direction.

Tamir (1982), for example, believes that her failure to find much evidence of mind-life crisis can be accounted for by socially desirable responding of old men. Herzog et al. (1982) also raise this as a possible explanation for the reported high life satisfaction or happiness or high well-being of the elderly. Because most research on well-being is conducted using self-reports (and must be so done if subjective well-being is the variable of interest).

Subjective well-being seems to be the most appropriate criterion for personal adjustment to ageing and much of the gerontological literature is replete with the findings on the conceptualization, measurement and prediction of subjective well-being. Gerontologists from the West have paid much attention to the topics of morale, life satisfaction and subjective well-being (Nydegger, 1977; Larson, 1978; George, 1981; Liang, 1985) possibly thinking that measures of these states are sensitive indicators of the quality of life. Furthermore, subjective well-being scores would be useful in documenting the needs of old persons and in identifying targets for intervention.

Though research on subjective well-being on aged has not aroused much interest in our country, some Indian observations are available. Sharma (1971) investigated the pattern of happiness and unhappiness among retired persons and their life activities. Chadha (1989) in his study observed that older persons in non-institutionalized setting were better on psychological well-being and less depressed as compared to older people in institutionalized setting. Aggarwal and Chadha (1990) also reported that old women rated high on hopelessness and were less satisfied with life as against men. Yet in an another study these researchers (Chadha and Aggarwal, 1991) observed that (a) the size of the social support network is stronger for the married as compared to the widow counterparts, (b) friendship support is one of the most important factors linked with positive changes among both men and women, and (c) two-third of network consisted of family members. Western studies have also showed that social support and network are important in maintaining independent living and well-being (Butler and Lewis, 1973; Litwak, 1980; Sherwood et al., 1981; Kastenbaum, 1983). Absence of enough Indian studies on the subjective well-being in aged and identifying targets for intervention in old population attracted the present researcher to take up this study.

More specifically, the present study was aimed at comparing subjective well-being or quality of life through different measures in old and middle-aged men in a limited sample.

Methodology

Sample

The sample of the present study was selected from the residents of Tilak Nagar Colony near University of Rajasthan, Jaipur.

Thirty old persons were selected with the following criteria of omission and inclusion:

(a) All the subjects must be males. (b) Age must be above 60. (c) All the subjects must be at least graduate by their education. (d) They must have retired from government jobs. (e) Persons retired from medical services must not be included in sample. (f) After retirement they must not be in reemployment.

Most of the these persons were retired from administrative, accounts and teaching services. Their age range was from 62 to 75 with mean age of 64.57 years.

A matched control of 30 subjects were taken from the same colony. Most of them were also in administrative, accounts and teaching services. All were males with minimum education of graduation. Their age range was from 35 to 45 years with mean age of 40.43 years. This matched control group of 30 subjects belonged to middle-age group.

Tools

Following psychological tests were administered to measure subjective well-being:

1. *Quality of life scale* (Kamman et al., 1979): It consisted of two items, one measuring general satisfaction and the other general happiness level on seven-point scale. It provides three scores, one each of the two items: general satisfaction level and general happiness level, and a total quality of life score. On this scale lower the score, better is the quality of life. For the present study, only total quality of life score was considered.
2. *Well-being scale* (Kassa et al., 1988): It is a 10 item scale. Each of 10 items has a five-point "Never"—"All the time" choice range. On this scale, higher the score, better is the subjective well-being.
3. *PGI general well-being scale* (Verma and Verma, 1988): It has 20 items giving a single score. Subject has to tick items applicable to him regarding how he felt during the month before. The score range is from 0 to 20, the scoring is done by adding the total number of items ticked.
4. *Self-esteem scale* (Rosenberg, 1965): It consists of 10 items, each with four point: strongly agree to strongly disagree. Agreement of items 1, 2, 4, 6 and 7 indicates high self-esteem while disagreement on items 3, 5, 8, 9 and 10 indicates high self-esteem. Scoring is done by adding the circled responses in a directed manner. On this scale, a high numerical score indicates low self-esteem, while a low score indicates high self-esteem. Range of scores is from 10 to 40 (i.e., score of 10 is minimum indicating highest possible self-esteem and score of 40 is maximum suggesting lowest possible self-esteem).
5. *Positive affect and negative affect scale* (Bradburn, 1969): It consists of 18 items–9 representing positive affect and another 9 negative affect. Range of score is from 0 to 9 for each of scales, i.e., PA and NA. Both PA and NA are independent.

Procedure

All the five scales (i.e., QOL, WB, PGWB, SE and PA and NA) were administered individually to subjects in both the groups. After giving required instructions to each subject individually, the scales were handed over to the subjects to be filled by him. Data so obtained were classified into six categories.

Results

The data obtained on various measures of subjective well-being for aged and middle-aged through different tests was summed up in two tables comprising total six measures. To examine the significance of difference between the two groups of subjects 't' test was computed for each measure. Detailed results are given in Table 1 and 2.

Table 1

Comparison between aged and middle-aged on different measures of subjective well-being

Measures	*Aged group (N=30)*		*Middle-aged Group (N=30)*		*t*	*P*
	X	*SD*	*X*	*SD*		
Quality of life (QOL)*	6.40	3.25	4.30	1.70	3.13	0.01
Well-being (WB)**	17.23	2.75	22.66	9.29	3.03	0.01
PGI general well-being (GWB)**	7.70	6.06	11.50	6.33	2.37	0.05
Self-esteem (SE)*	16.90	5.33	13.93	4.53	2.28	0.05

*On QOL and SE scales lower scores indicate QOL and self-esteem.

**On both the well-being scales (WB and PGWB) higher the scores, better is the subjective well-being.

Results presented in Table 1 disclose that aged and middle-aged subjects differ significantly on the above measures of subjective well-being (i.e., QOL, WB, PGWB and SE). Thus, it can be inferred that old men have poor quality of life, and self-esteem and poor subjective well-being (assessed through two independent scale of well-being) when compared to middle-aged men.

The Table 2 indicates that old men had scored significantly lower on PA than the middle-aged ones. The mean difference is significant at 0.1 level. On the other hand, the old men had scored significantly higher on NA than their middle-aged counterparts ($P < 0.01$). These observations strongly suggest that old people have very poor subjective well-being in terms of low positive affect and high negative affect.

Table 2
Comparison between aged and middle-aged on Bradburn's positive affect (PA) and negative affect (NA)

Measures	*Aged group (N=30)*		*Middle-aged Group (N=30)*		*t*	*P*
	X	*SD*	*X*	*SD*		
Positive Affect (PA)	5.20	2.51	6.97	2.11	2.95	0.01
Negative Affect (NA)	6.23	2.66	3.20	1.82	5.22	0.001

Discussion

On the basis of results of this study, old men are found to have poor quality of life, poor subjective well-being, low self-esteem, low positive affect and higher negative affect as against to their middle-aged counterparts. By and large all the measures of subjective well-being have demonstrated poor quality of life as well as poor subjective well-being in old men. Thus each measure of subjective well-being gets cross validated. These findings are in harmony with investigator's earlier observation (Rathore, 1991) that old men have more emotional problems than middle-aged ones.

The results of the present study also get support from the opinion that old people entertain rampant depression and despair. Lawton et al. (1980) for example, concluded from an extensive review of cross-sectional findings that scores on this scale are often elevated among the aged and Leon et al. (1979) confirmed this findings in a longitudinal design spanning the years from 50 to 80 years. Similarly, Feinberg and Carlson (1968) observed that as many as half of the people over the age of 65 years suffer from insomnia. Thus older people suffer from the entire spectrum of psychological problems.

All these observations are in line with present study's findings of poor quality of life, poor subjective well-being, low self-esteem, low positive affect and high negative affect in old men than middle-aged men. Results of the study can also be taken on face value as there are studies indicating consensus between objective and subjective health measures (Cambell et al., 1976; LaRue A. et al., 1979).

However, the results of the study are in conflict with some Western studies which have disproved negative stereotypes of aged (Andrews and Witeny, 1976; Herzog et al., 1982). It may be that other factors like personality and social support work against unhappiness in old persons. Thus all aged may not be unhappy and happiness is determined by several factors. Old age per se may not be alone responsible for unhappiness or poor subjective well-being. Be as it may, old men appear to be comparatively more unhappy than their counterparts who are young in age.

References

Aggarwal, V. and Chadha, N.K.: "Social Network and Aging". *Spectra of Anthropological Progress*, Vol. 12 (In press, 1990).

Andrews, F.M. and Witeny, S.B. (1976): *Social Indicators of Well-being: Americans' Perceptions of Life Quality*. New York: Plenum.

Bader, I.M. and Hoffman, A.M. (1966): "Research in Aging". *Journal of Home Economic*, 3, 117–125.

Bradburn, N.M. (1969): *The Structure of Psychological Well-being*. Chicago: Aldine.

Butler, R.N. and Lewis, M.I. (1973): *Aging and Mental Health*. Mosby. St. Louis, M.O.

Campbell, A., Converse, P.E. and Rodgers, W.L. (1976): *The Quality of American Life: Perceptions, Evaluations and Satisfactions*. New York: Russell Sage Fdn.

Chadha, N.K. (1989): Impact of Institutionalization on the Psychological Well-being and Depression among the Aged. Paper presented at the UGC National Symposium. "Stress, Anxiety and Depression in Modern Life". Patiala University, Patiala (3–4 November, 1989).

Chadha, N.K. (1990): "Aging and Related Problems: A Synoptic Review". In P.C. Joshi and A. Mahajan, (Eds.) *Studies in Medical Anthropology*. New Delhi: Reliance Pub. House.

Chadha, N.K. and Aggarwal, V.: "Hopelessness, Alienation and Life Satisfaction among Aged". Paper presented at the 78th session of Indian Science Congress, Indore (3–8 January, 1991).

Costa, P.T. Jr. and McCrae, R.R. (1984): "Personality as a Lifelong Determinant of Well-being". In C. Malatesta and C. Izard (Eds.), *Affective Processes in Adult Development and Aging*. Beverly Hill, CA: Sage Publications.

Costa, P.T. Jr. Zonderman, A.B., McCrae, R.R., Cornoni-Huntley, J., Locke, B.Z. and Barbano, H.E. (1987): "Longitudinal Analyses of Psychological Well-being in a National Sample: Stability of Mean Levels". *Journal of Gerontology*, 42, 50–55.

Feinberg, I. and Carlson, V.R. (1968): "Sleep Variation as a Function of Age in Men". *Archives of General Psychiatry,* 18, 239–250.

George, L.K. (1981): "Subjective Well-being: Conceptual and Methodological Issues". In C. Eisdorfer (Ed.), *Annual Review of Gerontology and Geriatrics* (Vol. 2), New York: Springer.

Herzog, A.R., Rodgers, W.L. and Woodworth, J. (1982): *Subjective Well-being among Different Age Groups.* Ann Arbor: Institute for Social Research, University of Michigan.

Kamman, R., Christie, D., Irwin, R. and Dixon, G. (1979): "Properties of Psychological Health". *New Zealand Psychology,* 8.1.

Kassa, S., Mastekassa, A. and Naess, S. (1988): "Quality of Life of Lung Cancer Patients in a Randomised Clinical Trial Evaluated by a Psycho-social Questionnaire", *Acta. Oncologica,* 27, 333.

Kastenbaum, R. (1983): "Can the Clinic Milieu be Therapeutic". In G.D. Rowles and R.J. Ohta (Eds.), *Aging and Milieu.* New York: Academic.

Larson, R. (1978): "Thirty Years of Research on the Subjective Well-being of Older Americans". *Journal of Gerontology,* 33, 109–125.

LaRue, A., Bank, L., Jarvik, K.L. and Hetland, M. (1979): "Health in Old Age". *Journal of Gerontology,* 34, 687–691.

Lawton, M.P., Whelihan, W.M. and Belsky, J.K. (1980): "Personality Tests and Their Uses with Older Adults". In J. Birren and R.B. Sloane (Eds.). *Handbook of Mental Health and Aging.* New York: Prentice-Hall.

Leon, R.R., Gillum, R. and Gouze, M. (1979): "Personality Stability and Change Over a 30 Year Period-Middle Age to Old Age". *Journal of Consulting and Clinical Psychology,* 23, 245–259.

Liang, J. (1985): "A Structural Integration of the Affect Balance Scale and Life Satisfaction Index A". *Journal of Gerontology,* 40, 552–561.

Litwak, E. (1980): "Research Patterns in the Health of the Elderly". In E.F. Borgatta and N.G. McCluskey (Eds.), *Aging and Society,* Beverly Hills, CA: Sage.

Nydegger, C.N. (Ed.) (1977): *Measuring Morale: A Guide to Effective Assessment.* Gerontological Society, Washington, D.C.

Pfeiffer, E. (1977): "Psychopathology and Social Pathology". In J.E. Birren and K.W. Schaie (Eds.), *Handbook of Psychology of Aging.* New York: Van Nostrand Reinhold.

Rathore, Saroj (1991): "A Comparative Study of Emotional Problems in Old and Middle-aged Men". *Indian Journal of Gerontology,* 5, 92–101.

Rosenberg, M. (1965): "Self-esteem Scale". In M. Rosenberg, *Society and the Adolescent Self-image.* Princeton: Princeton University Press.

Sharma, K.L. (1971): "A Survey of the Happiness and Unhappiness in Old Age". *Indian Journal of Gerontology,* 3, 76–77.

Sherwood, S., Greer, D.S., Morris, J.N. and Mor, V. (1981): *An Alternative to Institutionalization*. Cambridge, M.A.: Ballinger.

Tamir, L.M. (1982): *Men in Their Forties: The Transition to Middle Age*. New York: Springer.

Tisue, T. (1972): "Another Look at Self-rated Health among the Elderly", *Journal of Gerontology*, 27, 91–94.

Verma, S.K. and Verma, Amita (1988): *Manual for P.G.I. Well-being Measure*. Lucknow: Ankur Psychological Agency.

CHAPTER 4

Life Satisfaction in the Older Years

P.V. Ramamurti

The number of older people in India has been on the increase due to the growth in population and advances in medicine. The rapid strides in industrialization and urbanization and the tendency towards dissolution of the joint family system have resulted in the condition of the older people in India taking a turn for the worse. While studies on the problems of older people and the dynamics of their adjustment are well afoot in countries of the West, few noteworthy studies on any of the psychological or social aspects of ageing have been made in India. It is in this context that the present study was undertaken. It is the part of a series of investigations which the author is conducting. This is an attempt at investigation of aspects of life satisfaction in the older years.

Several studies have been reported on the life satisfaction of individuals. Of particular relevance in this context are the studies of Neugarten, Havighurst and Tobin (1961). Neugarten, Havighurst and Tobin developed two scales to measure life satisfaction. They are the Life Satisfaction Index. These two scales were derived from life satisfaction ratings which were the result of intensive clinical analysis. The scales have been clinically validated. They measure the happiness and satisfaction of an individual with his present life. Though they are not avowedly measures of adjustment still they have been considered by

IJG, 1970, Vol. 2, No. 3 and 4, pp. 68–70.

the authors as indicators (indirect) of the level of adjustment. These two scales were used in the present study.

Method

Life satisfaction index: It consists of twenty statements with a Yes-No answer. One has to read the statements and mark 'Yes' or 'No' depending on whether the statement applies to them or not. Favourable answers are scored one and unfavourable answers are scored zero. A maximum score of twenty is possible. The individual's life satisfaction score is a simple sum of his scores on both the indices. The higher the score, the greater the life satisfaction.

Validation and reliability: No exhaustive attempts at fresh validation have been attempted. However both the scales have discriminated at less than one per cent level (CR of 17.4 for index A and a CR value of 15.89 for index B) two groups, judged as well-adjusted and poorly-adjusted on the basis of an exhaustive interview (Ramamurti, 1968). The interview schedule was similar to the one used in the Berkeley investigations (Reichard, Livson and Petersen, 1962). The schedule deals with the various aspects of the day-to-day adjustment of the older person. As per reliability, a test-retest reliability with interval of 15 days was calculated. The retest coefficient was 0.88 and 0.84 for the LS index A and LS index B respectively.

Subjects: The subjects for the study were a random sample of 250 older men between 50 and 70 years of age belonging to Madras city. The basis for the sample was the latest available electoral rolls. All the individuals in the study sample knew how to read, write and understand English. These individuals were administered by the Life Satisfaction Indices.

Results and Discussion

The mean scores at each age level was calculated and is given in Table 1. It is 20.50 at 51 years. It reaches a low point of 17.10 at 56 years and then increases and reaches a high point of 20.17 at 62 years. Thereafter, there is a steady decline till the 70th year where it is 17.10. The standard error of the mean for the scores is 1.29.

Table 1

Scores on the Life Satisfaction Index-A and Life Satisfaction Index-B (combined score) of older individuals at each age level

Age	*Mean LSi-AAa+ LS 1-B scores*	*Age*	*Mean LS i-A+ LS 1-B scores*
51	20.60	61	19.61
52	19.80	62	20.17
53	19.66	63	19.40
54	18.73	64	19.20
55	17.82	65	19.30
56	17.10	66	18.70
57	17.61	67	18.89
58	19.14	68	18.40
59	19.41	69	17.80
60	20.51	70	17.10

There are two important facts the results have revealed. Firstly, there is a decline in life satisfaction around the 56th year which later improves. There is a decline again which commences at the 62nd year and continues till the 70th year.

The first trough of decline is around the 56th year. In the sample under study about 90 per cent of individuals below 55 years were employed and of those above 55 years of age only 20 to 25 per cent of the individuals were employed. Thus, most of the individuals of the sample around the 55th year were either retired or on the verge of retirement. Probably the onset of retirement and its apprehension might have been a source of concern to these people. This might have been reflected in the life satisfaction scores at the age. The increase of life satisfaction scores after the age of 56 is noteworthy. This may perhaps be due to getting used to the facts of retirement and reduced income, individual feels better and is less concerned. This feeling is reflected in the improvement of secures after the age of 56.

The gradual onset of decline of life satisfaction ratings beyond the age of 63 is again significant. This may be interpreted to reflect the deterioration in the physical capacities and the onset of aging effects. These become of increasing concern to the individual with advancing age. Thus the continuous decline in the life satisfaction ratings could be explained.

The findings of the present investigation, however, require to be taken with caution. For, though the sample is randomly drawn still the study is a cross-sectional study. It compares individuals at various ages from age 50 to 70. It is not a developmental study and hence it suffers from the well-known drawbacks of a cross-sectional investigation (e.g., the presence of generation differences to confound age differences). But developmental studies, it should be noted, at the fag end of the life span are caught with considerable difficulties of expenditure of time and energy and suffer from attrition of the sample originally taken.

To conclude, the results of this study have indicated a decline of life satisfaction first around the 55th year and again after the 61st year. The earlier decline may be attributed to effects of retirement and the latter decline may be attributed to the physical and psychological effects of ageing as such.

References

Neugarten, B.L., Havighurst, R.J. and Tobin, S.S. (1961): "Measurement of Life Satisfaction". *Journal of Gerontology,* 16 (2).

Ramamurti, P.V. (1968): A Study of Some Factors Related to Adjustment of Urban Aged Men, Unpublished Doctoral Dissertation, S.V. University.

Reichard, S., Livson, F. and Peterson, P.G. (1962): *Aging and Personality.* New York: John Wiley and Sons.

CHAPTER 5

Some Predictors of Satisfaction with Present Life in an Indian Sample

P.V. Ramamurti and D. Jamuna

Old age, life's last stage, has become in recent years the focus of attention in developing countries as the number of the aged is threatening to burst at the seams. With more people living to be old, and with the dependency ratio soaring high (Table 1), the issue became more public and governments need to take urgent steps to tackle the problem. The problem of the aged in India presents a dreadfully appalling scene with most of the elderly falling below the poverty line. In the more developed countries a substantial portion of the budget is devoted to elder care, while in India, care of the aged has a very low priority.

From times immemorial man has been trying his best to retain his youth and avoid the dread of old age. But none can escape it, save those who die young. The objectives of the science of gerontology is not so much to prolong life endlessly as it is to make it livable, manageable and more satisfying than what it would be otherwise. This has resulted in a sustained effort on behalf of the scientific community "add life to years in old age".

Though all behaviour has biological substrate, it is no less true that the mind has a substantial say over the body. The effect of stress on heart-disease and on the level of acidity in the stomach, and the whole gamut of psychosomatic diseases are cases in point.

IJG, 1993, Vol. 7, No. 3 and 4, pp. 96–103.

Psychologists are interested in keeping mental health and in finding out what are the psychological constituents of a happy, worry free old age.

Table 1

Percentage of population aged 60 and over in India 1981–2050

Year	*Percentage of Aged in*	*Nos.*	*Dependency Ratio*
1981	6.50	40 m	9.90
1991	6.20	50 m	10.80
2001*	7.10	70 m	12.00
2011*	8.13	—	13.10
2021*	10.15	—	15.70
2050*	21.12	—	—

*Population Projections (Medium).
Source: Registrar General of India, 1981.

International research for the last few years has been focusing on making life's last stage pleasant and satisfying. Some of these contemporary studies have shown that there are cultural contributants that determine our attitude to life and meaning in life, particularly in old age (Netting, 1986; Yee, 1986; Ramamurti, 1987). Several Western and Indian studies were reported on correlates of life satisfaction (Tobin and Neugarten, 1961; Williams and Wirths, 1965; Bortner and Hultsch, 1970; Adams, 1971; Palmore and Luikart, 1972; Edwards and Klemmack, 1973; Hutchison, 1975; Knapp, 1976; Medley, 1976; Wolk and Telleen, 1976; Larson, 1978; Palmore, 1979; Spreitzer and Snyder 1979; Markides and Martin, 1979; Toseland and Rasch, 1979–80; Fengler and Jensen, 1981; Baur and Okum, 1983; Dillard, Campbell and Chisolm, 1984; Levitt and Weber, 1986; Usui, Himmelfarb and Murrell, 1986; Ramamurti, 1989). Indian, with its hoary philosophical traditions and cultural practices of respect for old age may reveal a totally different set of constituents that contribute to a happy aging. It is in this context that we planned the present study of the constituents of happy ageing. Happy ageing is characterized by satisfaction with one's present life and a psychological state of happiness and content with existing condition.

Method

Sample

The sample for the present study consisted of 240 literate semi-urban elderly men (free from marked disability) in the age group 60–80 from the semiurban localities i.e., 89 towns of Andhra Pradesh belonging to middle income groups drawn by a multistage random sample using electoral rolls as basis.

The following independent variables were selected for the present study: general intellectual ability, span of interests, self-perception of health, perceived functional ability, self-acceptance of ageing changes, satisfaction with intergenerational, intrafamilial and social interaction, flexibility of behaviour, perception of social supports, spouse status and marital satisfaction, externality, activity level, economic well-being, emotional involvement, belief in after life and fate of *Karma*, death anxiety and attitude to individual ageing.

The variables were assessed through self-rated inventories. Life satisfaction (with present life) was assessed through the Life Satisfaction Inventory (Ramamurti, 1978). The total score on this inventory indicates the degree of happiness and satisfaction with aspects of present life. The independent variables were assessed by using standardized inventories i.e., I-E locus (Rotter 1966), Behavioural Rigidity (Schaie, 1955), Self-acceptance of Aging Changes (Jamuna and Ramamurti, 1989a), General Intellectual Ability (Raven, 1958), Self-perception of Disability and Self-perception of Health (Jamuna and Ramamurti, 1990). Activity level and the other variables were assessed by using appropriate inventories and scales which were standardized as part of a major Sandoz Projection on 'Markers of Successful Aging' (Ramamurti and Jamuna, 1991).

Results and Discussion

The contribution of the sixteen variables to the present life satisfaction was assessed through correlation analysis (Table 2). Of these, six variables were found to be relatively more significant. They were self-acceptance of ageing changes, self-perception of health, perceived functional ability (i.e., self-rating of capability in activities of daily living), belief in after life and Karma philosophy, satisfaction with family and social interaction and behavioural rigidity (flexibility).

Of the aforementioned, one of the more significant variables was self-acceptance of ageing changes. Becoming old is part of growing and is a stage of development that comes to one and all. The degree to which one accepts these changes as natural and takes them in the stride, to that extent he feels satisfied and contented. Therefore, it would be the task of psychologists and counsellors to help people who are ageing to accept these changes gracefully. It does help old people to accept these changes more easily if they would feel that even those who are in their youth today have to pass through old age tomorrow. They could maximize the assets that comes with old age like wisdom, experience, maturity, etc., and take pride in possessing them.

Table 2

Correlation coefficient of each independent variable with the dependent variable, present life satisfaction among the Indian aged

	Variable	*r values*
1.	Self-perception of health	0.38**
2.	Self-acceptance of ageing changes	0.41**
3.	Satisfaction with family and social interactions	0.24**
4.	Externality	0.12
5.	Perceive functional disability (ADL)	0.33**
6.	Flexibility of behaviour	0.22**
7.	Span of interests	0.13
8.	General intellectual ability	0.11
9.	Death anxiety	0.11
10.	Activity level	0.17*
11.	Marital spouse satisfaction	0.17*
12.	Belief in after life and karma	0.22**
13.	Economic well-being	0.11
14.	Perception of social supports	0.17*
15.	Emotional involvement	0.11
16.	Attitude towards ageing	0.13

** $P<0.01$, * $P<0.05$

An important variable contributing of happiness was not so much health itself but self-perception of health. Thus, "so you think, so you are" appears to be the critical factor. The degree to feeling of well-being, irrespective of how a person actually is really contributes much to happiness. It also means that those, who may not really have any serious physical malady but nevertheless 'feel' ill or sick cannot enjoy life or feel satisfied.

The extent to which one perceives of himself as functionally able (perceived functional ability) is important to satisfaction with present life (Ramamurti, 1987). This variable is closely related to self-perception of health. No doubt in old age, many people feel weak and experience several inabilities. But how a person feels about it and how he compensates for these drawbacks and accepts them or taken them in the stride as part of himself is the critical factor. So long as a person does not 'feel' severally disabled or feel that this wretched disability has cramped his life, his general satisfaction would be good. Counselling, therefore, ought to be directed to minimize the extent possible the 'disabiling' perception of functional disability.

Generally speaking most of the older people in India do not live alone. They attach themselves to their kith and kin in some way or the other. Thus, they find themselves in the web of a socio-familial matrix. Therefore, the extent to which these socio-familial interactions are perceived to be meaningful and satisfying to that extent they contribute in turn to general satisfaction. Therefore, relationship with children, peers and others if they are satisfying, would contribute to satisfaction with present life. Though India is getting industrialized, modernized and urbanized at a fast rate, familial and filial bondages are yet to be disrupted to a significant extent. Many children of aged parents have asserted that they would certainly care for their aged when they become invalidated in old age. This bondage seems to be more in existence between parents and their daughters than between parents and their sons. Yet, another Indian study had shown that the intergenerational antipathy between the old and young is more due to differences in interests rather than in values (Narsimha Reddy, 1985). Counselling should be directed to help the older individual, minimize ruptures with children or younger members and to keep their social relationship smooth and in constant repair.

Flexibility of behaviour doubtless contributes to happy ageing. The more flexible a person is in old age, the more he is psychologically adjusted. A person has to adapt to several changes that occur consequent to attaining old age, namely loss of old roles and adoption of new roles, like change in occupation, lifestyle, reduced income, physical disability, retirement, loss of parenting function, loss or reduction of social and familial status, reduced social contacts with kith and kin, loss of spouse and growing social distance in his relationship with other generations. The long years of settled, routine life during the adult years may habituate many to a routine and to a set of fixed expectations (Ramamurti, 1968). Flexibility and adaptability are of paramount importance for happy and contended old age. If one could have a control on life experiences it would be useful to avoid getting rooted into a set pattern of life and habits particularly during adulthood and middle-age. Getting used to a flexible way of life from early adulthood is perhaps the best way to prepare for the demands of new adjustments and changes in old age. In the middle years one could gradually get used to several possible changes in old age. Therefore, the dogged consistency of behaviour is perhaps a liability as far as adjustment to changes in old age is concerned. One should develop and get used to a variety of ways of responding to new situations and develop adaptability and flexibility as a trait. This would help the individual to make changes in his lifestyle easily if needed, in old age.

As an individual approaches the end of life's last stage, the future holds a gloomy outlook for many. A variable that is truly Indian and which is ingrained in Indian culture that may be considered as important in old age is belief-in-Karma philosophy. The belief that there is a continuity of life beyond death in an after life gives a meaning and purpose to life. Also, when the frustrations of life are threatening, belief in the inevitability of Karma offers succour and meaning to the helplessness that many experience (Ramamurti, 1989). It gives one's perception a certain stoicism to bear the difficulty with a smile on the face.

Several studies have gone to show that level of activity in old age is related to happiness (Ramamurti, 1972). The present study too has shown that individuals who kept themselves physically and mentally active were prone to feel more satisfied than those who did not. Therefore, it is useful to help old people develop a programme of activities like social work and extending various types of help in the household. It is indeed very true to say that in old age "an idle man's brain is the devil's workshop". Also in a follow up study (Ramamurti, 1976) carried out on a sample of surviving aged men, it was found that those who survived longer were individuals who had kept themselves physically and mentally active.

A satisfying husband-wife relationship is an important variable that contributes to happiness in old age. In fact, when children are married off, there is more scope for husband and wife to share over, the relationship between the spouses improves (Jamuna and Ramamurti, 1989b). Indian custom has it, that when a man completes 60 years of age the event is celebrated as 'second honeymoon' occurs involving a rediscovery of each other and are establishment of an intimate abiding relationship.

If the perception of these relationship are favourable they lead to greater satisfaction with present life (Ramamurti and Jamuna, 1991). Hence a satisfying husband-wife relationship adds to the joy of old age.

Old age is usually marked by a feeling of loneliness and unwantedness. At this point if the community is perceived as supportive and capable of extending care and attention, it is satisfying. The older person, like any other, is a social being, who lives in a social context. So much so he looks for supports in the community to his daily activities and needs, and when he has a feeling that he has social supports, it is a satisfying experience.

In sum, the favourable dimensions of the aforementioned variables together, contribute to a large extent to happiness in old age. To put it more explicitly, it is found that those persons who find life in old age satisfying are the individuals who have a positive self-perception of functional ability, intrafamilial and intergenerational amity, flexibility, belief in after life and Karma philosophy, those who engage in moderate activity, have marital satisfaction and positive perception of social supports.

The findings of this study have given us gleanings to some of the factors relevant in the Indian context (with a few of them specific to the culture) that significantly contribute. In most of the Third World countries of the Asian region the condition of the elderly is about the same or may be a shade better or worse than India. Therefore, the findings of the study may approximate those likely to be obtained in other Asian Third World countries. Nevertheless, similar studies on 'Successful Aging' of the elderly would give us a better understanding of the role of culture in other Third World and developing countries. In as much as some of these variables have been empirically demonstrated to be related to life satisfaction, intervention programmes may be planned to maximize the positive elements in these variables. These variables can be experimentally manipulated in welfare schemes such that the psychological problems of ageing can be minimized and we can add life to years in the real sense.

Acknowledgement

The research reported here was supported by a grant from Sandoz Foundation for Gerontological Research, Basle, Switzerland. The opinions expressed herein are ours and does not represent the Sandoz Foundation.

References

Adams, D. (1971): "Correlates of Satisfaction among the Elderly". *Gerontologist* 11: 64–68.

Baur, P.A. and Okum, M.A. (1983): "Stability of Life Satisfaction in Late Life". *Gerontologist* 23: 261–265.

Bortner, B.W. and Hultsch, D.F. (1970): "A Multiple Analysis of Correlates of Life Satisfaction in Adulthood". *Journal of Gerontology* 25: 41–47.

Dillard, J.M., Campbell, N. and Chisolm, G.B. (1984): "Correlates of Life Satisfaction of Aged Persons". *Psychological Reports* 54: 977–978.

Edwards, J.N. and Klemmack, D.L. (1973): "Correlates of Life Satisfaction: A Re-examination". *Journal of Gerontology* 28: 497–502.

Fengler, A.P. and Jensen, L. (1981): "Perceived and Objective Conditions as Predictors of the Life Satisfaction of Urban and Non-urban Elderly". *Journal of Gerontology* 36: 750–752.

Hutchison, I.W. (1975): "The Significance of Marital Status for Morale and Life Satisfaction among Lower Income Elderly". *Journal of Marriage and the Family* 37: 287–293.

Jamuna, D. and Ramamurti, P.V. (1989a): "Self-acceptance Inventory for the Aged". *Journal of Psychometry* 2: 32–34.

Jamuna, D. and Ramamurti, P.V. (1989b): "Age, Adjustment of a Husband-Wife Communication of Middle-Aged and Older Women". *Journal of Psychological Researches* 28: 145–147.

Jamuna, D. and Ramamurti, P.V. (1990): "Age Disability Scale". *Journal of Psychometry* 3: 21–26.

Knapp, M.R.J. (1976): "Predicting the Dimensions of Life Satisfaction". *Journal of Gerontology* 31: 595–604.

Larson, R. (1978): "Thirty Years of Research on the Subjective Well-being of Older Americans". *Journal of Gerontology* 33: 109–125.

Levit, M.J. and Weber, F.A. (1986): "Family Relationship, Personal Control and Well-being: A Three Generation Analysis". *Gerontologist*. 26: 166A.

Markides, K.S. and Martin, H.W. (1979): "A Casual Model of Life Satisfaction among the Elderly". *Journal of Gerontology* 34: 86–93.

Medley, M.L. (1976): "With Life among Persons of 65 Years and Older". *Journal of Gerontology* 31: 448–455.

Narasimha Reddy, K.L. (1985): Intergenerational Preferences as a Function of Values and Interests. M. Phil. Dissertation, S.V. University, Tirupati.

Netting, F.E. (1986): "Makers of Successful Aging: Gender and Cultural Sensitivities". *Gerontologist* 26: 62A.

Palmore, E. (1979): "Predictors of Successful Aging". *Gerontologist* 19: 427–431.

Palmore, E. and Luikart, C. (1972): "Health and Social Factors Related to Life Satisfaction". *Journal of Health and Social Behaviour* 3: 68–80.

Ramamurti, P.V. (1968): "An Adjustment Inventory for the Aged". *Indian Journal of Experimental Psychology* 4: 29–31.

Ramamurti, P.V. (1972): A Study of Role Availability, Role Utilisation and Problems of Adjustment among Middle aged and Older Individuals. Projects report submitted to Indian Council for Social Science Research, New Delhi.

Ramamurti, P.V. (1976): "Adjustment in Later Maturity: A Follow Up Study". *Psychological Studies* 21: 41–44.

Ramamurti, P.V. (1978): *The Sixth Decade and After*. Tirupati: S.V. University Press.

Ramamurti, P.V. (1987): "Empirically Derived Constituents for a Happy Aging" in *Aging: A Multifactorial Discussion*. K. Subha Rao and V. Prabhakar (eds.) 113–118, Hyderabad: AGI.

Ramamurti, P.V. (1989): "Correlates of Successful Aging among Elderly Men". In *Perspectives in Aging Research: Biological, Medical and Social*. Rameshwar Singh and G.S. Singhal (eds.) 237–239. New Delhi: Today and Tomorrow Printers and Publishers.

Ramamurti, P.V. and Jamuna, D. (1991): Makers of Successful Aging in an Indian Population. Project Report Submitted to Sandoz Foundation for Gerontological Research, Basle, Switzerland.

Raven, J.C. (1958): *Standard Progressive Matrices*. London: H.K. Lewis & Sons.

Rotter, J.B. (1966): "Generalised Expectations for Internal vs External Locus of Control of Reinforcement". *Psychological Monograph* 80.

Schaie, K.W. (1955): "A Test of Behavioural Rigidity". *Journal of Abnormal and Social Psychology* 51: 610–634.

Spreitzer, E. and Snyder, E. (1979): "Correlates of Life Satisfaction among the Aged". *Journal of Gerontology* 29: 454–458.

Tobin, S.S. and Neugarten, B.L. (1961): "Life Satisfaction and Social Interaction in the Aging". *Journal of Gerontology* 16: 344–346.

Toseland, R. and Rasch, J. (1979, 1980): "Correlates of Life Satisfaction: An Aid Analysis". *International Journal of Aging and Human Development* 10: 203–211.

Usui, W.M., Himmelfarb, S.Z. and Murrell, S.A. (1986): "Activity, Self-esteem and Life Satisfaction". *Gerontologist* 26: 113A.

Williams, R.H. and Wirths, C.G. (1965): *Lives Through the Years: Styles of Life and Successful Aging*. New York: Atherton Press.

Wolk, S. and Telleen, S. (1976): "Psychological and Social Correlates of Life Satisfaction as a Function of Residential Constraint". *Journal of Gerontology* 31: 89–98.

Yee, B.W.K. (1986): "Markers of Successful Aging among South-East Asian Refuges". *Gerontologist* 26: 82A.

CHAPTER 6

Time Structure and Well-Being Among Retired Persons

S.P. Sinha and Richa Singh

Retirement is a universal phenomenon, but by no means does it have the same effect on everyone. It has been suggested that personality types determine person's reactions to retirement (Nathawat and Rathore, 1996). Whether an individual reacts well or poorly to retirement is the result of a combination of different factors, viz., his outlook on life and work (Conner, Dorfman and Tomkins, 1987), his economic and marital status and health (Halpert and Zimmerman, 1986; Chadha, 1989, Aggarwal and Chadha, 1991; Ramamurti and Jamuna, 1993) and his personal history. If an individual has led an involved, highly active life, he is likely to carve out a busy retirement for himself. If he has led a disordered life, with little certain meaning, then retirement is apt to be unsatisfying and even dehumanizing.

Retirement may bring with it reduced goals and demands, leading to deficits in the perceived use of time that are linked to an explicit lack of purpose and a reduced structure in daily activities. Retirement involves psychological deprivation, the effects of which could show up in various ways e.g., psychological ill health and diminished well-being. Results of Feather and Bond's study (1983) showed that the unemployed group had lower time structure scores as compared to the employed group. Findings of this study also indicate that diminished time structure was associated with decrease in psychological well-being i.e., lower self-esteem and higher depression

IJG, 1997, Vol. 11, No. 3 and 4, pp. 72–77.

etc. Thus, how an unemployed person is able to fill his time was the best predictor of his mental health. Retirement also seems similar to the state of unemployment associated with depression and lower self-esteem. Retired people have difficulty in the filling their days and they may spend long periods without much activity, merely sitting, sleeping or watching TV. Those retired persons who engaged themselves in some sort of engagements/involvements in activities, whether obligatory or discretionary, perceived time as moving fast, showed less clinical depression, enhanced sense of purpose and control, while the opposite perceptions held true for subjects with lots of inactive spare time (Baum, Boxley and Sokolowski, 1984).

Individuals who perceived their use of time to be more structured and purposive experienced higher levels of psychological well-being (Bond and Feather, 1988). According to Kumar (1997) the way in which an individual orders and structures his life within the temporal context is a basic feature of personality. Present study was conducted on retired people to know how they utilize their time after retirement and how they structure their time and make a purposive life. Thus, it was hypothesized that higher the time structure the higher would be the subjective well-being.

Method

Sample

One hundred and twenty retirees (40 females and 80 males), at least graduates having a good understanding of English, having no liability with them, residing in Dayalbagh, Agra, age ranging from 58 to 90 years (mean age, 69 years 3 months), served as subjects. 60 subjects were engaged in employment/community participation after their retirement and 60 were not engaged in such activities. Stratification was done on the basis of years of retirement and economic status.

Tools

Time structure questionnaire (TSQ): This scale was developed by Bond and Feather (1988). This test consisted of 26 times to be answered on a seven-point scale. Possible scores for the TSQ could range from 26 to 182. The test-retest reliability for the total scores was 76. The correlation coefficients of item scores with the total use of time score for the TSQ were positive and statistically significant. TSQ item scores were intercorrelated and the resulting matrix of product moment correlations were factor analysed. Five interpretable factors viz., sense of purpose, structured routine, present orientation, effective organization, and persistence, were obtained accounting for 42.8 per cent of the total variance.

Subjective well-being inventory (SWBI): This inventory developed by Nagpal and Sell (1985) at WHO Centre, Delhi, measures feelings of well-being or ill-being as experienced by an individual or a group of individuals in various day-to-day life concerns. Different components of well-being covered by the test were – subjective well-being, positive affect, expectation achievement congruence, confidence in coping, transcendence, family group support, social support, primary group concern, inadequate mental mastery, perceived ill-health, deficiency in social contacts, general well-being and negative affect. SWBI has been reported to have high reliability coefficients. Statistically significant mean differences were observed in the comparison of high and low socio-economic groups which hinted at the validity of the inventory.

Results

The total scores on TSQ indicated the use of time. The mean and SD for the use of time scores for this sample were 132.9 and 21.20 respectively. The mean and SD of the well-being scores were 94.30 and 12.50 respectively. The coefficient of correlation between time structure (use of time scores) and well-being was 0.47, $p < 0.01$. This shows that higher the time structure the highest the well-being.

Table 1

Correlations between well-being and scores on different components of time structure questionnaire

Total TSQ scores	0.47**
Sense of purpose	0.41**
Structured routine	0.14
Present orientation	0.21*
Effective organization	0.46**
Persistence	0.15*

*P < 0.05, **P < 0.01

The coefficient of correlation between well-being scores and scores on different components of time structure scale were 0.41, 0.42, 0.21, 0.46 and 0.15 for sense of purpose, structured routine, present orientation, effective organization and persistence respectively. These values show that the correlation coefficients between sense of purpose, present orientation and effective organization are significant, the highest value was for effective organization followed by sense of purpose and present orientation. The coefficients of determination show that 16 per cent, 1 per cent, 4 per cent, 21 per cent and 2 per cent of the variance in well-being is to be accounted for by the various factors of TSQ respectively. Further analysis was done to compare the well-being scores of those retirees who have high time structure (scoring above median i.e., 132) with those who have low time structure (scoring below median). The well-being scores of the two groups were 101.1 and 87.89 respectively ($t=6.80$, $p < 0.01$). This shows that the two groups differed significantly. Thus, it may be concluded that the subjects who have a high time structure have high level of well-being.

Table 2

Correlations of time structure questionnaire (TSQ) scores with well-being and age

	Time Structure	*Well-being(Age)*
1. Time structure scores	—	—
2. Well-being	47**	—
3. Age	–0.24**	–0.19*

*P < 0.05, **P < 0.01

Age is usually thought of as an important variable that may affect the well-being of the subjects. An effort was made to partial out the effect of age variable on the coefficient of correlation between time structure and well-being. Here 1 stands for time structure, 2 for well-being and 3 for age. $r_{12}=0.47$, $r_{13}=-0.19$, and $r_{23}=-0.24$. r_{13} and r_{23} show that with the increase in age, there is a decrease in time structure and well-being among retired persons. r_{123} was found to be 0.44. This shows that had all of 120 subjects be of the same age, the correlation between time structure and well-being would have been 0.44 instead of 0.47.

Table 3
Mean, standard deviations and "T" values or tsq scores and well-being scores

Groups	*TSQ*		*Well-being*	
	Engaged (N=60)	*Non-engaged (N=60)*	*Engaged (N=60)*	*Non-engaged (N=60)*
Mean	137.6	128.17	97.63	92.03
SD	23.60	22.00	12.65	11.80
't'		2.24		2.07

$P < 0.05$

A comparison was also made after dichotomizing the time structure and well-being scores of the subjects on the basis of their being actively involved in some sort of activities in any formal or informal organization after their retirement. The engaged group was found to score significantly higher on both time structure and well-being ($M=137.67$ vs 128.17, $t=2.24$, $p < 0.05$ and $M=96.63$ vs 92.63 vs 92.03, $t=2.07$, $p < 0.05$ respectively).

Discussion

The results reveal that time structure and well-being are positively interrelated. As this is a correlational study, the findings of the present study do not allow any conclusion about causal direction i.e., whether high time structure induces high well-being or vice versa. The positive relationship between time structure and well-being shows that these results are in conformity with the results obtained by Bond and Feather (1988). In their study, more structure and purpose in use of time was found to be associated with more purpose in life, higher self-esteem, better general health, lower depression, less psychological distress, lower state and trait anxiety, lower neuroticism, less hopelessness, lower anomie, more optimism and more type A behaviour. In general, structure and purpose in use of time were found to be positively related to a wide range of variables concerned with psychological well-being.

An important feature of the present research is the obtained positive correlation coefficient between the sense of purpose scores and well-being. A higher proportion of variance in well-being is to be accounted for this factor. Retired persons who had more of a sense of purpose in their use of time showed better adjustment and well-being. These results supported Frankl's (1973) theory of logotherapy i.e., 'striving for meaning' and the 'realization of meaning' that brings enthusiasm, personal control and challenge to life. In Feather and Bond's (1983) study sense of purpose emerged as factor that accounted for most of the variance in factor analysis of the TSQ inter item correlations. Thus, it may be said that it had its own distinctive pattern of correlations with the variables related with well-being or health as compared to other factors.

The coefficient of correlation between the structured routine and well-being shows that both are positively related but to a negligible extent. Although orderly structure on daily activities has its healthy consequences and is an essential aspect of planning, but it has stability and there is no flexibility to change from time to time depending on the circumstances. Hence, it may lead to the manifestation of obsessive compulsive neuroses in some extreme cases.

The third component of time structure i.e., present orientation correlated positively with well-being scores of the persons. It is found by Kastenbaum (1987) that the capacity to integrate past experiences with the pulse of ongoing life is a significant variable of adjustment among elderly. Those who do not repent or broad over for the past are the best adjusted person (Whitbourne and Power, 1994).

The fourth component of the time structure i.e., effective organization and well-being were found to be positively correlated to a significant extent. This shows that having planned activity pattern help the individual to be free from stress and strains of life and this results in increased well-being. The correlation coefficient between fifth factor of time structure i.e., persistence and well-being showed that maintenance of activity and persistence are not effectively related with well-being.

Age was found to be negatively correlated separately with the use of time and well-being. Bond and Feather (1988) found positive relationship between age and time structure for the adult samples. But in contrast to their findings negative correlation was found in the present sample of elderly people. Bond and Feather have suggested that the positive correlation that they have found between time structure and age might not hold across the entire life span. At key transition points in life cycle, one would expect to find decreases in perceived use of time. The findings of the present study confirmed the predictions put forth by Bond and Feather (1988). Similarly the correlation between age and well-being was found to be negative. Rodin (1986) found that with the increasing age health or well-being sometimes has negative consequences such as stress and worry. Retirement is the period when psychological ageing starts to take place. Such people have to face threats to their well-being from two directions, firstly, the deterioration of his bodily functions and secondly, from social expectations that he will become useless on account of his age, irrespective of his real capacities. The findings that engagement in some sort of activities whether honorary/paid in formal/informal organization leads to better time structure and greater well-being is in consistency with the results obtained by Sastry and Pandey (1991) that retired occupied and retired non-occupied groups differed in terms of neuroticism and loneliness. This also found support from Sach's (1975) activity theory. According to this theory, the role of social interactions in the life of the elderly is important for maintaining satisfaction. It has been found that those elderly people who use their time more effectively and meaningfully scored highest on emotional well-being i.e., showed better psychological functioning (Baum, Boxley and Sokolowski, 1984; Sinha, 1994). With the increasing age people have to undertake different roles. These new roles introduce new sets of purposes and routines in the organization of daily life. It has been found that dissatisfaction with life among elderly is related to a mismatch between desired and actual activity patterns. The findings of the present study confirmed the findings of Elliot and Borris' study (1987), that life satisfaction is dependent on number of roles performed and the level of involvement in meaningful roles.

Retirement is a normal part of most people's experience as they grow older. There is the need for further studies that highlight the interrelations between these variables in relation with compulsory retirement (forced early retirement), early voluntary retirement and time due retirement.

Thus, the results of the present study have clinical implications for the retirees. These implications indicate enhanced well-being, i.e., elimination of geriatric depression, loneliness and hopelessness. They must have a structure of purposive use of time.

References

Aggarwal, V. and Chadha, N.K. (1991): Hopelessness, Alienation and Life Satisfaction among Aged. Proceedings of the Seventy-Eighth Session of the Indian Science Congress, Indore.

Baum, S.K., Boxley, R.L. and Sokolowski, M. (1984): Time Perception and Psychological Well-being in the Elderly. Annual Convention of the American Psychological Association, *56* (1), 54–61.

Bond, M.J. and Feather, N.T. (1988): "Some Correlates of Structure and Purpose in the Use of Time". *Journal of Personality and Social Psychology,* 25, 321–329.

Chadha, N.K. (1989): Impact of Institutionalization on Psychological Well-being and Depression among the Aged. Paper presented at the National Seminar on Anxiety, Stress and Depression in Modern Life, Punjab University, Patiala.

Conner, K.A., Dorfman, L. and Tomkins, J.B. (1987): "Life Satisfaction of Retired Professors: The Contribution of Work, Health, Income and Length of Retirement". *Educational Gerontology,* 11 (4–6), 337–347.

Elliot, M.S. and Borris, R. (1987): "Occupational Role Performance and Life Satisfaction in Elderly Persons". *Occupational Therapy Journal of Research,* 7 (4), 215–224.

Feather, N.T. and Bond, M.J. (1983): "Time Structure and Purposeful Activity among Employed and Unemployed University Graduates". *Journal of Occupational Psychology,* 56, 241–254.

Frankl, V. (1973): *Man's Search for Meaning.* New York: Pocket Books.

Halpert, B.P. and Zimmerman, M.K. (1986): "The Health Status of the 'Old-old': A Reconsideration". *Social Science and Medicine,* 22 (9), 89–899.

Kastenbaum, R. (1987): "Past Versus Future Orientation in Psychotherapy for Elderly". *Psychotherapy in Private Practice,* 5 (1), 115–121.

Kumar, S.V. (1997): "Pre-retirement Plans and Post-retirement Adjustments". *Research and Development Journal,* 3 (2) 12–22.

Nagpal, R. and Sell, H. (1985): *Subjective Well Being.* World Health Organization, Delhi.

Nathawat, S.S. and Rathore, S. (1996): "Influence of Hardiness and Social Support on Well Being in Elderly Men and Woman". *Indian Journal of Clinical Psychology,* 23 (2) 92–101.

Ramamurti, P.V. and Jamuna, D. (1993): "Psychosocial Dimensions of Aging in India". *Indian Journal of Social Science,* 6 (4), 309–332.

Rodin, J. (1986): "Aging and Health: Effects of the Sense of Control". *Science,* 233 (4770), 1271–1276.

Sachs, D.A. (1975): "Behavioral Techniques in a Residential Nursing Home Facility". *Journal of Behaviour Therapy and Experimental Psychiatry*, 6, 123–127.

Sastry, N. and Pandey, S. (1991): Aging, Neuroticism, Loneliness and Adjustment: An Exploratory Study. Proceedings of the Seventy Eighth Session of Indian Science Congress Association, Indore.

Sinha, S.P. (1994): "Old Age Depression Intervention Strategies". *Indian Journal of Gerontology*, 8 (1–2), 24–28.

Whitbourne, S.K. and Powers, C.B. (1994): "Older Women's Construct of Their Lives: A Quantitative and Qualitative Exploration". *International Journal of Aging and Human Development*, 38 (4), 293–306.

CHAPTER 7

Hopelessness, Alienation and Life Satisfaction Among Aged

N.K. Chadha, Vandana Aggarwal and A.P. Mangla

In the traditional Indian pattern of living, many of the concomitants of ageing were cushioned by extended family. Besides life expectancy was much shorter. Those who were not struck down in their prime had their children and grandchildren to take care of them. But lifestyles are changing fast and in the professional mobility the old are very often left to fed for themselves. And yet, this is not the only face of ageing. What is it like to be ageing in young India, perceptions vary. There are professionals all over India who have taken radical decisions to reorient their lifestyles following retirement. A couple who spent their working lives, engaged in medical service in Delhi retired and resettled in Pune, where they rendered medical aid to the rural communities nearby. There are many such instances of a confident redirection of one's life. However, for each of these well-adjusted aged, there are perhaps a hundred or more lonely, infirm traumatized elderly who have to see sun go down on their helplessness.

It is a dreary scene for which society has shown little concern. The problem has enormous ramifications. According to 2001 Census, the number of those in 60+ age group went up to over eight crores. This constitutes nearly eight per cent of the population in India. The percentage is increasing.

India is happy to perpetuate the myth of respect and consideration for old age, thus washing its hand off a sensitive problem that has acquired an explosive potential.

IJG, 1992, Vol. 6, No. 3 and 4, pp. 82–92.

Even academic research is discarding the aged to the insignificance of the unimportant and the unnecessary. A spokesperson of the Indian Council for Social Science Research confirmed that barely a handful of social scientists in the country are studying gerontological issues.

Changes in the interests and activities of the aged reflect, the changing position of the older adults in their environment as well as motivation of their long established patterns of behaviour. The one stable element in the behaviour is personal values, although these too may be modified, if cognitive load placed on the individuals becomes excessive or if the values are in dramatic conflict with the changes and drift in the content of individual's life.

The adaptive person modifies his behaviour thus 'ageing successfully'. The internal habit system that promotes the adaptation are not fully known.

Although, there are many issues to be explored more fully in relation to ageing but it was not possible to study them all in such a short span of time.

Life satisfaction among the aged is an important concept, as it has far-reaching implications and it can give us overall view as to how much adjusted an individual is, or how the person is 'ageing successfully'.

The level of satisfaction among aged not only effects the psychological adjustment but also physical, social and financial adjustments.

The psychological problems faced by the aged are simply numerous, of which 'hopelessness' is one. Maladjustment or reacting to a transition to an unknown state often leads to hopelessness, which is found to be a common outcome of old age.

Owing to the changes brought about in our society due to modernization and industrialization, the joint family system has broken into nuclear family system which is more economical and practical. The aged are isolated unit. Thus, the problem of aged being 'alienated' is another very common problem taken into account in this study.

The two psychological variables – hopelessness and alienation are inversely related to life satisfaction i.e., subject higher on hopelessness and alienation will be lower on life satisfaction and vice versa.

Surveys indicate that older persons tend to be in a disadvantageous position in society with regard to income and services. With their declining physical, psychological and social resources, old people find themselves unable to maintain relationship adequately and perceive themselves as inferior.

Objectives of the Study

This study is based on following objectives:

1. The see the differences, if any, between married vs widowed group on psychological variables like hopelessness, alienation and life satisfaction.
2. To find the significant differences, if any, between FM and FW (FM=Female Married; FW=Female Widow) on psychological variables like hopelessness, alienation and life satisfaction.
3. To see the significant differences if any, between MM and MW (MM=Male Married; MW=Male Widow) on psychological variables like hopelessness, alienation and life satisfaction.
4. To find the significant differences, if any, between male and female groups on psychological variables like hopelessness, alienation and life satisfaction.
5. To find the significant differences, if any, between FM and MM on psychological variables like hopelessness, alienation and life satisfaction.
6. To find the significant differences, if any, between FW and MW on psychological variables like-hopelessness, alienation and life satisfaction.

Method

Hypothesis

The study is based on following hypothesis:

1. Married, male or female are low on hopelessness, less alienated and are high on life satisfaction level, as compared to widow/widower counterparts.
2. Males are low on hopelessness, less alienated and high on life satisfaction level as compared to their female counterparts.

Design of the Study

The present study takes into account the psychological aspect of ageing.

The psychological variables are viz., life satisfaction, hopelessness and alienation.

The sample size was one hundred and nine (N=109), from age group of fifty five years and above (55+).

The aged involved in the study were basically taken from four groups.

Group-A: Female Married (FM), Group-B: Female Widows (FW), Group-C: Male Married (MM), Group-D: Male Widowers (MW).

Becoming old means facing a time of transition. Most elderly people are giving up a comfortable role for one that is essentially devalued in society. Thus, the most common problem of the elderly is learning a new role. The aged males and females have different kind of problems and adjustments which are demanded from them. Similarly married and widowers/widows have different kind of experiences. The lifelong loss which widows/widowers have to cope with, is specially very traumatic. Basically distinction has been made between married and widows/widowers and males and females.

Sample

The voting list of Adarsh Nagar area (Delhi) was taken and incidental sampling technique was applied and first individual available for the sample was chosen from the given population, for the study.

The sample thus consisted of 109 individuals chosen from Adarsh Nagar residential area. 30 female married, 30 female widows, 30 males married and 19 males widower.

Although an attempt was made to make the sample of the last group (male widowers) as also thirty, but male widowers were much less on the list. The investigators tried their best to interview maximum, male widowers available.

According to Census of India (1991), the marital status of the population 60+ shows a fairly large proportions of the population that has a widowed status, the incidence of which, as may be expected, is much higher among females than among males. While two-third of the aged men have their spouses living only one-third men are widowed. This is due to the fact that as a rule men marry women who are younger than themselves. Hence, there are more widows than widowers.

In a study like this, which deals with personal and confidential matters, it is perhaps impossible to avoid altogether all sampling errors. Hesitation to putting down facts on paper is a part of human nature. People were hesitant in departing with information like income and also information which deals with inner conflicts and feelings. Thus, interview was taken by asking one question in several to welcome anyone to do it. However, there were some who showed interest and were cooperative with the interviewer. They really encouraged the investigation by welcoming and also by introducing to some of their friends and neighbours in the colony. In such a questionnaire, another problem faced was the 'social desirability' factor, subjects tend to give socially desirable answers, which were cross-checked in the interview itself and correct answer was filled in by the investigator, making a judgement between correct answer and socially desirable answer.

Table 1

Description of the characteristics of the sample

Characteristics	*Female (60)*		*Male (49)*	
	Married (N=30)	*Widow (N=30)*	*Married (N=30)*	*Widower (N=19)*
Age range	55–81	55–87	55–76	55–80
Socio-economic status	MIG*	MIG	MIG	MIG
Retired (R)	1	1	10	11
Non-Retired (NR)	29	29	20	8
Middle income group				

The tools used in the study were:

1. The Beck Hopelessness Scale (Beck, 1979).
2. The Alienation Scale (Kureshi and M. Dutt, 1979).
3. The Lifescale (Chadha and Van Willigen, 1995).

Results

In this section, t-test was employed to find out the significant differences, if any, between different groups of subjects on the chosen variables taken in the present study.

Table 2

Comparison between male vs female on psychological variables

Variables	*Female (N=60)*		*Male (N=49)*		*'t' Value*
	Mean	*SD*	*Mean*	*SD*	
Hopelessness	14.99	9.47	10.89	6.03	2.74**
Alienation	104.20	10.77	102.20	9.51	1.03
Life satisfaction	225.33	45.19	246.77	39.92	2.62**

*Significant at 0.05 level, ** Significant at 0.01 level.

Table 2 reveals that males significantly differ from females on hopelessness and life satisfaction at 0.01 level of significance. Two groups did not show any statistically difference on alienation. Further it was found that mean scores of females were higher for hopelessness, whereas mean score for life satisfaction were higher for males. The results of the t-test between FM and MM on given variables are presented in Table 3.

Table 3

Comparison between female married and male married

Variables	*GPA (FM) (N=30)*		*GPC (MM) (N=30)*		*'t' value*
	Mean	*SD*	*Mean*	*SD*	
Hopelessness	7.26	4.86	4.26	2.97	2.89**
Alienation	53.2	5.97	51.73	5.05	1.02
Life satisfaction	119.2	21.48	136.6	22.59	3.03**

*Significant at 0.05 level, **Significant at 0.01 level.

Table 3 depicts same results as Table 2 which indicates the FM differ significantly on hopelessness and life satisfaction at 0.01 level of significance from MM.

It was noted that mean value of hopelessness was higher for female married where as life satisfaction score was found to be higher for male married. Results of t-test between female widowed and male widower are shown in Table 4.

Table 4 reveals that female widowed group do not differ significantly from male widower group on any of the psychological variable in present study. Result of t-test between married and widowed groups are given in Table 5.

Table 4

Comparison between female widowed and male widowers on given variables

Variables	GPB (FW) (N=30)		GPD (MW) (N=19)		't' value
	Mean	SD	Mean	SD	
Hopelessness	7.73	4.61	6.63	3.09	1.00
Alienation	51.0	4.80	50.47	4.46	0.39
Life satisfaction	106.13	23.71	110.3	17.33	0.71

Table 5

Comparison between married and widowed groups on given variables

Variables	Married (N=60)		Widowed (N=19)		't' values
	Mean	SD	Mean	SD	
Hopelessness	11.52	7.8	14.36	7.7	1.96*
Alienation	104.93	11.2	101.47	9.26	1.78
Life satisfaction	255.66	44.07	216.44	41.04	4.20**

**P < 0.01, *P < 0.05.

Table 5 indicates that married differ significantly from widowed sample on hopelessness at 0.05 level of significance and on life satisfaction at 0.01 level of significance.

Further it was observed that mean scores of widowed group was higher on hopelessness whereas for life satisfaction mean scores were found to be higher for married. The results of t-test between female married (FM) and female widow (FW) are presented in Table 6.

Table 6

Comparison between female married and female widows on given variables

Variables	Female Married (N=30)		Female Widow (N=30)		't' value
	Mean	SD	Mean	SD	
Hopelessness	7.26	4.86	7.73	4.61	0.38
Alienation	53.2	5.97	51.0	4.80	1.97*
Life satisfaction	119.2	21.48	106.1	23.71	2.23*

*P<0.05

Table 6 reveals that female married significantly differ from female widows on alienation and life satisfaction.

Further, it was noted that mean scores of female married were higher for both alienation and life satisfaction. Results of t-test between married male and male widower on given variables are presented in Table 7.

Table 7

Comparison between MM and MW on given variables

Variables	*Male Married (N=30)*		*Male Widower (N=19)*		*'t' value*
	Mean	*SD*	*Mean*	*SD*	
Hopelessness	4.26	2.94	6.63	3.08	3.03*
Alienation	51.73	5.05	50.47	4.46	1.02
Life satisfaction	136.46	22.59	110.23	17.33	4.57**

**P < 0.01, *P < 0.05.

Results in Table 7 reveals that male married differ significantly from male widower on hopelessness and life satisfaction at 0.01 level of significance. It was found that mean scores of male widowers were higher for hopelessness whereas for life satisfaction mean scores were higher for male married.

Discussion

Hopelessness and Marital Status

It was seen that male married and male widower group differ significantly at P.01 corresponding to at value of 3.03. Also a comparison between female married and female widows is made which corresponds to a value of 0.38, thus showing no significant differences among the female married and female widows on hopelessness in old age. Lastly, an aggregate score between married and widowed is compared which again shows significant differences, giving a score of 1.964 (P 0.05).

The findings in the present study are supported by Greene et al. (1986) in which they gave the levels of hopelessness prevalent in a general adult sample for 396 randomly selected adults. According to this study, hopelessness was found to be closely related to age and marital status. Widowed, separated and divorced respondents who described themselves to be more pessimistic than married persons.

As hopelessness is positively related with many mental illnesses, a higher score on this variable, achieved by widowed sample of elderly is related to the fact that widowed, single and divorced, constitute the largest group of first admissions to mental hospitals and they do not constitute the largest group in the hospitals for their death rates as high. These findings, however, do not fully represent the frequency of mental disorder amongst the older people. Populations differ in their capacity to tolerate the old deviant person.

However, the non-significant t-value which was obtained in case of female married and female widow can be explained in a typical Indian context. There are various cultural reasons for which probably, the married population of the elderly females does not differ significantly from widows samples. The reason could be attributed to the fact that there are larger number of widows than widowers (Census of India, 1991). Two-third women and one-third men are widowed, thus when a woman becomes widow, the changes takes place in the roles and status. The case with which this transition is carried out will depend on the willingness of the widow to accept these changes. Since there are greater number of widows, it is easier for them to adjust to the roles of a widowhood than men.

Hopelessness and Sex Differences

The t-values were compared between male married and female married groups which show a significant difference corresponding to a value of 2.89 (P.01). The second comparison was made between male widowers and female widows which shows an insignificant value of 1.00. Lastly, an aggregate comparison between male and female group is made, which again shows a significant difference of score 2.74 (P.01).

The findings in the present study do not agree with the findings from Greene et al. (1986) study. According to this study, there is no significant correlation between hopelessness score and sex. However in their study, the hopelessness score between female widows and male widowers is found to be non-significant, giving an insight into cross-cultural differences. The non-significant score between female widows and male widowers clearly shows that female widows and male widowers are equally hopeless.

The results obtained in Indian sociocultural setting can be explained by the fact that a non-significant value of both female widows and male widowers can be attributed to the lower social status of the widowed group.

Significant differences are found in case of female married and male married and also an overall male and female score can be explained by the social fact that in our Indian society, the social roles have a very strict boundary, which enables an individual to adjust to the new role more swiftly. Although role transition to old age is very traumatic experience, especially the three role shifts as-retirement, widowhood and death. But, sex differences are prominent because males and females have a very different type of experience going through these role shifts and transition to the old age.

Alienation and Marital Status

The inferential findings to the t-test is applied to the obtained data which yields the results, making a comparison between male married and male widower which shows no significant differences among the sex groups. The second comparison group between FM and FW shows a significant differences amongst themselves with t-value being 1.97 (P.05). Lastly, the comparison made between the aggregate group of married vs widowed again shows insignificant score. The value of t-test being 1.78. Thus, MM vs FW shows significant results.

The results can be interpreted in terms of simply, the aged being socially isolated units, since no previous research indicates that older people differ on the basis of marital status on alienation, but almost all the studies indicate the fact that aged population gets alienated.

Alienation in the elderly is generally characterized by emptiness, loneliness and isolation. Although some men and women are favoured with large and loving families or have developed friendships and other associations which guarantee against loneliness, however many ageing people grow old in isolation. Families have drifted apart, friends have died, and no one has taken their place.

Often older people are treated as though they were an alien race, to which the young and the middle-aged are unrelated and will never belong.

A study of bereaved people showed disturbances of sleep and appetite, as well as increased use of alcohol, tobacco and tranquilizers compared to a group of non-bereaved persons. Those who had lost a spouse spent more days sick in bed and had more admissions to hospitals. Morever, they more often sought help for emotional problems (Weiss, 1971). This study clearly indicates the fact that widowed group is in worse condition than married one, though results found in this study do not conform to this study.

Alienation and Sex Differences

The results comparing the sex differences on alienation indicates that the first group compared viz. FM vs MM does not show any significant differences. Similarly the second comparison group i.e., FW vs MW also does not show any significant differences. Similarly the second comparison group i.e., FW vs MW also does not show any significant differences and lastly when aggregate group of males vs females was compared that also does not show any significant t-values. The values being 1.02, 0.39 and 1.03 respectively. Although a very interesting phenomena to be noted is that the mean values of all the groups lie above the mid score, i.e., 42, on the alienation scale. Thus, indicating the fact that although all groups are quite alienated, but they show no significant differences among themselves.

The modern era is characterized by rapid industrialization and modernization of the Indian society, thus the aged have become an isolated unit and the caring traditions of the youth have changed into an attitude of indifference towards the elderly citizens of the society.

Majumdar (1985) in a survey on the elderly in New Delhi, found that after retirement there is a feeling among the aged that everyone's attitude towards them has changed. The old people felt lonely and perceived void in their life after retirement. Almost all had financial problems. Bose (1982) in a study of aged men and women found that the cause for the perceived loss of status were economic dependence, physical weakness and domestic events.

It was observed while collecting the data that the older people complained of losing grip on the younger persons. They also feel that they are neither properly cared for when they are ailing nor they are well fed and clothed by their sons and relatives.

Dube (1955) showed in his study that respect is shown to the older people in rituals only, but in everyday life we ignore these considerations. He further said that parents dominate the family till their middle age (40–45), but with approaching old age they recede into the background.

All these studies done in India clearly show, how and why the aged are becoming increasingly alienated strata of Indian population.

Life Satisfaction and Marital Status

Inferential findings were applied to the data obtained differing on marital status. The various group combinations and results suggest that there is a relationship between life satisfaction and the marital status of an individual. The score for FW vs FW found to be 2.23 (P.05) is, in accordance to the score of MW vs MW group, which was found to be, t=5.03 (P.01) and also an aggregate score of married vs widowed is found to be depicting significant value of t=4.80 (P.01).

The findings of the present study are supported by a study done by Gaven (1949). He studied the relationship between life satisfaction and marital status in old age, concluded that married older people are more satisfied with their lives than unmarried and widowed people.

The reasoning which could be provided for married being more satisfied than widowed sample, could be that during old age an individual starts withdrawing from the active role played at work and at home. There is a dynamic change in an individual. One goes through a total biological, psychological and social change which takes time to adjust. During this period of transition and learning a new role, the support of spouse plays an important role. It is only the spouse who can understand and with whom can share all the feelings and also lot of leisure time could be spent talking and doing activities together with the spouse. There could be individual differences depending upon the interrelationship between the two.

Widowed group is not endowed with this support and, in fact, they go through a personal trauma which increases manifold on losing their spouse. Chatfield (1974) states similar results.

Life Satisfaction and Sex Differences

The inferential findings of various groups on life satisfaction suggests that when sample is differed on the variable of sex the results achieved were – firstly, FM vs MM group depicts at score=3.07 (P.01) which shows a very significant differences. Secondly, the score achieved by FW vs MW group does not show significant differences while an aggregate score on male vs female group shows a significant difference with at =2.62 ($p < 0.01$) with man scores higher for males than for.

These findings are supported by the study of Palmores (1980), who found that older men tended to show almost no overall reduction in their activities on life satisfaction while older women tended to have a small reduction in both activities and life satisfaction.

Russell (1987) in his study, concluded that a positive relationship is found between variables like gender, marital status, annual income, self-related health, religiosity, retirement choice and mobility.

The differences found on the basis of gender were prominent which could be explained by sociocultural differences, and the roles which are fixed for males and females separately in Indian context. The reason for females having a lower life satisfaction score, could be attributed to the fact that, women's field is restricted to home and homely responsibilities, has a smaller field of activities outside home and when during old age, they retire from homely duties, the activities and social life become all the more smaller for females than for males. Males still have friends and old pals and colleagues with whom they can spend some time after retirement but women have a narrower circle, in which they move about. Thus restricting them at home, leading to social isolation, alienation and hopelessness in turn leading to a low life satisfaction.

Thus, the problem of aged, specially with women (as observed in this study), is to maintain or develop substantial levels of social physical and mental activity, if the ageing experience is to be successful.

References

Beck, A.I. (1979): *Hopelessness Manual*. New York: Harcourt Brace Jovanovich Inc.

Bose, A.B. (1982): "Aspects of Aging in India". Monthly Publication, *Opinion Survey*, 27 (2), 6–16.

Chadha, N.K. and Willigen, J. Van (1995): "The Development of A Measure of Successful Aging", *Indian Journal of Gerontology*, Vol. 9, 3 and 4, 83–90.

Chatfiled, W. (1974): "Economic and Sociological Factors Influencing Life Satisfaction of the Aged". *Journal of Gerontology*, 32 (4), 593–595.

Dube, C. (1955): "A Study of Prevalence and Basocial Variables in Mental Illness in Rural and Urban Community of U.P." *Acta Psychat Scand*, 46, 327.

Gaven, R.S. (1949): *Personal Adjustment in Old Age*. Chicago: Science Research Association, 125–127.

Greene, G., Adelman, R., Charon, T. and Hoffman, S. (1986): "Ageism in the Medical Encounter: An Exploratory Study of the Doctor Elderly Patient Relationship". *Language and Communication,* 6 (1–2), 113–124.

Havinghurst, J. and Albrecht, R. (1953): *Older People,* New York: Longman.

Kureshi, A. and Dutt, M. (1979): "Dimensions of Alienation: A Factor Analytic Study". *Psychologia,* 22, 205–230.

Maddox, G. (1970): "Adaptation of Retirement". *Gerontologist,* 10, 14–18.

Majumdar, C. (1985): "The End of the Road". *Hindustan Times,* Sunday Magazine, Oct. 6.

Palmore, E. (1980): *International Handbook of Aging*. London: Macmillan Press Ltd.

Rusell, R.V. (1987): "Importance of Recreational Satisfaction and Activity Participation to the Life-Satisfaction of Aged". *Journal of Leisure Research,* 19 (4) 275–283.

Weiss, R. (1971): Mental Health Implications of Conjugal Bereavement. Final Report NIMH Grant MH-12042, USA.

Section B

Personality and Adjustment

The phrase personality trait has a special meaning in personality psychology that is narrower than the everyday usage of the term. Motivation, emotion, attitudes, abilities, self-concepts, social roles, autobiographical memories, and life stories are just a few of the other 'units' that personality psychologists study. Some of these other units may have theoretical or empirical relationships with the Big Five traits, but they are conceptually distinct.

The Big Five are five broad factors (dimensions) of personality traits. They are:

- *Extraversion.* The broad dimension of extraversion encompasses some more specific traits such as talkative, energetic and assertive.
- *Agreeableness.* This dimension includes traits like sympathetic, kind and affectionate.
- *Conscientiousness.* People high in conscientiousness tend to be organized, thorough and planful.
- *Neuroticism* (sometimes reversed and called emotional stability). Neuroticism is characterized by traits like tense, moody, and anxious.
- *Openness to Experience* (sometimes called intellect or intellect/imagination). This dimension includes having wide interests and being imaginative and insightful.

It is also worth noting that there are many aspects of personality that are not subsumed within the Big Five.

Five Factors Theory, formulated by Robert (Jeff) McCrae and Paul Costa (see, for example, their 1999 *Handbook of Personality*), is an explanatory account of the role of the Big Five factors in personality. Five-Factors Theory includes a number of propositions about the nature, origins, and developmental course of personality traits, and about the relation of traits to other personality variables. Five-Factors Theory presents a biological account of personality traits, in which learning and experience play little, if any part is influencing the Big Five.

Although they are related, the terms 'Big Five' and 'Five-Factors Theory' refer to different things. Some researchers use the term Five-Factor Model instead of 'Big Five'. In scientific usage, the word 'model' can refer either to a descriptive framework of what has been observed, or to a theoretical explanation of causes and consequences; the Five-Factor Model (like the Big Five) is a model in the first sense only. The term 'Big Five' was coined by Lew Goldberg and was originally associated with studies of personality traits used in natural language. The term 'Five-Factor Model' has been more commonly associated with studies of traits using personality questionnaires. The two research traditions yielded largely consonant models (in fact, this is one of the strengths of the Big Five/Five-Factor Model as a common taxonomy of personality traits), and in current practice the terms are often used interchangeably. A subtle but sometimes important area of disagreement between the lexical and questionnaire approaches is over the definition and interpretation of the fifth factor, called intellect/imagination by many lexical researchers and openness to experience by many questionnaire researchers.

The Big Five are an empirically-based phenomenon, not a theory of personality. The Big Five factors were discovered through a statistical procedure called factor analysis, which was used to analyse how various personality traits are correlated in humans. The original derivations relied heavily on American and Western European samples, and researchers are still examining the extent to which the Big Five structure generalizes across cultures.

Both cross-sectional and longitudinal studies have shown consistent changes between college age subjects and middle adulthood subjects. There appear to be declines in three of the five major factors of personality – neuroticism, extraversion, and openness – and increases in agreeableness and conscientiousness. Cross-cultural studies have suggested similar patterns of age differences for both men and women. Common trends were also seen for the more specific traits that define the major factors. These notions may differ culturally and recent history also plays an important role in shaping but results of this study suggest the hypothesis that these are universal maturational changes in adult personality.

What causes such a maturational trend, and how widely is it found? We might hypothesize that age changes in personality are dictated by cultural demands and expectations.

If personality maturation is determined by culture, then different cultures might shape personality in different ways. For example, Eastern cultures such as China and India tend to place very high demands on their children, so perhaps in those cultures children would already have reached the full development of conscientiousness by the beginning of adolescence. In other cultures adolescents might develop lower levels of agreeableness as they entered the fiercely competitive world of work. Perhaps adult responsibilities would lead to higher levels of anxiety and depression or opportunities for leadership would encourage the growth of extroversion.

All of these speculations could have been plausibly entertained only a few years ago, because virtually no data on adult personality development had been collected outside of the United States and Western Europe. During the past decade, though, researchers from around the world have started assessing personality using translations of a new measure, the revised neo-Personality Inventory (neo-pi-r), is the first inventory designed to assess the five personality factors.

Cross-sectional comparisons of adolescents and older adults have now been reported in a dozen cultures, from Italy to Russia and to Japan. With only minor variations, all have shown the same age trends, with declines in neuroticism, extroversion and openness, and increases in agreeableness and conscientiousness as people mature. It is true that younger people everywhere have had more exposure to the mass media and generally better health care than their grandparents did – but it would be hard to explain why that would lead to lower agreeableness or higher neuroticism in today's youth.

Instead, it seems likely that these more or less universal age changes are biologically based. Personality traits from all five factors are heavily influenced by genetics, and many genes show their effects at different points in the life span. Declines in neuroticism and increases in conscientiousness may be as natural a part of the human experience as the graying of hair.

Although cross-sectional data from multiple cultures makes a persuasive case for universal maturation in personality, more direct evidence would come from longitudinal studies in non-Western societies. Such studies would also be useful in establishing whether there are culture-specific generational differences in addition to the common developmental changes. Future studies tracing earlier phases of development (from early adolescence or childhood) and extending the range of cultures to developing nations also will deepen our understanding of ageing, personality and culture.

The meaning of adjustment was borrowed from biology (the concept of adaptation in biology). But from the psychological point of view the term adjustment refers to the individual's struggles to survive in his/her surroundings. In other words, it refers to the changes (political, economic, developmental changes – all of these changes effect our lives) we must make in ourselves and our environment in order to achieve a satisfying relationship with others and with our surroundings. Yet each time we change the world around us, we also modify the environment to which we have to adapt, thus creating a vicious circle of ever-increasing instability.

How people are effected by change depends upon their: (1) Attitudes, (2) Needs, (3) Values, (4) Lifestyles, (5) Reception to changes, (6) Tolerance to stress and (7) Openness to change.

Hopefully adjustment will lead to personal growth – the process by which the individual changes his/her thoughts, feelings, and/or behaviour. Adjusted person is that who develops new capacities, adaptive qualities and growth forces. The crises in adjustment are due to destructive forces, pathologies and restriction of development.

According to Maslow adjustment is a process of: (1) moving towards self-actualization, (2) life must be experienced fully in the present moment, (3) choices must be made to enhance growth, (4) be honest in your relationships, (5) be assertive in expressing your needs and (6) strive to do your best in achieving tangible goals.

Karl Rogers is of the view that a well-adjusted person is one who discovers true values and feelings and strives to achieve his own full potential. Adjustment means striving to become what we visualize ourselves to be capable of becoming. It challenges individuals to set goals and change their behaviour. The humanistic perspective stresses the holistic characteristics of human experiences. People act on the basis of perceived reality – how they see themselves and their surroundings, affirms the importance of their inner freedom and try for self-actualization (although it is rarely achieved). Finally adjustment is interpreted in terms of growth tendency with no sharp separation between growth and adjustment.

Personality and adjustment are placed squarely within a life-span context. This permits us to consider more fully the notion of individual development and to counter the traditional and biologically-based view of ageing as an inevitable time of decline. We now know, for example, that observations of how people perform in natural contexts give us a far more accurate picture of the abilities of older people than do traditional laboratory experiments and texts; moreover, some psychologists contend that the differences in older people's test performances often reflect their different ways of approaching tasks, as opposed to any deficits in their abilities. A life-span perspective is important in helping us to come to terms with the complexity of individual development over the life course. It also leads us to a reassessment of what is meant by that very commonly used term – 'adjustment in old age'. As Peter Coleman himself states: "every change that occurs in the life course requires adjustment" and, again contrary to popular belief, the evidence is that older people's capacity to adjust is not diminished with age.

People differ in their *capacity for pleasure*. A high capacity here means the ability to enjoy a great many things and to enjoy them a lot. Its basic level depends both on brain chemistry and on heredity. Its level can vary depending on general health, sleep, nutrition, and exercise and level of stress. A low capacity can be increased by antidepressant medication.

People with a high capacity for pleasure will be better able to enjoy activities with low levels of stimulation such as those allowed by the restrictions of very old age.

People also have a *physical pain threshold* that may be independent of their pleasure threshold. This threshold may increase or decrease with age, and is of course affected by medication. New medications are constantly being developed and aggressive treatment for pain is becoming the norm. Pain is also affected by environmental and psychological factors.

Trying to predict your response to the increasing pains of ageing is difficult because you may become less or more sensitive as you get older. It appears that some people can adapt to almost anything, so you may be able to get used to a lot more than you think. Also, pain is a complicated response that is affected by psychological and social, as well as physiological factors. Still you may have developed a sense of your responsiveness to pain that may have some relationship to your potential for suffering from the changes of ageing.

Because so many people are living so much longer than previously, it is probably time to talk about a new life stage, called 'Very Old Age'. There is *middle age* which has now been pushed to later period in life to encompass the active years late in one's career or early in retirement. Next is *old age,* when dying brain cells and the wearing out of the physical body result in some changes in the type and level of activity.

In *very old age,* individual's mobility and functioning are restricted to the point that many of the activities that gave him pleasure or a sense of accomplishment are no longer possible. In addition, he must spend a lot more energy and money on body maintenance. There may be things he must do each day to deal with chronic health conditions or with physical and emotional pain. His life expectancy may be less than five years; it may be zero or less. Of course, the conditions of *very old age* can be brought on by an accident or by serious illness, as well as by advancing years. As with other life stages, *very old age* presents both positive possibilities and some new challenges.

There are several personality characteristics that can make a difference in the way you react to *very old age:*

People differ in their *response to adversity,* such as that which is presented by being very old. Some people are fighters. They rise to a challenge and are energized by struggle. If there is nothing to fight, they will look around for something to attack and overcome. Others seek security and a life that proceeds at an even, predictable pace. They avoid challenges or try to find the way around them that takes the least energy for the fighters, very old Age is just another problem that they will meet as they have done in the past: head-on and with confidence. Some security seekers may find solace in leading a restricted life. Others might want to escape by leaving life.

Summary of Papers

This section of the book contains four papers. The paper entitled "A Study of Some Personality Factors and Contributors to Old Age Adjustment" written by Shamshad Hussain and Priyadarshini Narain tries to test the assumptions that the problems of aged relating to adjustment will have their relation with the four main personality variables: extraversion, neuroticism, dependence proneness and authoritarianism. Extraversion would facilitate the process of adjustment, while neuroticism, dependence proneness and authoritarianism would negatively contribute to these problems. The co-relational findings of this study indicate that neuroticism had significant negative co-relation with adjustment whereas other factors did not have significant relationship with adjustment areawise and overall. However, dependence proneness had significant negative co-relation with health and overall adjustment.

The paper "Life Stress and Personality Adjustment Among Aged Persons" written by S.K. Srivastava and Anshika Gupta, aims to find out the impact of age on life stress and personality adjustment and to see the significant differences, if any, between high and low stress groups on personality adjustment.

The study Social Correlates of Adjustment in Aged conducted by Saraswati Mishra is based on the data collected from 720 retired persons. She found that interactions with friends, relatives' membership of voluntary organizations and others increase life adjustment in older persons. Leisure time activities and other activities and adjustment are also positively correlated. No significant relation was found between family members, separated children living in the same city. A similar study "Some Factors Related to Adjustment Among the Rural Aged" was conducted by M. Easwaramoorthy. He found that adjustment is better around sixties and it is poor after sixty. Education, personal problems, deprivations and happiness affect adjustment in later life among the rural aged.

References

Goldberg, L. R. (1990): "An Alternative 'Description of Personality': The Big-Five Factor Structure". *Journal of Personality and Social Psychology*, 59, 1216–1229.

Harold Maslow, Abraham (1987): *Motivation and Personality*.

McCrae, R.R. and Costa, P.T., Jr. (1999): "A Five-Factor Theory of Personality". In L.A. Pervin and O.P. John (Eds.): *Handbook of Personality Psychology*. New York: Guilford, 139–153.

Rogers, Karl (1961): *On Becoming a Person.*

CHAPTER 8

A Study of Some Personality Factors and Contributors to Old Age Adjustment

Shamshad Hussain and Priyadarshini Narain

Old age is taken to be a period of decline in the life of an individual. Although it is primarily a physiological phenomenon, it gets reflected in an individual's economic, psychological and social aspects and affects them substantially. This phase is marked by a constant loss in adaptability, leading to increased problems for the individual.

A number of studies point to certain age-related changes in personality (Bhaduri, 1993). Older people exhibit a tendency to become more conservative. This tendency takes the form of behavioural rigidity, unyieldingness and greater consistency in social and political attitudes (Dibner, 1975). They are often viewed by the younger generations as feeling lonely and rejected. At the same time, they are seen to perceive themselves as losers (Stone and Kailash, 1973). However, this attitude results more from realistic appraisals of obstacles that society puts in the way of older people rather than from any pessimism inherent in the ageing process. At the same time they also become wiser with age as a result of their experiences (Butler, 1975). This is the time when they attain a sense of the entire life cycle. They understand what life is about and get a subjective awareness of death.

Despite these age-related change, research shows that personality is more continuous than discontinuous through life. At any point in time, a person is more like he has always been than he is likely

IJG, 1996, Vol. 10, No. 1–4, pp. 25–33.

others of his age group, both in terms of self-reported personality traits and ratings by others (Costs McCrae and Arenberg, 1980; Costa and McCrae, 1988). Neugarten and her colleagues (1964) found that adoptional process such as coping styles, life satisfaction and strength of goal-oriented behaviour remained stable in adults over a 10-year span, for ages 40–80. However, they did discover a shift from active mastery to passive mastery.

It appears that adjustment to the various problems that life throws up is not so much a matter of the age group to which an individual belongs (Larsen, 1978). Successful ageing has been found to be associated with several factors such as socio-economic status (Kaur and Khumar, 1993), physical and mental health, marital status (Eisdorfer and Lawton, 1973; Ramamurti and Jamuna 1993) and size of the social support network (Arora and Chadha, 1995). Moreover, the active pursuit of leisure activities is critical to satisfactory adjustment.

There is some evidence that personality traits determine the adjustment that an individual makes in different areas of life. McCrac and Costa found that neuroticism and extraversion were related to happiness. Men high in neuroticism were more likely to feel dissatisfied and unhappy, and men high in extraversion were more likely to feel satisfied and happy. Again, people having an internal locus of control (LOC) appear to make a better adjustment than those with an external LOC (Thomae, 1980). However, this relationship was reversed in the case of institutionalized elderlies, those having an external LOC showing better adjustment (Felton and Khanna, 1974).

The present research is an attempt to study old age adjustment in relation to some personality variables. Old age adjustment was studied in terms of health, home, social, emotional, marital, financial and overall adjustment. These areas of adjustment were sought to be related to the dimensions of extraversion, neuroticism, dependence proneness and authoritarianism. An attempt was made to assess the nature of relationship between the personality variables and old age adjustment. Further, the contributions of these variables, jointly to the different areas of old age adjustment were also assessed. The researchers proceeded on the basis of some specific hypotheses which were as follows:

Neuroticism would have its adverse effect on the individual's adjustment. There would be a negative correlation between the personality dimension of neuroticism and the different areas of old age adjustment as well as overall adjustment.

Extraversion would positively contribute to adjustment, i.e., the correlation between the dimension of extraversion and the different areas of adjustment, particularly social adjustment, would be positive.

The greater the dependence proneness, the poorer the adjustment would be. The correlation would be negative not only in respect of overall adjustment, but with respect to the different areas as well.

Authoritarianism would be negatively correlated with the level of adjustment.

Method

Sample

The sample selected for the study was a purposive-cum-incidental sample. It consisted of 100 elderly males falling in the age group of 55 years and above, and residing in the city of Patna or its neighbouring areas. Some of the respondents were leading a retired life and others were on the verge of retirement. The reason for taking 55 as the cut-off age was that people of this age group, if not already retired, have at least started preparing for retirement. A number of studies have been conducted taking 55 as the cut off age (Soodan, 1975). Socio-economic status of the respondents was controlled by selecting the sample from the middle-income group. Respondents from small families were selected in order to control various extraneous variables.

Research Tools

The instruments used for measuring the different variables were

1. Hindi Adoptation of Eysenck Personality Questionnaire (Adult) – De and Thakur.
2. Indian F-Scale – Bhushan, L.I.
3. Dependence Proneness Scale – Sinha, J.B.P.
4. Shamshad-Jasbir Old Age Adjustment Inventory – Hussain, S. and Kaur, J.

Procedure

The selected measurement tools were administered to the respondents for obtaining responses on the different variables. As the sample consisted of old people, the respondents were contacted individually in their homes. Report was maintained for ensuring correct responses.

After the data were collected, the scoring was done with the help of standard procedures and were tabulated for the analysis. Statistical techniques, like correlation and multiple regression analysis were used with a purpose not only to find out a simple relationship between the scores on adjustment and those on personality factors, but also to estimate the joint contribution of the personality variables towards adjustment (areawise as well as overall). The presumption of normality was not considered for the application of parametric tests because of the large sample.

Results and Discussion

Correlational Analysis

Table 1

Correlation Matrix showing Pearson Production-Moment Correlations between personality variables: extraversion (X9), neuroticism (X8), dependence proneness (X10), and authoritarianism (X11) and different areas of old-age adjustment, health adjustment (X1), home adjustment (X2), social adjustment (X3), emotional adjustment (X4), marital adjustment (X5), financial adjustment (X6) and overall adjustment (X7)

Variables	*X8*	*X9*	*X10*	*X11*
X1	0.16	–0.51*	–0.29*	0.06
X2	0.19	–0.31*	–0.12	–0.04
X3	0.30	–0.46*	–0.14	0.18
X4	0.09	–0.05	–0.15	0.17
X5	–0.01	–0.57*	–0.16	0.03
X6	0.05	–0.28*	–0.11	0.08
X7	0.17	–0.51*	–0.23**	0.10

*Significant 0.01 level of confidence.
**Significant at 0.05 level of confidence.

Table 1 depicts the correlations between the four personality variables taken up for study of adjustment in the different areas of life that go to make up the overall adjustment of an elderly individual. It clearly indicates that neuroticism and dependence proneness are negatively related to adjustment. Neuroticism has been found to be significantly related to every areas of adjustment except emotional adjustment. Individuals high in neuroticism tend to misevaluate adjustive demands. They are unable to assess the real significance of interpersonal relations. This, coupled with their overriding anxiety prevents them from getting the true picture of life circumstances and leads them to show maladaptive behaviours. Whether it be in the home or the work place, with family members or companions, they generally end up taking the wrong foot forward. Those interacting with them are also at a loss about how to handle them properly. The result is a strained relationship and a poor adjustment on the part of the individual. His overconcern and anxiety in health matters is also an irritant for his companions.

In the case of dependence proneness, it is seen that except health adjustment, it does not have a significant relationship with any of the other areas. In the absence of significant relationship nothing definite can be said. However, the overall adjustment correlation coefficient is found to be significant, indicating that dependence proneness does adversely affect the adjustment an individual makes. The fact that the correlation coefficient of health adjustment is significant has immense implications. The more dependent an elderly person is in matters relating to health, the more his health is going to suffer. Old age is a time of infirmity and failing health and matters relating to these aspects come to play a significant role in his life. Minor ailments keep cropping up everyday which need to be attended to. Despite their best intentions, the younger companions are hard pressed for time, and so are unable to do much to help the elderly with their problems. In such circumstances the elderly individual who is dependent upon the younger member and who expects to be helped out in attending to health matters will find himself the loser, probably his dependence does not matter much in his relations with others, with spouse or even in emotional and financial matters. In fact in some spheres his dependence might even be welcomed. But in the health areas, it will lead to maladjustment rather than adjustment.

Extraversion is not seen to have significant relationship with old age adjustment, neither with any of the areas nor with overall adjustment. Probably, being an extrovert may not facilitate the process of adjustment. It is generally thought that the extrovert individuals, because of their outgoing nature and readiness to get involved with others, may find it much easier to adjust in life than an introvert. But the fact is that an extrovert is rather impulsive by nature and is not able to carry his enthusiasm for long. So he may not enjoy an advantage over the introvert as far as adjustment is concerned. Here it is to be noted that the correlation between extraversion and marital adjustment, although very low and insignificant, is nonetheless negative. The fact of extraversion in an individual probably does not go down well with the spouse, leading to marital problems.

Authoritarianism, too, has not been found to have any significant relationship with adjustment and, as such, nothing definite can be said. However, contrary to the hypothesis, it has not been found to have negative correlation with any of the areas of adjustment except home adjustment.

Regression Analysis

Tables 2 to 8 show regression analyses of different areas of adjustment as functions of the four personality variables extraversion, neuroticism, dependence proneness and authoritarianism.

Table 2

Dependent Variable—Health Adjustment

Variables	*Regression coefficient*	*S.E.*	't'
X11*	0.03834	0.1634	2.346**
X10	–0.16073	0.8867	–1.813
X8	0.15206	0.13497	1.127
X9	0.58477	0.09894	–5.910*

R^2=0.345

Table 3

Dependent Variable—Home Adjustment

Variables	*Regression coefficient*	*S.E.*	't'
X11	1.849752E-03	0.01487	0.124
X10	–0.02650	0.08066	–0.329
X8	0.22328	0.12277	1.819
X9	–0.26462	0.08999	–2.940*

R^2=0.132

Table 4

Dependent Variable—Social Adjustment

Variables	*Regression coefficient*	*S.E.*	*'t'*
X11	0.03974	0.01180	3.367*
X10	1.361214E-04	0.06403	0.002
X8	0.25427	0.09747	2.609**
X9	–0.45081	0.07144	–6.310*

$R^2=0.376$

Table 5

Dependent Variable—Marital Adjustment

Variables	*Regression coefficient*	*S.E.*	*'t'*
X11	0.02828	0.01603	1.763
X10	–0.12107	0.08699	–1.392
X8	0.03757	0.13241	0.284
X9	–0.96524	0.09706	–0.672

$R^2=0.060$

Table 6

Dependent Variable—Emotional Adjustment

Variables	*Regression coefficient*	*S.E.*	*'t'*
X11	0.04114	0.01447	2.842*
X10	–0.01322	0.07852	–0.168
X8	–0.11067	0.11953	–0.926
X9	–0.064442	0.08762	–7.355*

$R^2=0.381$

Table 7

Dependent Variable—Financial Adjustment

Variables	*Regression coefficient*	*S.E.*	*'t'*
X11	0.01804	0.01044	1.729
X10	–0.02416	0.05662	–0.427
X8	2.569039E-03	0.08619	0.030
X9	–0.19269	0.06318	–3.050*

$R^2=0.108$

Table 8
Dependent Variable—Overall Adjustment

Variables	*Regression coefficient*	*S.E.*	*'t'*
X11	0.16738	0.05761	2.905*
X10	–0.34554	0.31255	–1.106
X8	0.55907	0.47575	1.175
X9	–2.20256	0.34874	–6.316*

R^2=0.355
*Significant at 0.01 level of confidence
**Significant at 0.05 level of confidence

The analysis of the findings given in Tables 2, 3, 4, 5, 6, 7 and 8 shows that the joint contributions of the personality variables towards health, home, social, marital, emotional, financial and overall adjustment are 35 per cent, 13 per cent, 38 per cent, 6 per cent, 38 per cent, 11 per cent and 36 per cent respectively (as given by the R^2 value). This indicates that the highest contributions of personality factors are towards social and emotional adjustments, i.e., 38 per cent each round up value (Tables 4 and 6). The joint contribution of the personality variables towards overall adjustment is also quite high, i.e., 36 per cent (Table 8), followed by health adjustment, 35 per cent (Table 2). The lowest contributions are towards financial and marital adjustments, 11 per cent and 6 per cent respectively (Tables 7 and 5). Thus it is clear that this set of personality variables is able to account for quite a high percentage of variances in social adjustment, emotional adjustment, health adjustment and overall adjustment. But it explains very little of the variance in marital adjustment. Marital adjustment is probably affected more by other factors.

As far as the independent contributions of the four personality variables towards adjustment (areawise and overall) are concerned, neuroticism seems to be making a significant contribution to all areas, except to marital adjustment. In fact none of the personality variables is contributing separately to marital adjustment. As already noted, their joint contribution to this area is also very low, i.e., only 6 per cent (Table 5). Authoritarianism is found to be making significant contribution to health adjustment, social adjustment, emotional adjustment and to overall adjustment. Extraversion is seen to be contributing significantly to social adjustment only. This supports the hypothesis that extraversion would be positively correlated with social adjustment. Dependence proneness is not seen to be contributing significantly to any of the areas of the adjustment.

In the light of the findings and their discussion it can be observed in general that personality variables have their role in determining the level of adjustment of an individual. However, their relative strength varies from one area to another. In general, the overall contribution to these personality variables have been identified in the present study.

The findings of this study on Indian population, especially those of Bihar, will help the researchers, counsellors and clinical psychologists in diagnostic appraisal and further research.

References

Arora, M. and Chadha, N.K. (1995): "Social Support and Life Satisfaction of Institutionalized Elderlies". *Indian Journal of Gerontology,* 9 (3–4), 74–82.

Bhaduri, M. (1993): The Effect of Life Stresses on Ego-strength in Middle and Old Age Males and Females. Paper presented at XXXI AAP Conference, Jodhpur.

Butler, R.M. (1975): "Man Does Not Die, He Kills Himself", *International Journal of Aging and Human Development,* 6 (4), 367–370.

Costa, P.T. Jr. and McCrae, R.R. (1988) "Personality in Adulthood: A Six-year Longitudinal Study of Self-reports and Spouse Ratings on the MEO Personality Inventory". *Journal of Personality and Social Psychology,* 54, 853–863.

Costa, P.T. Jr., McCrae, R.R. and Arenberg, D. (1980): "Enduring Dispositions in Adult Males". *Journal of Personality and Social Psychology,* 38, 793–800.

DeCaro, T.J. (1974): "Recreation Participation Patterns and Successful Aging". *Journal of Gerontology,* 29, 416–422.

Dibney, A.S. (1975): "The Psychology of Normal Aging". In M.G. Spencer and C.J. Dorr (Eds.) *Understanding Aging: A Multidisciplinary Approach.* New York: Appleton-Century-Crofts.

Eissdorfer, C. and Lawton, M.P. (Eds.) (1973): *The Psychology of Adult Development and Aging.* Washington, D.C.: American Psychological Association.

Felton, B.J. and Kahana, E. (1974): "Adjustment and Situationally Bound Locus of Control among Institutionalized Aged", *Journal of Gerontology,* 29, 295–301.

Kaur, P. and Khumar, S.S. (1993): "Stressful Life Events, Distress and Socio-economic Status in the Study of Life Satisfaction of Elderly". Paper presented at XXXI AAP Conference, Jodhpur.

Larson, R. (1978): "Thirty Years of Research on the Subjective Well-being of Older Americans". *Journal of Gerontology,* 33, 109–125.

Neugarten, B.L. and Associates (Eds.) (1964): *Personality in Middle and Late Life.* New York: Atherton.

Ramamurti, P.V. and Jamuna, D. (1993): "Some Predictors of Satisfaction With Present Life in Indian Sample". *Indian Journal of Gerontology,* 7 (3 and 4), 96–103.

Soodan, K.S. (Ed.) (1955): *Aging in India.* Calcutta: Minerva Associates.

Stone, K. and Kailash, R. (1973): "Of Poker, Rols and Aging: Description, Discussion and Data". *Aging and Human Development,* 4, 1–13.

Thomae, H. (1980): "Personality and Adjustment to Aging". In J.E. Birren and R. Bruce Sloane (Eds.) *Handbook on Mental Health and Aging.* Englewood Cliffs: N.J. Prentice Hall.

CHAPTER 9

Life Stress and Personality Adjustment Among Aged Persons

S.K. Srivastava and Anshika Gupta

As we know, there are many obstacles, both environmental and personal, which place adjustive demands or stress on the individual. Our life would have been happier if our biological, psychological and social needs and motivations were easily met. But this is not always the case with us. We have to face many impediments in the fulfilment of these needs. Stress is a type of pressure which an individual feels in the process of achieving his particular goals. All of us face different type of situations everyday in our life, and ordinarily we succeed in meeting them to our full satisfaction. However, in some cases our adjustive resources are severely taxed so much so that we are almost at the point of breakdown.

Adjustment is a harmonious relationship with the environment in which most individual needs are satisfied in socially acceptable ways, and resulting in forms of behaviour which may range from passive conformity to vigorous action. According to Singh (1983) adjustment is a precarious and ever-changing balance between the needs and desires of the individual on the one hand and the demands of the environments or society on the other. Well adjusted people tend to have a fairly realistic level of aspiration. Maladjusted people, on the other hand, tend to be unrealistic to set their aspiration either too high or low leading to inevitable failure or to wasted opportunities and, in either case, to unhappiness.

IJG, 1994, Vol. 8, No. 1 and 2, pp. 37–41.

Anantharaman (1976) reported that persons belonging to upper social class were better in adjustment (life satisfaction) than other belonging to lower social classes. Duckitt and Broll (1982) found that social support and life event stress were directly related to psychological distress, and only the life event stress was related to physical health. Shejwal and Ram (1983) found that there is no sex difference in the perceived stress (readjustment) related to events threatening personal attachment and the only exception was the case of broken heart. Males reported significantly higher readjustment than females for this event. Differences in the evaluation of stress by married and unmarried persons were not significant. Death of spouse and the son-daughter leaving home was perceived as more stressful by married subjects.

The findings of Kumari and Prakash (1986) revealed that the various age groups significantly differed in terms of the number of life events experienced. Female subjects experienced more life stress than male subjects. A significant negative correlation ($r=-0.243$) was found between life events score and general health score indicating a negative relationship between life stress and mental health. Goodyer, Kolvin and Gatzanis, (1986) findings indicate that with the possible exception of severe emotional disorders, neither age nor sex substantially influenced the association between events and psychiatric disorder. These findings also suggest that girls may be more likely than boys to develop a severe emotional response to recent events. Chadha (1991) shows that males and females differ significantly (at 0.01 level) in regard to self-concept and life satisfaction. Aged male subjects scored higher than female on self-concept and life satisfaction.

Bose and Mukhopadhyay's (1993) results revealed that the highly stressed male group proved to be emotionally unstable and emotionally regressive than the low stressed male patients. Highly stressed female cancer patients on the other hand were found to be emotionally unstable, emotionally regressive, socially maladjusted and lacking independence than low stressed female patients. Kaur (1994) found the impact of stressful life events, distress and socio-economic status on the life satisfaction of the elderly. Results also indicate that the level of life satisfaction rises with the rise in the socio-economic status, and socio-economic status and distress have a significant correlation. Distress and life satisfaction are negatively correlated. Several studies, e.g., Hough, Fairbank and Garcia (1976),

Clearly and Mechanic (1983), Singh, Kaur and Sharma (1983), Chovan (1985), Dewe (1989), Verma (1989), Jaiswal (1993) and Srivastava (1994) have been carried out on life stress and related variables, but no study has compared personality adjustment in terms of life stress among two different age group of elder persons. Keeping this in the mind, the present study sought to understand the impact of age on stress and personality adjustment and find out the role of life stress in personality adjustment. The following objectives have been formulated for this study:

- To study the effect of age factor on life stress and personality adjustment.
- To see the significant differences, if any, between high and low stress groups on personality adjustment.

Method

Sample

The present study was carried out on a sample of 150 employees. Seventy-five employees were taken from 35–40 years age group and other seventy-five employees from 50–60 years age group. Sex factor, socio-economic status and family size and structure of the employees were controlled. The employees were selected from a government sector concern viz. Indian Drugs Pharmaceuticals Limited (IDPL). The selection was done using the purposive sampling technique.

Test Materials Used

Two tests were administered on each employee. Life Stress Scale by Gunthey and Gadakari (1987) and Personality Adjustment Inventory by Sharma (1974). In life stress scale maximum score indicates high stress and minimum score indicates low stress, while in personality adjustment inventory low scores indicate better adjustment and high scores indicate maladjustment.

Results and Discussion

In Table 1 and 2 't' test was employed to find out the significant differences between different age groups of employees on life stress and personality adjustment. Table 1 reveals that group-A (35–49 years employees) employees significantly differ from group-B employees (50–60 years employees) on life stress.

Table 1

Comparison between two age groups of employees on life stress

Different age group of employees	*Life stress scores*		*'t' value*
	Mean	*SD*	
35–49 years (Group-A) (N=75)	26.63	10.16	
			2.77**
50–60 years (Group-B) (N=75)	30.78	8.05	

Table 2

Comparison between two age groups of employees on personality adjustment

Different age group of employees	*Personality adjustment scores*		*t-value*
	Mean	*SD*	
35–49 years (Group-A) (N=75)	18.15	7.78	
			2.17**
50–60 years (Group-B) (N=75)	20.56	5.65	

*Significant at 0.05 level.
**Significant at 0.01 level.

It was found that mean scores of group-B employees were higher in comparison to group-A employees on life stress. It means, age factors are playing significant role in the life stress and aged persons (Group-B) feel high stress as compared to elder persons (Group-A) in the life. The findings of Kumari and Prakash (1986) revealed that the various age groups significantly differed in terms of the number of life events experienced. Bhaduri's (1993) findings show that female subjects and old age people are having higher life stresses and less ego strength. The Table 2 clearly revealed that group-A (35–49 years employees) differs significantly (t=2.17, p. 0.05) from group-B (50–60 years employees) on personality adjustment. The mean scores of the personality adjustment among group-A and group-B employee was 18.15 and 20.56 respectively (Table 2). It was noted that mean value of personality adjustment was higher for group-A employees. They show better adjustment in comparison to group-B employees because low scores indicate better adjustment and high scores indicate maladjustment. As per our results, further, we have concluded that aged persons feel some problems in the adjustment than elder persons in the society. On the basis of the present findings (see Tables 1 and 2) it can be said that better adjustment shows lesser stress.

Table 3

Comparison between high and low stress groups on personality adjustment in two different age groups of employees

Level of stress	*Different age group of employees*	*Personality adjustment scores*		*t-value*
		Mean	*SD*	
High stress (N=20)	Group-A 35–49 years	32.51	4.74	7.45**
Low stress (N=15)		20.73	4.54	
High stress (N=19)	Group-B 50–60 years	40.50	6.10	11.44**
Low stress (N=16)		19.90	4.46	

**Significant at 0.01 level.

In the present study, the second objective was to see the significant differences, if any, between high and low stress groups on personality adjustment. Table 3 depicts that high stress groups on personality adjustment in both the groups of employees (Groups A and B). Mean scores indicate that highly stressed employees were highly maladjusted than less stress employees ($t=7.45$, $p=0.01$ and $t=11.44$, $p<0.01$ respectively among the group-A and group-B employees). Highly adjusted persons are likely to be less stress. This is because for proper adjustment in society or an organization one should establish harmony with the outside world and should develop close sympathetic relationships with others. This personality trait is found more in less stress persons than in high stress persons among both group-A and group-B employees. We can say that stress leads to maladjustment – no matter whether the employees are elder or aged persons. Vishnoi (1974) found that better adjusted persons have high achievement tendency and poor adjusted persons have low achievement tendency. Hussain's (1991) correlational findings showed higher adjustment with greater ego-strength and lesser anxiety, the high and low adjusted groups significantly differed on ego-strength and anxiety.

References

Anantharaman, R.N. (1976): "Psychology of Aging: A Study in Adjustment". *Indian Dissertation Abstracts.* January-June Issues, 174–176.

Bhaduri, N. (1993): The Effect of Life Stresses on Ego Strength in Middle and Old Age Males and Females. Paper abstracted in 30th Annual Conference of Indian Academy of Applied Psychology at J.N.V. University, Jodhpur.

Bose, Swapna and Mukhopadhyay, A. (1993): An Attempt to Trace the Emotional Maturity Factor and its Impact on Stress among Male and Female Cancer Patients. Paper abstracted in 30th Annual Conference of Indian Academy of Applied Psychology at JNV University, Jodhpur.

Chadha, N.K. (1991): "Self Concept and Life Satisfaction among Aged". *Indian Journal of Gerontology,* 5 (No. 1 and 2), 47–54.

Chovan, M.J.R. and Chovan, W. (1985): "Stressful Events and Coping Responses among Older Adults in the Socio-cultural Groups". *Journal of Psychology,* 19, No. 3, 253–260.

Cleary, P. and Mechanic, T. (1983): "Sex Differences in Psychological Distress among Married People". *Journal of Health and Social Behaviour,* 24, 111–121.

Coleman, J.C. (1988): *Abnormal Psychology and Modern Life.* Bombay: D.B. Taraporevala Sons and Company, Private Limited.

Dowe, P.J. (1989): "Examining Nature of Work Stress: Individual Evaluation of Stressful Experience and Coping". *Human Relations,* 42, 993–1013.

Duckitt, J. and Broll, Teresa (1982): "Life Events Stress, Social Support and Health". *Journal for Research in the Human Science,* 8(4), 377–383.

Goodyer, I.M., Kolvin, I and Gatzanis, S. (1986): "Do Age and Sex Influence the Association between Recent Life Events and Psychiatric Disorder? A Controlled Enquiry". *Journal of Child Psychology and Psychiatric,* 27(5), 681–687.

Gunthey, R.K. and Gadakari, P. (1987): Life Stress Scale (Hindi Adaptation of Coleman). Unpublished Scale, Department of Psychology, J.N.V. University, Jodhpur.

Hough, R.L., Fairbank, D.T. and Garcia, A.M. (1976): "Problems in the Ratio Measurement of Life Stress". *Journal of Health and Social Behaviour,* 17, 70–82.

Hussain, S. (1991): A Study of Adjustment, Anxiety and Ego Strength in Context of Mental Health. Paper abstracted in 28th Annual

Conference of Indian Academy of Applied Psychology at Utkal University, Bhubaneswar.

Jaiswal, Smita (1993): Reaction to Frustration and Life Stresses in Cancer Patients. Paper abstracted in 30th Annual Conference of Indian Academy of Applied Psychology at J.N.V. University, Jodhpur.

Kaur, Paramjit (1994): Impact of Stressful Life Events, Distress and Socio-economic Status on the Life Satisfaction of the Elderly. Paper abstracted in 81st ISCA, Rajasthan University, Jaipur (Young Scientist Award Programme).

Kumari, H. and Prakash, I.J. (1986): "Life Stress and Mental Health: A Study of Age and Sex Differences". *Journal of Personality and Clinical Studies,* 2(2), 103–107.

Mangal, S.K. (1984): *Abnormal Psychology*. New Delhi: Sterling Publishers Private Limited.

Sharma, C.P. (1974): *Manual for Personality Adjustment Inventory.* Agra Psychological Research Cell.

Shejwal, B.R. and Ram, U. (1983): Sex Differences in the Perception of Stressful Life Events Threatening Personal Attachment. Paper presented at the Seminar on Stress, University of Pune, Pune.

Singh, A. (1983): "Personality Adjustment". *School Education,* 9(4), 15–17.

Singh, Gurmet, Kaur, Dalbir and Sharma, H.R. (1983): *Handbook for Presumptive Stressful Life Events Scale.* Agra: National Psychological Corporation.

Srivastava, S.K. (1994): "Anxiety and Adjustment among Industrial Workers". *Management and Labour Studies,* 19(2), 99–103.

Verma, N. (1989): Life Stress, Social Support and Coping in Individuals with Psychological Distress, Ph.D. Thesis, Bangalore University.

Vishnoi, K. (1974): A Study of Personality Adjustment in Relation to High and Low Achievers". *Journal of Education and Psychology,* 31(4), 212–216.

CHAPTER 10

Life Stress and Personality Adjustment Among Aged Persons

Saraswati Mishra

In the pre-industrial agrarian set-up, most of the aged people used to remain financially independent till they lived. The traditional social and cultural values also did not permit the grown-up children to leave their financially and physically insecure old parents alone. The sons used to serve their parents as feet, hand, ears and eyes. Moreover, the prevailing economic, political and value systems of the pre-industrial social order, which were based on the preservation of inherited inequality, enabled the aged people to enjoy leadership roles and powerful positions of decisions makers and advisers in the joint family, caste group and village community (Bhatia, 1964; D'Souza, 1971).

Information available in some studies indicates that the status of the old people is now declining gradually and creating many problems for them (Jagjit Singh, 1962; Indra, 1963; Gursharan Kaur, 1964; Marula Siddaiah, 1966; Narang, 1968; Ramamurti, 1968; Kurian, 1972; Soodan, 1972; Desai and Naik 1973; Bose, 1982; D'Souza, 1982; Hardikar and Bhatia, 1983).

There are two contrasting views regarding the successful ageing. According to one view (i.e., engagement theory) continuation of activities and attitudes of middle years into old age is conducive to happiness and successful ageing (Havighurst, 1963). The other view (disengagement theory) the individual prefers to give up his earlier

IJG, 1993, Vol. 7, No. 1 and 2, pp. 43–47.

activities and social roles and society takes away his earlier professional and social responsibilities both not minding but mutually and willingly seeking the engagement (Cumming and Henery, 1961). The retirement should be perceived as a process which should be understood as a transition from one system to another. The phenomenon of transition may be explained in terms of engagement and dis-engagement theories of ageing. The period of retirement consists of constructive and destructive elements for the individual and the system. Engagement and disengagement needs oscillate in every individual development. The timely and proper guidance at this period leads to better adjustment of the individual (Sharma, 1972).

The empirical findings (Sharma, 1969) have shown that demographic variables play an important role in determining the pattern of life in terms of life activities of older individuals. It has also been reported (Sharma, 1971) that various patterns of life activities leading to social as well as personal adjustment are discernable in old age. The happiness to a great extend depends upon busy life, good health, feeling of paucity of funds having spouse and social context etc.

The purpose of this study was to find out the social correlates of good adjustment in old age.

Method

Sample

Seven hundred and twenty retired government employees (living in Chandigarh and Jabalpur city of India) were randomly selected for this study. These subjects belong to different family structures viz., joint family (N=214); nuclear family (N=453) and quasi-nuclear family (N=53).

Tool and Procedure

These subjects were interviewed personally and life satisfaction scale (Havighurst, 1963) was also administered to measure their degree of adjustment. To find out the significance of difference between different variables Goodman and Kruskals' Gama (r) test was used and the value of 'r' was converted into the value 'z'.

Good adjustment and successful ageing have been used here synonymously. It is operationally defined as having harmonious living, feeling of happiness and satisfaction with one's life, present status and activities.

Results and Discussion

The amount of relationship that exists between the retirees' life satisfaction, which is the indicator of their social adjustment and consequently the successful ageing, on one hand, and the different situational, attitudinal and behavioural factors, on the other, are given in the Table 1.

The Situational Factors

In this category, the variables showing the intellectual, social, economic and physical status of the retirees are included. Regarding these variables, we found that educational level, pre-retirement occupational status, present monthly income and the health condition, all have strong positive association with their present life satisfaction. Respectively, the value of 'r' comes to 0.52, 0.58, 0.52 and 0.55, and the values of 'z' is 3.27, 3.66, 3.9 and 3.61 which are significant statistically at 0.01 level. This finding seems quite obvious as the situational factors show the resourcefulness of the human being, which helps in achieving the happiness even in old age. Age itself had no significant association with their happiness in any direction although it was found in negative direction.

Table 1

*Association between the retirees degree of successful ageing and level of different factors**

Sl. No.	*Name of the variables*	*The value of its association with successful ageing value of 'r'*	*The value of the association's statistical significance value of 'z'*	*Significance level*
1.	Education	0.52	3.27	0.01
2.	Pre-retirement occupational status	0.58	3.66	0.01
3.	Monthly income at present	0.52	3.93	0.01

Cont'd...

Cont'd...

4. Present health condition	0.55	3.61	0.01
5. Seniority by age	–0.14	–1.65	N.S.**
Attitudinal Factors			
1. Positive attitudes towards social changes	0.59	3.76	0.01
2. Non-interfering attitudes regarding the personal affairs of grown-up children	0.42	2.70	0.01
3. Strength of religious beliefs	–0.14	–1.08	N.S.
A. Behavioural Factors (Activities)			
1. Occupational activity	0.64	4.02	0.01
2. Hobbies or special interests	0.63	4.99	0.01
3. Religious activities	–0.17	–1.14	N.S.
4. Other household activities	–0.10	–0.97	N.S.
5. All the activities	0.61	3.86	0.01
B. Behavioural Factors (Interactions)			
1. Family members	0.15	1.20	N.S.
2. Separated children in the city	0.20	1.07	N.S.
3. Friends in the city	0.35	2.48	0.01
4. Neighbours	0.27	1.73	N.S.
5. Relatives in the same city	0.30	1.98	0.05
6. Members of voluntary organizations of city	0.50	2.94	0.01
7. All the social interaction with non-family members	0.41	2.61	0.01

* The value of 'r' upto 3.3 to 0.4 and above 0.4 indicates the weak, moderate and strong association between two variables. The value of 'z' equal to 1.97 and 2.33 are considered statistically significant at 0.05 and 0.01 levels respectively.

** N.S.=Not significant at 0.05 level. Due to the qualitative nature of data 0.05 was considered appropriate level of significance for any association between two factors.

Attitudinal Factors

These factors are concerned with the thinking of retirees towards new values and norms of the present society. In this category we found that, while positive attitudes towards various social changes in the Indian society, and the non-interfering attitudes association with life satisfaction, having the value of 'r' as 0.59 and 0.42, and the value of 'z' as 3.18 and 2.70 respectively, both significant at 0.01 level; the strength of religious beliefs has weak negative association with it, which is not statistically significant even at 0.05 level. This finding is also quite understandable considering the young generations expectations from the older generation in the todays society.

Behavioural Factors

These factors are connected with the retirees' various types of activities and their social interactions with various groups of people.

(a) *Activities:* Regarding the activities, we find that while the occupational activity, hobbies and total activeness of the retirees, in terms of the time budgeting i.e., total time daily devoted by them; have quite strong positive association with their happiness, having respectively, the value of 'r' as 0.64, 0.63 and 0.61 and the value of 'z' as 4.02, 4.99 and 3.86 are significant at the level of 0.01; the religious activities and other household activities have quite weak negative association with it, which is not significant in both the cases. It shows that the retirees derive pleasure in earning even after retirement and the special interests or hobbies have a very important role in providing satisfaction to the aged people.

(b) *Interactions:* In this category of factors, we found that while the interaction with friends, members of voluntary organizations in the city and the overall interaction level of the retirees, in terms of the frequency of meetings with the group members, have either moderate or strong positive association with their happiness, having the value of 'r' as, 0.35, 0.50 and 0.41 and the value of 'z' as 2.48, 2.49 and 2.61 respectively, all are significant at 0.01 level; their interaction with family members, separated children, neighbours and relatives, have comparatively the weaker positive association with it, having respectively the value of 'r' as 0.15, 0.20, 0.27 and 0.30, and the value 'z' as 1.20, 1.07, 1.73 and 1.98. Only in the case of relatives, this association was found statistically significant at 0.05 level. It shows that while the people enjoy interaction with the group of their own liking, they do not cherish it when it is forced.

References

Bhatia, H.S. (1964): "Rural Social Change and the Problem of the Aged", *Social Welfare*. XI (July): 5–6.

Bose, Ashish (1982): "Aspects of Aging in India", *Social Action* 32 (1), January-March 1–19.

Cumming, E. and Henery, H. (1961): *Growing Old: The Process of Disengagement*. New York: Basic Books.

D'Souza, Alfred (1982): "The Social Organization of Aging among the Urban Poor", *Social Action* 32 (1) January-March, 53–54.

D'Souza, Victor S. (1971): "Changing in Social Structure and Changing Roles of the Older People in India", *Sociology and Social Research*, 555 (April), 297–304.

Desai, K.G. and Naik, R.D. (1973): *Problems of Retired People in Greater Bombay*. Tata Institute of Social Sciences Series No. 27, Bombay.

Hardikar, S.N. and Bhatia, G.G. (1983): "Old Age: A Medical and Social Review" in *Disabled in India* (Ed.) S.N. Gajendragadkar, Bombay: Somaiya Publications Pvt. Ltd.

Havighurst, R.J. (1961): "Successful Aging", *The Gerontologist*, Vol. 1, 1961, 8–13.

Indra, Rajinder (1963): Problems of Old Women in a Village. Unpublished Master's Thesis, Punjab University, Chandigarh.

Kaur, Gursharan (1964): The Problems of Aged Women in Batala. Unpublished Master's Thesis, Punjab University, Chandigarh.

Kurian, George (1972): "Aging in India and Canada: A Comparative Perspective", *Social Action* 22 (July), 222–230.

Marula, Siddaiah, H.M. (1966): "The Declining Authority of Old People", *Indian Journal of Social Work* XXVII (July), 175–195.

Narang, Taranjit (1968): Adjustment of the Aged with Special Reference to Family Types. Unpublished Master's Thesis, Punjab University, Chandigarh.

Ramamurti, P.V. (1968): A Study of Some Factors Related to Adjustment of Urban Aged Men. Ph.D. Thesis, Srivenkateswara University, Tirupati.

Sharma, K.L. (1969): "Leisure Time Activities of Retired Persons", *Indian Journal of Gerontology*, 1, 1, 32–37.

Sharma, K.L. (1971): "A Survey of the Happiness and Unhappiness in Old Age", *Indian Journal of Gerontology* 3, 3 and 4, 67–69.

Sharma, K.L. (1972): "Education for Senior Citizens". *Indian Journal of Gerontology*, 4, 3 and 4, 89–91.

Singh, Jagit (1962): Problems of the Oldmen in Burail. Unpublished Master's Thesis, Punjab University, Chandigarh.

Soodan, Kirpal Singh (1972): "Changing Roles of the Aged". *Indian Journal of Gerontology*, 4, 3 and 4, 89–91.

CHAPTER 11

Some Factors Related to Adjustment Among the Rural Aged

M. Easwaramoorthy

Ageing is the final phase of human development, and must be seen as part of a continual process of change (Hamilton, 1991). The fact that life is a continuous process of growth beginning from infancy and coming to old age through childhood and adulthood and that it ultimately terminates with the death of an individual is an obvious phenomenon and need not be emphasized (Bhatia, 1983).

The Indian society has been undergoing rapid transformation under the impact of several forces like industrialization, urbanization and education, consequently the traditional system of values and institutions are in the process of adaptation (Gangrade, 1989). India is in the process of industrialization. There is a growing shift in the means of livelihood from rural to urban and semiurban occupations. Hitherto, most people lived in rural areas in joint families. In a sense, many of them were self-employed in business or agriculture and retirement was for the most part gradual and voluntary. In the large joint family, even at home, there was division of labour and the aged individual had some role or other to play. This kept him occupied and made his life more meaningful while his maintenance was not an undue burden on the family (Ramamurti, 1970).

IJG, 1993, Vol. 7, No. 1 and 2, pp. 37–42.

Old age is inevitable and the number of old people is increasing all over the world due to the intervention programme's for the control of diseases, better health care and nutrition, and improved public awareness of health problems and needs (Mathur, 1988). The need for researches in Gerontology in developing countries is emphasized by Lin (1983). In fact the need for studies in psycho-social aspects of the aged and retired is stressed in Indian context by recent evidences (Bose and Gangrade, 1988 and Lakshiminarayanan 1988). The psycho-social aspects of the rural aged population remain unclear (McGhee, 1984). Moreover it is obvious that only scientifically designed survey's and studies can alone give a clear picture about the aged and the retired especially about their psychological well-being. Hence a study was carried out to find out some of the factors related to adjustment among the rural aged.

Method

The sample of the study consist of 80 elderly individuals drawn randomly from rural areas of Coimbatore district. Life Satisfaction Index-Z (Havighurst, 1971) was found to be proper for the study and reliability and validity of this tool as an adjustment inventory among the Indian sample, has already been established by Anantharaman (1980). The Life Satisfaction Inventory is in self-explanatory form and can be answered in three choices, viz., Agree, Disagree and "?", each correct answer has to be given one mark and the total maximum score possible is 18. The more the score the better will be one's adjustment. In addition to this tool, personal data sheet were used to identify the factors related to adjustment. The tools of the study was personally administered to the sample of the study to collect the needed data. Quartile deviation was applied to the scores of Life Satisfaction Index to categorize the sample as poorly, moderately and better adjusted. The information obtained through the personal data sheet were analysed by simple percentage.

Results and Discussion

The data of the study as mentioned earlier was subject to percentage analysis. The results are presented in self-explanatory tables. Numbers in parentheses indicate percentage.

Table 1

The trend of adjustment in relation to age

Age in years	*Adjustment category*			*Total (N)*
	Poorly adjusted	*Moderately adjusted*	*Better adjusted*	
58–60	10 (31.25)	9 (28.13)	13 (40.62)	32
61–63	4 (57.14)	3 (42.86)	0 (0.00)	07
64–66	6 (50.00)	5 (41.67)	1 (8.33)	12
67–69	1 (25.00)	2 (50.00)	1 (25.00)	04
70–72	7 (50.00)	6 (42.86)	1 (7.14)	14
73–75	2 (66.67)	1 (33.33)	0 (0.00)	03
76+	5 (62.50)	2 (25.00)	1 (12.50)	08

Table 2

Adjustment with reference to education

Education	*Adjustment category*			*Total (N)*
	Poorly adjusted f(%)	*Moderately adjusted f(%)*	*Better adjusted f(%)*	
Primary	2 (12.50)	6 (37.50)	8 (50.00)	16
Secondary	0 (0.00)	2 (40.00)	3 (60.00)	05
Uneducated	33 (55.93)	20 (33.90)	6 (10.17)	59

Table 3

Relation between adjustment and personal problems

Problem Area	*Adjustment category*			*Total (N)*
	Poorly adjusted f(%)	*Moderately adjusted f(%)*	*Better adjusted f(%)*	
Financial	35 (58.33)	20 (33.33)	5 (8.33)	60
Utilization of time	3 (25.00)	5 (41.67)	4 (33.33)	12
Settlement of children in life	21 (47.73)	12 (27.27)	11 (25.00)	44
Other problems (includes health)	21 (72.41)	5 (17.24)	3 (0.35)	29
No problems	1 (12.50)	3 (37.50)	4 (50.00)	08

Table 4
Relation between adjustment and deprivations in life

Deprivations	Adjustment category			Total (N)
	Poorly adjusted f(%)	Moderately adjusted f(%)	Better adjusted f(%)	
Income	36 (62.07)	17 (29.31)	5 (8.62)	58
Friendship	7 (38.89)	5 (27.78)	6 (33.33)	18
Authority and status in family	16 (44.44)	9 (25.00)	11 (30.55)	36
Social engagement	21 (46.67)	14 (31.11)	10 (22.22)	45
Usefulness to family and relatives	23 (46.00)	19 (38.00)	8 (16.00)	50
Status in social life	10 (33.33)	11 (36.67)	9 (30.00)	30
Other deprivations	8 (57.14)	4 (28.57)	2 (14.29)	14
No deprivations	0 (0.00)	3 (30.00)	7 (70.00)	10

Table 5
Relation between adjustment and happiness in life

Status of happiness	Adjustment category			Total (N)
	Poorly adjusted f(%)	Moderately adjusted f(%)	Better adjusted f(%)	
Happiness	3 (17.67)	6 (35.29)	8 (47.06)	17
Blend of happiness and uhappiness	10 (34.48)	12 (41.38)	7 (24.14)	29
Unhappiness	22 (64.71)	10 (29.41)	2 (5.88)	34

Table 6
Adjustment in relation to number of dependents

Number of dependents	Adjustment category			Total (N)
	Poorly adjusted f(%)	Moderately adjusted f(%)	Better adjusted f(%)	
1 – 3	15 (41.67)	16 (44.44)	5 (13.89)	36
3 – 6	16 (48.49)	10 (30.30)	7 (21.21)	33
6 +	4 (44.45)	2 (2.22)	3 (33.33)	09
No. of dependents	0 (0.00)	0 (0.00)	2 (100)	02

The results of the present study indicate that adjustment is better around sixties and adjustment in latter life is progressively deteriorating (Table 1). This may be due to the deterioration of health, consequent reduction in financial and social support. John Van Willigen (1989) illustrates this with the help of exchange theory. According to the exchange theory "interaction is maintained because individuals find such interaction rewarding for whatever reasons". The decrease in social interaction that characterizes social ageing is a manifestation of decreasing power resources (Bengston and Down, 1980). Interaction with aged person decreases because it is less rewarding and consequently leads to a reduction in the size of social support network resulting in poor adjustment. It can be observed (Table 2) that education influences adjustment in later life, better the education better the adjustment. This finding supports the findings of Bhatnagar and Randhawa, (1987) who reported that education as a factor for better adjustment. It is seen from Table 3 that financial problems and settlement of children interferes with adjustment. This is quite evident because the job opportunities are too less for the rural population in India as compared to the urban population. Elderlies experience deprivation in various aspects of life (Table 4) and seems to be an important deprivation to interfere with adjustment. The data (Table 6) suggest an obvious fact that the number of dependents have no effect on the adjustment of elderlies in the rural setting. This may be due to the joint family system in rural areas where the resources are pooled together to meet the needs of the family members.

The findings of the present study fall in line with mainly existing evidences (Ramamurti, 1970, 1972; Fengler and Jensen, 1981; Bhatia, 1983).

The causes behind the results of the present study may be many. Rural elderly are relatively more disadvantaged with respect to personal resources such as income and health. Recently Chadha and Easwaramoorthy (1992) have illustrated with research evidences, that the life of rural elderlies is characterized by less income, poor housing, poor health, poor access to health care and transportation. Moreover due to industrialization and urbanization the sons and daughters of elderlies have to migrate to urban and industrial areas for seeking jobs and education, leaving the elderlies in villages. Thus, the care received by the rural elderly is less when compared to their urban counterparts. Apart from these factors, the rigidity in old age may also negatively affect the elderlies in their adjustment.

The results of the present study illustrate the vulnerability of the rural elderly and imply the need to devise ways and means to create better and conducive environment for optimal harnessing of their life. It is also suggested to carry out further researches in this area by considering other personal, psychological and socio-economic variables and taking various sub groups like the tribals and socially backward groups into consideration.

Acknowledgement

The author gratefully thanks Dr K.K. Chadha, Department of Psychology, University of Delhi, Delhi for reviewing this article and for providing many valuable suggestions in the preparation of this article.

References

Anantharaman, R.N. (1980): "Reliability and Validity of Life-satisfaction Questionnaire". *Indian Journal of Clinical Psychology*. 7, 59–61.

Bengston, V.L. and Dowd, J.J. (1980): "Sociological Functionalism, Exchange Theory and Life Cycle Analysis: A Call for More Explicit Theoretical Bridges". *International Journal of Aging and Human Development*. 12 (1), 55–73.

Bhatia, H.S. (1983): *Aging and Society: A Sociological Study of Retired Public Services*. Udaipur: Arya's Book Centre Publishers.

Bhatnagar, G.S. and Randhawa, M. (1987) "Social Adjustment among Retired Persons". In M.L. Sharma and T.M. Dak (Eds.), *Aging in India: Challenge for Society*. New Delhi: Ajanta Publications.

Bose, A.B. and Gangrade, K.D. (1988): *The Aging in India, Problems and Potentialities*. New Delhi: Abinav Publications.

Chadha, N.K. and Easwaramoorthy, M. (1992): "Aging: Issues and Rehabilitation Strategies" in N.K Chadha and S.S. Nath (Eds.), *Issue and Trends in Rehabilitation Research*. New Delhi: Friends Publications (In Press).

Fengler, A.P. and Jensen (1981): "Perceived and Objective Conditions as Predictors of the Life Satisfaction of Urban and Non-urban Elderly". *Journal of Gerontology*. 36, 750–752.

Gangrade, K.D. (1989): "Emerging Conception of Aging in India. A Socio-cultural Perspective". *The Eastern Anthropologist*. 42(2).

Hamilton, I.S. (1991): *The Psychology of Aging: An Introduction*. London: Jessica Kingsley Publishers.

Havighurst (1971): *Life Satisfaction Index Z, Age and Ageing*, Vol. 3, No. 2, pp. 113–121.

Lakshminarayanan, T.R. (1988): An Exploratory Study on Pensioners in Coimbatore District. Unpublished Doctoral Thesis. Bharatpur University, Coimbatore.

Lin, T.V. (1983): "Mental Health in Third Worlds". *The Journal of Nervous and Mental Disease*. 171 (2), 71–78.

Mathur, G.C. (1988): "Housing for Aging". In A.B. Bose and K.D. Gangrade (Eds.), *Aging in India: Problems and Potentiality.*

McGhee, J.L. (1984): "The Influences of Qualitative Assessment of Social and Physical Environment of Morale of the Rural Elderly". *American Journal of Community Psychology*. 12 (4), 709–723.

Ramamurti, P.V. (1970): "Attitude Towards Personal Futurity. Across Sectional Analysis of Age-span 20–70". *Indian Journal of Gerontology*. 3 (1 and 2).

Ramamurti, P.V. (1972): An Empirical Investigation of Roles and Problems of Middle-Aged and Older People. ICSSR Project. S.V. University, Tirupati.

Van Willigen, J. (1989): *Getting Some Age on Me*. Kentucky: University Press of Kentucky.

Section C

Attitude towards the Elderly

It is widely recognized that we live in a youth-oriented society. Little attention is paid to the resulting ageism, towards older adults or how this affects our personal and professional relationships.

The term 'ageism' was coined in 1969 by Robert Butler, the first director of the National Institute on Aging. He likened it to other forms of bigotry such as racism and sexism, defining it as a process of systematic stereotyping and discrimination against people because they are old. Today, it is more broadly defined as any prejudice or discrimination against or in favor of an age group (Palmore, 1990). Erdman Palmore, who has written extensively about ageism, lists the basic characteristics of stereotyping which forms the basis of ageism in his 1990 book *Ageism* (151–152):

Ageism is manifested in many ways, some explicit, some implicit. The following piece by Edith Stein illustrates some graphic examples of negative ageism (Palmore, 1990: 3–4):

- "Older persons falter for a moment because they are unsure of themselves and are immediately charged with being 'infirm'.
- Older persons are constantly 'protected' and their thoughts interpreted.
- Older persons forget someone's name and are charged with senility and patronized.
- Older persons are expected to 'accept' the 'facts of aging'.
- Older persons miss a word or fail to hear a sentence and they are charged with 'getting old', not with a hearing difficulty.

- Older persons are called 'dirty' because they show sexual feelings or affection to one of either sex.
- Older persons are called 'cranky' when they are expressing a legitimate distaste for life as so many young do.
- Older persons are charged with being 'like a child' even after society has ensured that they are as dependent, helpless, and powerless as children."

Ageist attitudes are perpetuated in many ways, for example, the lack of positive images of the elderly in advertisements and on TV programmes, and the widespread use of demeaning language about old age are noticed nowadays. In addition, institutions perpetuate ageism. Businesses frequently reinforce ageist stereotypes by not hiring or promoting older workers even when they are physically and mentally fit. Another example is the use of state welfare funds which are often targeted at children and adolescents, women (who are of productive age) excluding equivalent services for older adults such as adult protective services (such as pension and other services) and geriatric physical and mental health services.

Human service professionals also perpetuate ageism. This is done more covertly by denying or limiting services, by not including aging issues in their schedule of activities. The same criticism can be made about training of professional social workers who receive little information about the ageing process although many of their clients will be elderly.

Underlying these attitudes are myths and stereotypes about old age which are deeply entrenched in all the societies who claims themselves modern. Even those who would not say that they are ageist probably have some ageist attitudes based on distorted or inaccurate information.

The most common of these negative myths and stereotypes about ageing are as follows:

1. *Illness:* Perhaps the most common prejudice against elders is that most are sick or disabled (Palmore, 1990).
2. *Impotency:* A related stereotype is the belief that most elders have no sexual desire and no longer engage in any sexual activity. The few who do, are morally perverse or at least abnormal (Golde and Kogan, 1958). Even physicians, who should know better, often assume that sexuality is unimportant in late life (Butler, 1975, 1975a, 1975b).

3. *Ugliness:* Another stereotype is that old people are ugly. Beauty is associated with youth, and many people, especially women, fear the loss of their beauty as they age. The following terms reflect this stereotype of ugliness: crone, fossil, goat, hag, witch, withered, wizened, wrinkled.
4. *Mental Decline:* Another common stereotype is that mental abilities begin to decline from middle age onwards, especially the abilities to learn and remember, and that cognitive impairment (i.e., memory loss, disorientation, or confusion) is an inevitable part of the aging process (Palmore, 1988).
5. *Mental Illness:* A similar stereotype is that mental illness is common, inevitable, and untreatable among most aged. Both elders themselves and many health professionals think that most mental illness in old age is untreatable, which partially explains why few mental health professionals choose to specialize in geriatric mental health and also why elders use mental health facilities at one-half the rate of the general population.
6. *Uselessness:* Because of the beliefs that the majority of old people are disabled by physical or mental illness, many people conclude that the elderly are unable to continue working and that those few who do continue to work are unproductive. This belief is the main basis for compulsory retirement policies and discrimination in hiring, retaining, and promotion.
7. *Isolation:* From a third to half of respondents to Palmore's facts on aging quiz think "The majority of old people are socially isolated and lonely" and "The majority of old people live alone" (Palmore, 1988). Two-thirds of persons under 65 think that loneliness is a 'very serious problem' for most people over 65.
8. *Poverty:* Views about the economic status of elders range from those who think most elders are poor, to those who think the majority are rich. At present those thinking elders are poor tend to outnumber those thinking elders are rich.
9. *Depression:* Since many believe that the typical older person is sick, impotent, senile, useless, lonely, and poor, they naturally conclude that the typical old person must also be depressed.
10. *Political Power:* Another stereotype is that the elderly are a "potent, self-interested political force". The assumption is that the political power of the elderly hamstrings our politicians from undertaking needed reforms.

The studies have shown that these stereotypes are not true in most of the cases.

Although much less prevalent, *positive stereotypes* about ageing are also held by some people. Although they are usually far less damaging than negative stereotypes, (which are based on inaccurate information that reinforces a distorted view of the elderly). An example of positive age stereotyping is that wisdom, dependability, kindness and compassion invariably accompany old age.

The consequences of ageism are similar to those associated with all attempts to discriminate against other groups: persons subjected to prejudice and discrimination tend to adopt the dominant group's negative image and to behave in ways that conform to that negative image (Palmore, 1990: 91). The dominant group's negative image typically includes a set of behavioural expectations or prescriptions which define what a person is to do and not to do. For example, the elderly are expected to be asexual, intellectually rigid, unproductive, forgetful, and happy, enjoy their retirement, and also be invisible, passive, and uncomplaining.

Palmore identifies four common responses of elders to these prescriptions and expectations: acceptance, denial, avoidance, or reform (Palmore, 1990: 96–102). All of these responses can have harmful effects on the individuals. For example, an elderly person who accepts the negative image may 'act old' even though this may be out of keeping with their personality or previous habits. This may mean that they stop or reduce social activities, do not seek appropriate medical treatment, or accept poverty. In essence, this internalization of a negative image can result in the elderly person becoming prejudiced against him/herself, resulting in loss of self-esteem, self-hatred, shame, depression, and/or suicide in extreme cases.

Denial of one's status as an elderly person can also have negative consequences. One example, lying about one's age may not seem significant, but it can further erode morale. Avoidance of ageist attitudes may also take many forms. Examples include moving into age-segregated housing, self-imposed isolation, alcoholism, drug addiction, or suicide.

The reform response, Palmore's last response pattern, is the antithesis of the avoidance response in that the person recognizes the discrimination and attempts to eliminate it. This attempt may be an individual one or a collective one through membership in an advocacy group such as powerful associations of senior citizens are coming up all over the world.

Ultimately, stereotypes are dehumanizing and promote one-dimensional thinking about others. Elders are not seen as human beings but as objects who, therefore, can be more easily denied opportunities and rights. For example, elders are frequently misdiagnosed or denied medical treatment because they are seen as 'old' and, therefore, incurable. Elders are also frequently denied employment or promotion opportunities because they are 'old' and less productive. Such discrimination is also evident on the social policy level where the elderly are blamed for having medical problems and consuming public resources rather than seeing them as having human needs requiring appropriate social responses. Seeing people as objects also increases the likelihood that they may be subjected to abuse and other cruel treatment.

Thus, ageism devalues this segment of the population, a vital human resource is lost. This is contrary to Indian values which entail respect for human worth and dignity. Cumulatively, the elderly represent a vast amount of experience, skill, and knowledge which this country needs to remain strong and true to its ideals.

Rodeheaver (1990) suggests that in order to counteract ageism, changes must be made in the systems which perpetuate it. Some of these systems mentioned earlier are the media, popular culture, and institutions such as business, government, and human service systems. Underlying all of these systems are ageist attitudes held by individuals who participate in these systems. Therefore, changing individual ageist attitudes is a fundamental approach to reducing ageism.

A first step in this process is identifying personal attitudes which are ageist in nature. This can be difficult since most people will deny that they are prejudiced. However, until a person is aware of this or her own attitudes, little progress can be made.

Another approach which can modify ageist attitudes is personal contact with older adults. This is often an effective way to prevent or reduce the development of ageism, especially among young children. Many innovative intergenerational programmes have been created which not only benefit children in this way, but also benefit the older adults. During these programmes, positive aspects of ageing can be emphasized so that the children will have a balanced picture of the older adults-and of themselves as they grow older. A good example of an intergenerational programme is the recording of older adults' oral history by students.

More formal instruction and education about ageing is also needed in professional schools whose graduates will inevitably serve the elderly. This is also true for schools of journalism whose graduates will have significant power in shaping public perception and opinion. In addition, continuing education and in-service training programmes in all fields should also include the ageing process and related issues.

Social action and reform is another approach to counteracting ageism. This approach is particularly effective when directed at institutions.

Summary of the Papers

This part contains five papers. P.V. Ramamurti studied "Attitude Towards Personal Futurity: A Cross-sectional Analysis of Age Span 20–70" and found differences between successive age groups 20–30,30–40,40–50,50–60,and 60–70 in the attitudes towards future. In old age, the individual suffers shrinkage in the perception of his future. There is a decrease in positive and favourable attitude towards future.

K.L. Sharma and Prabha Bhandari's findings show a predominance of negative attitudes and beliefs about the ageing and the aged. On the basis of these findings it may be stated that statements like "old people dislike any changes or interfere with established ways of doing things", "old people are conservatives", etc., are associated with older people. This negative attitude indicates a minority group position for the aged and more emphasis on youth orientation in India.

K.L. Sharma in his another paper "Images of Ageing" has tried to find out the degree of ageism, in 600 college going students of both the sexes. A questionnaire containing a set of six problems: not having enough money to live comfortably, poor health, lonelines, lack of proper housing, not having work to keep oneself busy and fear of criminal attack on oneself was given to the subjects. The subjects were asked how they rate themselves and older persons on the same problems. It was found out that both males and females differ in their stereotypes towards ageing (for degree of ageing). It was also noticed that respondents having older family member were realistic rather than fancy attitude in comparison to the respondents not having older members in their families.

Akbar Husain et al. made "A Comparative Study of Retired and Pre-retired Elderly on Life Attitude Profile", and found that for pre-retired subjects as compared to retired subjects life seems more purposeful and prone to optimism and hope.

In her study – "Attitude Towards Helping Elderly People: An Indian Study" Indira Jai Prakash assessed the attitudes of Indian subjects towards the elderly and compared to those of British and Canadian subjects. Indians were found to attribute blame to the elderly for their poor health and low income in old age.

References

Butler, R.N. (1969). "Ageism: Another Form of Bigotry". *The Gerontologist*, 9, 243–246.

Butler, R.N. (1975a). "Psychiatry and the Elderly: An Overview". *American Journal of Psychiatry*, 132, 893–900.

Butler, R. N. (1975b).*Why Survive? Being Old in America*. New York: Harper & Row.

Golde, P. and Kogan, N. (1958). "A Sentence Completion Procedure for Assessing Attitudes Toward Old People". *Journal of Gerontology*, 14, 355–363.

Gutmann, D. (1985). "The Cross-cultural Perspective: Notes Toward a Comparative Psychology of Aging". In R. H. Binstock and E. Shanas (Eds.), *Handbook of Aging and the Social Sciences* (2nd ed.), New York: Van Nostrand Reinhold.

Palmore, E. (1977). "Facts on Aging: A Short Quiz". *The Gerontologist*, 17, 315–320.

Palmore, E. (1981). "The Facts on Aging Quiz": Part II. *The Gerontologist*, 21, 431–437.

Palmore, E. (1990). *Ageism: Negative and Positive*. New York: Springer.

Rodehearver, D. (1990). "Ageism" in *Social Gerontology* (Eds.) David E. Redbum and Robert P. Menamara, Springer Publishing Company.

CHAPTER 12

Attitude Towards Personal Futurity

A Cross-Sectional Analysis of Age Span 20–70

P.V. Ramamurti

In recent years there has been an increasing interest in an altogether different dimension viz., an individuals' perception of futurity, cognitive and personal. From the time of the studies of Israeli (1933) there has been sporadic but persistent interest in this field as could be seen from the literature reported (e.g., Israeli, 1933; Lewin 1935; Frank 1939; Abbutt, 1943; Freud, 1953; Hartman 1958; Kastenbaum, 1956, 1961 and 1966). Many variables have been studied in relation to future time perspective, e.g., Academic Achievement (Teahan, 1958), Schizophrenia (Wallace, 1956), Aging (Wallach and Green, 1961), Death Attitude (Kastenbaum, 1959) and Socio-economic Class (Leshan, 1952). In the light of these studies it was considered useful to conduct an investigation to examine age trends in attitudes to personal futurity. In view of the fact that the available years to an individual's life go on decreasing as one grows older, it was felt that changes in one's attitude to future might occur. Accordingly the present investigation was planned to study the attitude towards future across the life span 20–70. A null hypothesis was accordingly set up that there are no differences in the attitudes to future between successive age groups of the life span.

IJG, 1971, Vol. 3, Nos. 1 and 2, pp. 33–35.

Method

In order to study changes in attitude across the life span 20–70 a developmental method ought to be utilized. But for obvious reasons of having to wait for a very long period and the need for considerable effort, a cross-sectional analysis was undertaken. Even in developmental studies time differences may confound age or maturational changes.

An inventory consisting of twenty statements representing attitudes towards future (ten statements representing a favourable outlook to future and ten statements representing an unfavourable outlook towards (future) was prepared. The inventory yielded a test-retest reliability co-efficient of 0.94. With an interval of 15 days on a sample of 75 individuals. The inventory was prepared in connection with a doctoral dissertation (Ramamurti, 1968). The inventory, yields a maximum score of 20 and a minimum score of zero and the score is a measure of the degree of favourable attitudes of the subject.

The sample consisted of 300 individuals (150 men and 150 women). The sample was drawn through a two stage random sample using the electoral rolls of Tirupati town as the basis. There were 60 individuals (30 men and 30 women) at each of the following stages: 20–30, 30–40, 40–50, 50–60 and 60–70. They were individually interviewed and tested.

Results and Discussion

The mean scores at each level 20–30; 30–40; 40–50; 50–60 and 60–70 were computed. As there were no significant sex differences at each stage, the groups were considered as a whole for purposes of studying age trends (the test of sex differences is not reported here). The mean scores of the age groups are provided in Table 1.

Table 1

Mean attitude scores of individuals in the various age groups 20–70

Age groups	*Mean attitude source*	*Mean difference*	*F. value*
20–30 (N=60)	13.55	0.51	
30–40 (N=60)	13.01	1.23	
40–50 (N=60)	11.88	1.75	10.05*
50–60 (N=60)	10.13	1.92	
60–70 (N=60)	8.21		

* Significant at 0.01 level.

The data in Table 1 clearly indicate that there is a gradual reduction of the favourable attitude in the higher age groups. The differences between the groups are generally significant as indicated by the 'F' test. The decrease in the positive attitude seems to set in significantly after the 30 years and thereafter it accelerates to reach a low of 8.72 in the age group 60–70. These results reject the hull hypothesis set up earlier stating that there are no differences in the attitude towards future among the successive age groups.

The results indicate that individuals in the younger ages exhibit a generally favourable attitude towards future. But in the older ages, particularly late in middle-age or early in old age, the individual suffers a shrinkage in the perception of his future. There is a decrease in the positive and favourable attitude towards future.

The individual's visualization of his personal future, while young in years, is liable to be rosy and full of hope. But later in life as the number of years that are left to live becomes lesser than those already spent and as the signs of the onset of old age show themselves up his conception of future shrinks and his fantasy of the future perhaps becomes dim and punctuated with apprehensions. It may be characterized by growing emptiness of outlook for the future with increasing apprehension of the proximity of death as there may not be anything extraordinary to look forward to in life at that stage. The feeling of the proximity of the end of existence, the growing physical incapacity due to onset of old age may unfavourably influence his attitude towards the perception of his personal futurity.

References

Abbutt, C.E. (1943): "The Apparent Time Acceleration with Age". *Science,* 58: 307–408.

Frank, L.K. (1939): "Time Perspective". *Journal of Social Psychology,* 4: 293–312.

Freud, S. (1953): "Formulations Regarding the Two Principles of Mental Functioning" in *Collected Papers,* Vol. IV, London: Hogarth.

Hartman, H. (1958): *Ego Psychology and the Problem of Adaptation.* Translated by David Rapaport, New York: Intern. Univ. Press.

Israeli, N. (1933): "Measurement of Attitudes and Reactions to the Future". *Journal of Abnormal Social Psychology.* 28: 181–193.

Kastenbaum, R. (1959): "Time and Death in Adolescence" in H. Feifel (Ed.) *The Meaning of Death,* McGraw-Hill, New York, pp. 99–113.

Kastenbaum, R. (1961): "The Dimensions of Future Time Perspective: An Experimental Analysis". *Journal of Genetic Psychology*. 65, 203–218.

Kastenbaum, R. (1966): On the Meaning of Time in Later Life. *Journal of Genetic Psychology*, 109: 9–25.

Leshan, L.L. (1952): "Time Orientation and Social Class". *Journal of Abnormal Social Psychology* 47: 589–592.

Lewin, K. (1935): *A Dynamic Theory of Personality*, New York, McGraw Hill.

Ramamurti, P.V. (1968): A Study of Some Factors Related to the Adjustment of Urban Aged Men. Unpublished Doctoral Dissertation, S.V. University.

Teahan, J.E. (1958): "Future Time Perspective, Optimism and Achievement". *Journal of Abnormal Social Psychology*. 57: 370–380.

Wallace, M. (1956): "Future Time Perspective in Schizophrenia". *Journal of Abnormal Social Psychology*. 55: 240–245.

Wallach, M.A. and Green, L.R. (1951): "On Age and Subjective Speed of Time". *Journal Gerontology*, 16: 71–74.

CHAPTER 13

A Study of Students' Stereotypes Towards Ageing

K.L. Sharma and Prabha Bhandari

The aged and the ageing were a problem in primitive society, a problem in pre-industrialized society, remains a problem in modern society and will become more so in the future. The ageing process and the aged themselves, whether a minority or a majority group, are integrally involved in total society. Their roles, statuses, care and functions are intimately related to the economics and politics of the society.

Societies tend to be age-graded with expectations and appropriate roles determined by tradition and social functions and far less by individual assessment and actual capabilities. The roles, statuses and physical and psychological characteristics of different stages and physical and psychological characteristics of different stages in the life cycles are soon learned and incorporated into ones belief system and personal economy. The beliefs themselves play a role in setting the stage for the person to behave in the manner expected by these over-generalized behavioural expectation.

Ageing is accompanied by many stereotyped beliefs and these in turn are dominantly negative in outlook, regardless of country involved (Arnhoff et al., 1964). It appears to be difficult for anyone to see ageing as anything but a 'negative process' with the old viewed as more conservative, less active and less fit by students (Axelord and

IJG, 1970, Vol. 2, No. 1 and 2, pp. 20–27.

Eisdorfer, 1961; Eisdorfer and Altorcchi, 1961), by working people (Meltzer, 1960) and even by gerontologists (Arnhoff and Lorge, 1960).

The purpose of the present study was to find out students' stereotypes towards ageing. It was hypothesized that males and females do differ in their stereotypes towards ageing. It was further hypothesized that subjects having older people in their families have realistic rather than fancy attitude in comparison to the subjects not having older members in their families.

Method

200 unselected students (100 males and 100 females) of the University of Rajasthan, Jaipur (India) were the subjects of this study.

The "Attitude towards old people questionnaire" (Arnhoff et al., 1964), consisting of a 100 statements about old people, was administered individually, the 100 statements of the questionnaire reflect misconceptions, stereotypes and over-generalized beliefs about old people.

These 100 items may be classified under 12 areas viz.:

(1) Conservatism (5 times), (2) Activities and interests (5 items), (3) Financial (8 items), (4) Physical (12 items), (5) Family (9 items), (6) Personality (27 items), (7) Attitudes towards the future (5 items), (8) Best time of life (5 items), (9) Insecurity (4 items), (10) Mental deterioration (10 items), (11) Sex (4 items), (12) Interference (6 items). The respondent was asked to check either 'yes' or 'no' for each item indicating his agreement as to whether he accepts or rejects the statement as being generally true to old people.

The mean present agreement (True) was calculated for each item by males and females (Table 1). The percentage then served as the basic data for all further analysis.

Mean for all the 12 areas was computed separately for both the sexes (Table 4). To see the sex difference in the amount and degree of emphasis to each area, rank-order-correlation and chi-square value for each area was found out. To measure the difference in the degree of factuality and fancy in stereotypes of the subjects having older people and the subjects not having older people in their family, χ^2 values on the basis of total mean of scores were computed.

Results and Discussion

Table 1

Showing the per cent agreement (Yes) for each item by males and females

Item No.	For all the respondents		χ²
	Male N=100	Female N=100	
1	2	3	
1. Conservative			
40	75	82	1.416
57	71	79	1.707
70	78	76	0.113
74	56	61	0.515
39	75	68	1.202
2. Activities and interest			
17	77	85	0.208
21	49	50	0.208
36	67	68	0.228
76	60	69	1.769
79	70	85	7.885*
3. Financial			
19	30	63	21.887
23	54	54	0.000
25	30	31	2.359
37	75	78	2.503
61	55	55	0.202
67	59	33	13.607*
78	67	67	0.000
86	50	56	0.723
4. Physical			
18	53	71	6.877*
28	69	75	0.893
35	51	57	0.725

Cont'd...

Cont'd...

	53	64	59	0.665
	66	57	75	7.219*
	77	54	58	0.325
	87	54	60	0.735
	88	69	69	0.000
	89	64	74	3.693
	90	59	57	12.180
	98	63	75	4.140*
	100	57	70	3.645
5. Family				
	8	78	86	2.168
	10	32	35	0.210
	13	51	55	0.020
	14	77	81	0.482
	31	60	64	0.567
	41	66	61	0.539
	45	77	86	2.685
	54	65	83	8.420*
	91	69	82	4.565*
6. Personality				
	4	84	80	0.7484
	6	70	67	0.092
	7	34	38	0.3473
	9	82	80	0.1298
	11	65	75	0.1488
	16	47	66	7.3460*
	29	72	70	0.0971
	30	67	71	0.3741
	33	46	60	3.9330*
	43	70	73	0.228
	47	79	80	0.0307
	48	60	74	4.5000*

Cont'd...

Cont'd...

	51	71	71	0.0000
	58	66	67	0.0224
	59	50	63	3.438
	63	46	60	3.933*
	64	60	61	0.020
	68	59	57	0.082
	71	31	34	0.192
	81	62	47	0.504
	82	67	63	0.411
	85	55	69	4.159*
	93	69	80	3.196
	95	65	61	0.396
	96	67	80	4.609*
	97	75	80	0.716
	99	68	74	1.190
7. Attitudes towards the future				
	24	54	71	6.163*
	32	67	79	3.653
	54	69	76	1.228
	60	67	81	5.093*
	65	58	62	0.333
8. Best time of life				
	2	34	33	0.355
	34	57	71	4.253*
	69	47	48	0.480
	84	57	63	0.750
	94	40	41	0.025
9. Insecurity				
	12	71	81	2.742
	20	53	56	0.181
	80	75	80	0.717
	83	36	38	0.086

Cont'd...

Cont'd...

10. Mental deterioration			
1	42	40	0.080
5	53	58	0.506
15	50	65	4.603
26	43	61	6.486
27	74	75	0.026
50	62	69	3.767
52	60	50	2.020
53	64	59	0.527
75	67	75	1.554
92	50	64	3.997*
11. Sex			
42	51	55	0.321
49	51	60	1.690
56	48	69	9.080*
73	61	64	0.190
12. Interference			
3	35	45	2.080
22	59	60	0.020
38	70	76	0.910
46	55	62	1.009
62	71	80	2.180
72	41	47	0.700

*Significant at the level of 0.05

Table 2

Showing mean per cent agreement (Yes) for the total scale

Variables compared		*Mean yes (%)*	χ^2	*Level of significance*
1. All respondents	(N=200)	61.95	5.70	0.05
2. Male	(N=100)	59.05	0.35	ns
3. Female	(N=100)	64.86		

Cont'd...

Cont'd...

4. Having older persons in the family	(N=140)	63.12	0.058	ns
5. Not having older persons in the family	(N=60)	57.85		
6. Males having older persons	(N=68)	59.79	0.06	ns
7. Males not having older persons	(N=32)	57.33		
8. Females having older persons	(N=72)	66.45	0.69	ns
9. Females not having older persons	(N=28)	58.37		
10. Males having older persons	(N=68)	59.79	0.66	ns
11. Females having older persons	(N=72)	66.45		
12. Males not having older persons	(N=32)	57.33	0.006	ns
13. Females not having older persons	(N=28)	58.37		

Table 3

Showing mean per cent agreement (Yes) for the 12 areas covered by the questionnaire

Areas	*Male N=100*	*Female N=100*	*χ^2 value for females and males**
1. Conservatives	71.00	73.20	1.20
2. Activities and interest	64.60	73.40	1.81
3. Financial	52.50	54.75	0.12
4. Physical	59.50	66.66	1.08

Cont'd...

Cont'd...

5.	Family	64.22	70.22	0.11
6.	Personality	62.70	66.14	0.25
7.	Attitudes towards the future	63.00	73.80	2.68
8.	Best time of life	47.00	51.20	0.35
9.	Insecurity	58.75	63.75	0.05
10.	Mental deterioration	57.40	61.60	0.36
11.	Sex	52.75	62.00	1.74
12.	Interference	55.18	61.66	0.86

*not significant.

The findings of the present study (see Table 2) show a predominance of negative attitudes and beliefs about the ageing and the aged [Mean per cent agreement (yes) for all the respondents (N<200)=61.95; No=38.05, χ^2=5.70, P=0.05]. The areawise analysis of the data (see Table 3) reveals that the highest degree of negative attitude has been shown in the area of conservatism. On the basis of these findings it may be stated that statements like "Old people dislike any changes or interference with established ways of doing things" (Item No. 40). "Old people respect tradition" (Item No. 70) etc., are generally associated with older persons. This negative attitude indicates a minority group position for the aged and more emphasis on youth orientation in India. In psychological theory man is seen as constructing his future, behaving and moving in direction calculated to fulfil his expectations (Kelly, 1955). Viewed from this angle, old people are the people who are thought to be more inactive type, having no hope from the future and having other worldly attitude. Both the orientation as mentioned above and changing nature of social bond due to social factors like family disintegration, and economic factors like unemployment etc., are responsible for the devalued and low status for the aged.

Table 2 further reveals that the group comprising of subjects (both males and females) who had older members in their families showed a more negativistic attitude towards old and ageing (M=63.12) than the subjects who did not have any old member in their family (M=57.85). The inter-group and intra-group calculations for sex differential reveals that the females have more negative attitudes (M=64.5) than males (M=59.05). The means for females having old people in their family and not having them are respectively – 66.45 and 58.37. The respective mean for the males are 59.79 and 57.33. The obtained data hints that the attitude towards old people are formed not only on the basis of hearsay but even more pronounced is the effect of personal contact. This is more true, possible, for female subjects who have to spend more time around old persons than male subjects who are away from the home for longer hours than their female counterparts. Even when they are at home there is very little communication with the old person in the family.

Table 2 also indicates that there are mean differences in the negativistic attitudes towards old people between those having old persons in the family and those not having them but the difference is not significant.

References

Arnhoff, F.N. and Lorge, I. (1969), "Stereotypes about Aging and the Aged". *Sch. Soe.*, 88, 70–71.

Arnhoff, F.N., Leon Henery V. and Lorge Irving (1964), "Cross-cultural Acceptance of Stereo-types towards Ageing", *J.Soc. Psychol*, Vol. 63, pp. 41–58.

Axelrod, S. and Eisdorfer, C. (1961), "Attitudes towards Old People: An Empirical Analysis of the Stimulus". *J. Gerontol.* 16, 340–43.

Eisdorfer C. and Altrochhi, J. (1961), "A Comparison of Attitudes toward Old Age Mental Illness". *J. Gerontol.* 16, 340–443.

Kelly, G.A. (1955), *The Psychology of Personal Constructs.* Vol. 1. New York: Norton.

Meltzer, H. (1960), "Workers Perceptual Stereotypes of Differences". *Percept. Mot. Skills,* 11, 89.

CHAPTER 14

Images of Ageing

K.L. Sharma

What we think about a person influences how we will perceive him. How we perceive him influences, how we will behave towards him and how we behave towards him ultimately shapes who is. Ageing is accompanied by many stereotyped beliefs, which usually, are dominantly negative in outlook, regardless of culture and country in consideration. When someone misjudges another person because of his age, this is known as inequality or *ageism*. The term ageism was coined by Robert Butler (1969), to describe "a process of systematic stereotyping or discrimination against people because they were old". He linked it to other forms of bigotry such as racism and sexism. Traxler (1980) defined ageism "as any attitude, action, or institutional structure which subordinates a person or group because of age or any assignment of roles in society purely on the basis of age". Today, it is more broadly defined as any prejudice or discrimination against or in favour of an age group (Palmore, 1990). Attitudes and values provide foundations for the beliefs that shape and guide our perceptions of and responses to social groups like the aged.

Ageist images of the elderly such as: senile, sedentary, sexless and spent-force are generally taken for granted as facts (Hess, 1974; Boone, 1985). Commonly used phrases such as "don't be an old fuddy-buddy" denote old age as a period of impotency and incompetency (Nuessel, 1982).

Persons subjected to prejudice and discrimination tend to adopt the dominant group's negative image and to behave in ways that

IJG, 2002, Vol. 16, Nos. 3 and 4, pp. 286–297.

confirm to that negative image (Palmore, 1990). Furthermore, the dominant group's negative image typically includes a set of behavioural expectation or perceptions, which define what a person is to do and not to do. For example, the elderly are expected to be asexual, intellectually rigid, unproductive, forgetful, happy, enjoy their retirement and also be invisible, passive and uncomplaining. Palmore (1990) identifies four common responses of elders to these prescriptions and exceptions: acceptance, denial, avoidance or reform. All these responses can have harmful effects on the individuals. For example, they stop or reduce social activities, refuse to take appropriate medical treatment or accept poverty. In essence, this internalization of a negative image can result in the elderly person becoming prejudiced against him/herself, resulting in loss of self-esteem, self-hatred, shame, depression and/or suicide in extreme cases. Ultimately stereotypes are dehumanizing and promote one-dimensional thinking about others. Elders are not seen as human beings but as objects who, therefore, can be more easily denied opportunities and rights. A final consequence of ageism is that by devaluating this segment of the population, a vital human resource is lost. This is contrary to Indian values or many other countries, which entail respect for human worth and dignity. Cumulatively, the elderly represent a vast amount of experience, skill and knowledge which present generation needs to remain strong and true to their ideals.

Ageist myths and stereotypes are perpetuated in many ways, such as by family influences, lack of education and the popular media (Keith, 1977). The young and old rarely have meaningful interactions outside the family (Peacock and Talley, 1984). As a result, the young are inclined to view the old stereotypically and do not appreciate that they too would get old some day. It is also to be noted that we are tempted to apply developed labels from one setting or culture to elsewhere without much introspection. If these labels are consistently employed by the majority of people, especially by those with greater social standing, then these labels become self-fulfilling prophecies (Rodin and Langer, 1980). The irony is that the old persons are the most heterogeneous of any age groups as well as age differently biologically, psychologically and sociologically. It is significant to note that some time the old also share this same homogeneous stereotype even though generally perceiving them to be exceptions.

The unfounded myths about the ageing process or stereotypes of older people need to be exposed and it is important for the younger generation to develop healthy and realisitic views of the elderly (Tibbitts, 1979; Peacock and Talley, 1984). According to the National Academy for Teaching and Learning about Ageing of the United States, three areas of focus for an ageing education are involved: attitudes, the ageing process and issues of an ageing society. Younger generation in general need practical understanding of ageing that is applicable to daily life. The way younger generation view old people can effect the way they view their own ageing process.

As we have seen that much research has been conducted concerning ageism. However, the empirical evidence is inconclusive. Some research demonstrates the existence of ageist attitudes (Tuckman and Lorge, 1953; Gold and Kogan, 1959; Kastenbaum and Durkee, 1964a, 1964b) and other research does not (Brubaker and Power, 1976; Schonfield, 1982). This discrepancy is most likely the result of methodological differences and in particular, methodological error. Another problem with much of ageism research is that it only examines the negative stereotypes of old age. More recent studies have suggested that while attitudes towards the aged are increasingly positive, they are still stereotypic (Austin, 1985).

The present study was conducted on the unselected 600 college going students (300 male students and 300 female students) of Jaipur (Rajasthan, India) to find out the degree of ageism in these students. For this purpose these students were asked how they rate themselves and older persons on the same problem. It was hypothesized that males and females differ in their stereotypes towards ageing (degree of ageism). It was further hypothesized that subjects having older persons in their family have realisitic rather than fancy attitude in comparison to the subjects not having older members in their families.

Method

A questionnaire containing a set of six problems: (1) Not having enough money to live comfortably, (2) Poor health, (3) Loneliness, (4) Lack of proper housing, (5) Not having work to keep oneself busy and (6) Fear of criminal attack on oneself. The questionnaire contained the following two sets of instructions:

"Below are given six problems that other people have mentioned to us. You please put a mark of right against each problem to indicate that it is a serious problem, somewhat a problem or not a problem *for you personally*."

"Please read these problems again and put a mark of right against each problem indicating how serious a problem you think is *for most of people over 65+*."

To find out the level of difference between the perception of self and the perception of people 65+ only the responses given as "a serious problem" to each problem were considered for analysis. Percentages of responses were calculated for each problem for self and for other 65+. The same procedure was adopted to see sex difference and differences in the responses of those respondents who had elderly person in the family and who did not have elderly in their family. To find out the degree of ageism, differences (in terms of percentages) between two degree of groups (in terms of percentages) were calculated.

Results and Discussion

The data presented in Table 1 shows a clear-cut difference in the perception of problems for oneself and for elderly persons. The respondents are of the view that elderly persons have more financial problems, they *do not have enough money to live comfortably* (the seriousness of this problem for self is 29% and for 65+ or elderly is 38% and the difference between these two groups is 9%) and *have poor health* (difference between the perception of seriousness of problem for self and for 65+ is 22%), they are *lonely* (difference between the perception of seriousness of problem for self and for 65 + is 15%), *have nothing to do* (difference between the perception of seriousness of problem for self and for 65+ is 10%). The difference between self and other 65+ for other two problems (lack of proper housing 9%) and fear of criminal attack on oneself (3%) is not very significant. These findings support Richard Kalish's (1979) notion of the New Ageism "... ageism stereotypes the elderly in terms of the characteristics of the least capable, least healthy, lonely, inactive ... it perceives the older persons as, ineffective, relatively helpless dependent individual who receives the support services of agencies ... it encourages the development services without adequate concern as to whether the outcome of these services contributes to reduction of freedom for participants to make decisions controlling their lives."

Table 1

Per cent of subjects (N=600) saying the problem is very serious for oneself and for elderly (65+)

	Problems	Responses		
		Self (%)	Elderly (%)	Diff. (%)
1	not having enough money to live	172 (29)	225 (38)	9
2	poor health	112 (19)	245 (41)	22
3	loneliness	119 (20)	211 (41)	15
4	lack of proper housing	57 (10)	104 (17)	7
5	not having work to keep busy	101 (17)	160 (27)	10
6	fear of criminal attack	80 (13)	95 (16)	3

It is interesting to note that the respondents not having old persons in their family have greater degree of stereotype in comparison to those who have older persons in their family (see Table 2).

Table 2

Per cent of subjects having elderly persons in the family (N=360) and subjects not having elderly person in the family (240), Saying the problem is very serious for themselves and for others (65+)

Problems	Having elderly			Not having elderly		
	Self (%)	Elderly (%)	Diff. (%)	Self (%)	Elderly (%)	Diff. (%)
1	104 (29)	117 (33)	4	68 (28)	108 (45)	17
2	74 (21)	156 (43)	22	38 (16)	134 (56)	40
3	71 (20)	128 (36)	16	48 (20)	115 (48)	28
4	54 (15)	58 (16)	1	43 (18)	55 (23)	5
5	68 (18)	95 (26)	8	36 (15)	81 (34)	19
6	36 (10)	50 (14)	4	44 (18)	45 (19)	1

The difference between the perception of seriousness of the problem for self and for other 65+ in the respondents having elderly family member is less in comparison to the respondents not having elderly family member. For the respondents having elderly member in family the difference between perception of seriousness for self and other 65+ (or elderly) is there for some problems such as poor health (difference 22%), loneliness (difference 16%) and have nothing to do (8%) but this difference is greater for the respondents not having elderly family member (poor health difference 40%, loneliness 28%, have nothing to do 19%). Similarly, the difference for not having enough money is 17 per cent for not having elderly group and 4 per cent for having elderly group. The obtained data hint that, the attitudes towards old people are formed not only on the basis of hearsay but even more pronounced is the effect of personal contact. It seems that the not having group's attitude are based on the myths of ageism prevalent in the society. It is generally noticed in big cities that the young and old rarely have meaningful interactions. In a study conducted by the Centre on Ageing at the University of Maryland, it was found that children of all ages had limited knowledge and negative attitudes about old people. In fact, only 39 of the 180 children surveyed were able to name an older person they know outside of the family. As a result, the young are inclined to view the old stereotypically and do not think about their own ageing.

Table 3

Per cent of male subjects (300) and female subjects (300) saying the problem is very serious for themselves and for others (65+)

Problems	*Having elderly*			*Not having elderly*		
	Self (%)	*Elderly (%)*	*Diff. (%)*	*Self (%)*	*Elderly (%)*	*Diff. (%)*
1	85 (28)	120 (40)	12	87 (29)	105 (35)	6
2	46 (15)	172 (57)	42	66 (22)	73 (24)	2
3	58 (19)	141 (47)	28	61 (20)	70 (23)	3
4	53 (18)	63 (21)	3	44 (15)	41 (14)	1
5	55 (18)	121 (30)	12	46 (16)	39 (13)	3
6	41 (14)	54 (18)	4	39 (13)	41 (13)	0

The Table 3 reveals that in comparison to female subjects male subjects perceive elderly more stereotypically. The difference in the perception of seriousness of the problem is greater for male respondents in comparison to female respondents. For problem 1 the difference between self and other 65+ (or elderly) for female respondents is 6 per cent and for male respondents this difference is 12 per cent. In the similar way for other problems this difference is greater (see Table 3). The perception of less negative image of elderly by female respondents is due to the fact that in India female members of the family spend more time around the elderly family member. The male members of the family are away from the home for longer period of time than their female counterparts. Even when male members are at home there is very little communication with the old person in the family. The data presented in the table below substantiates this view. The female respondents not having elderly persons in their family perceived elderly more negatively than the female respondents having elderly persons in their family (see Table 4).

Table 4

Per cent of female subjects having elderly persons in the family (N = 182) and not having elderly person in the family (N = 118) saying the problem is very serious for themselves and for others (65+)

Problems	*Having elderly*			*Not having elderly*		
	Self (%)	*Elderly (%)*	*Diff. (%)*	*Self (%)*	*Elderly (%)*	*Diff. (%)*
1	56 (31)	52 (29)	2	31 (26)	53 (45)	19
2	51 (28)	60 (33)	5	15 (13)	58 (49)	36
3	46 (25)	47 (26)	1	15 (13)	55 (47)	34
4	27 (15)	25 (14)	1	17 (14)	24 (20)	4
5	32 (18)	30 (16)	2	14 (12)	25 (21)	9
6	18 (09)	21 (11)	2	21 (18)	21 (17)	1

It is interesting to note that for female respondents having elderly family member the difference in the perception of seriousness of problem for oneself and for other 65+ (or elderly) is to a great extent similar. The data suggest that there is not much difference in the perception of seriousness of problem for self and elderly in having elderly member in family group. It suggests a similarity in sexism and ageism. The female respondents not having elderly members in the family perceived that elderly have poor health (difference between the perception of seriousness of problem for self and for other 65+ is 36%), they are lonely (difference 34%) do not have financial security (difference 19%) and have nothing to do (difference 9%). For other two problems this difference is not significant.

The same is not completely true for the male respondents having elderly family member and not having elderly family member. The difference between the responses of the subjects having elderly in the family and not having elderly in family is not very significant in the perception of some problems (see Table 5).

Table 5

Per cent of male subjects having elderly persons in the family (N = 178) and not having elderly person in the family (N = 122) saying the problem is very serious for themselves and for others (65+)

Problems	*Having elderly*			*Not having elderly*		
	Self (%)	*Elderly (%)*	*Diff. (%)*	*Self (%)*	*Elderly (%)*	*Diff. (%)*
1	48 (27)	65 (37)	10	37 (30)	55 (45)	15
2	23 (13)	96 (54)	41	23 (19)	76 (62)	43
3	25 (14)	81 (46)	32	33 (27)	60 (49)	22
4	27 (15)	32 (16)	1	26 (21)	31 (25)	4
5	33 (19)	65 (37)	18	22 (18)	56 (46)	28
6	18 (10)	29 (16)	6	23 (19)	25 (20)	1

On the basis of the difference between perception of seriousness of problem for self and for other 65+ it may be said that the male respondents, not having elder family member, are of the view that elderly persons have poor health (62%), have nothing to do (46%) are lonely (49%) and not have enough money to survive (45%). Almost 25 per cent of these respondents are of the view that older people do not have proper living facilities and 20 per cent believe that older persons have threat to their lives. The difference in the perception of seriousness of these problems for self and for other 65+ (or elderly) is for these six problems also indicate that these respondents are of the view that older persons have poor health (difference 43%), are one (difference 22%) have nothing to do (difference 28) and have financial problems (15%). For remaining two problems the difference in their perception is not very significant.

According to the male respondents having elderly family member, old persons have poor health (54%), are lonely (46%), have nothing to do (37%), not have enough money to survive (37%) and have threat for life (16%). The degree of difference in the perception of seriousness of problem for self and for elderly in decreasing order is as follows: elderly are lonely (difference 32%), have poor health (difference 41%), they have nothing to do (difference 18%), not have enough money to live (difference 10%) fear of criminal attack (6%). The difference in the responses for last problem (elderly do not have proper living space) is only one per cent. It is interesting to note that for this group the difference for elderly have fear of criminal attack is 6 per cent while for respondents not having elderly this difference is one per cent only.

Respondents, both male and female having elderly member in the family perceive these problems for self approximately in similar way. 28% female respondents of this group feel that they have poor health while only 13 per cent male respondents reported that they have poor health. For problem of loneliness the difference between male and female respondents is 11 per cent. Female respondents (25%) feel loneliness. About 31 per cent female respondents reported that they lack money to live comfortably and for 27 per cent male respondents this problem is serious. The difference between male and female is only 4 per cent. It means both the groups think alike about these problems for self. Both male and female subjects of having 65+ group have different opinion about the seriousness of problem for elderly. The maximum difference is about the health of elderly (difference is 21%). Next comes loneliness (20%), no work to keep busy (difference 11%), lack of money to live comfortably (difference 8%). For other remaining problems this difference is not significant. The male respondents have greater degree of stereotyping.

Both male and female subjects not having elderly family member differ in their opinion about the seriousness of problem for self. Almost 30% male subjects and 26% female subjects feel that they lack money to live comfortably. It is surprising to note that 27% male and 13% female subjects have serious problem of loneliness. For no work to keep busy male (18%) and female (12%) subjects also differ. Both male and female subjects of this group equally feel that they have fear of criminal attack. Only 19 per cent male subjects reported that they have poor health and on the other hand for female this percentage was only 13 per cent. Male respondents also reported that they do not have proper housing facilities. On scrutiny of the questionnaire it was found that most of the male respondents were not residents of Jaipur and were living in rented accommodations away from their families.

Both male and female respondents not having elderly family member also have different opinions about the seriousness of problem for elderly. Fifty-five per cent of male respondents think that elderly people do not have enough money to live comfortably. Sixty two per cent of these respondents believe that elderly have poor health, 49 per cent feel loneliness, 25 per cent do not have proper housing, 48 per cent have no work to keep busy themselves and 20 per cent have fear of criminal attack. The female respondents of this group (not having elderly in family) in comparison to male respondents have lesser degree of ageism. For 45 per cent elderly lack money, 49 per cent poor health, 47 per cent loneliness, 20 per cent do not have proper housing, 21 per cent do not have work to keep themselves busy and 17 per cent feel that older persons have fear of criminal attack.

The present data reveal that those respondents having elderly member in the family do not have significant negative image of elderly in comparison to the respondents not having elderly family member. These findings have great similarity with the findings of studies conducted by the author (Sharma, 1970, 1972), which showed that the treatment older members of the family receive ranges from extreme reverence and respect to deprivation. In a sense ageism is not a universal, cross-cultural phenomenon. There appears to be a great variation as to the treatment that old people receive in different societies. Number of empirical studies suggest that attitudes towards the elderly are most favourable in primitive societies and decrease with increasing modernization to the point of generally negative view in industrialized western nations. In other words, the more 'civilized' (so-called) the societies the more likely they are to be ageist and maintain negative attitudes about the aged (McTavish, 1971). Slater (1964) has mentioned that the world 'sheikh' originally meant 'old men'. In Middle East men are viewed as having attained high status and prestige. The old age is life's summit. In India also, older persons were given great respect in societies. A Sanskrit verse says that one who serves and respects older persons is blessed with four things: knowledge, wisdom, power and wealth.

The cross-cultural differences in attitudes towards the aged may in part be due to difference societal perspectives (Jensen and Oakley, 1982–83). For example, those societies which view life and death as a continuous process exhibit fewer ageist attitudes in comparison to those societies which do not view death as natural part of life cycle. For example, in western societies death is not viewed as natural part of the life cycle. In traditional societies old person is not considered as non-productive. The societies like Japan, Middle East and India fewer ageist attitudes are exhibited towards older persons because in these societies older individuals are viewed as productive in many ways. Their voices are heard in decision-making processes. In western societies older persons are viewed as non-productive and therefore, negative attitudes towards older people are very common. Busse (1968) has described American society as maintaining a stereotypic and often negative perception of older adults. This negative and stereotypic perception of ageing and aged individuals is apparent in the areas of language, media and humor. All societies are not youth oriented, therefore, in such societies negative attitudes towards older persons are not very common. The increasing youth oriented trend in societies is one of the important causes of ageism.

References

Austin, D.R.: "Attitudes Towards Old Age: A Hierarchical Study". *The Gerontologist,* 25: 431–434, 1985.

Boone, D.R.: "Ageism: A Negative View of the Aged". *ASHA,* 27: 51–53, 1985.

Brubaker, T.H. and Power, E.A.: "The Stereotype of 'Old': A Review and Alternative Approach". *Journal of Gerontology,* 31: 441–447, 1976.

Busse, I.W.: "Viewpoint: Prejudice and Gerontology". *The Gerontologist,* 8:66, 1968.

Butler, R.N.: "Ageism: Another Form of Bigotry". *The Gerontologist,* 9:243–246, 1969.

Goldge, P. and Kogan, N.: "A Sentence Completion Procedure for Assessing Attitudes Towards People". *Journal of Gerontology,* 14: 355–363, 1959.

Hess, B.B.: "Stereotypes of the Aged". *Journal of Communication,* 24: 76–85, 1974.

Jensen, G.D. and Oakley, F.B.: "Ageism Across Cultures and in Perspective of Sociobiologic and Psychodynamic Theories". *International Journal of Aging and Human Development,* 15: 17–26, 1982–1983.

Kastenbaum, R. and Durkee, N.: "Elderly People View Old Age". In R. Kastenbaum (ed.), *New Thoughts on Old Age,* New York: Springer, 1964a.

Kastenbaum, R. and Durkee, N.: "Young People View Old Age". In R. Kastenbaum (ed.), *New Thoughts on Old Age,* New York: Springer, 1964.

Keith, P.M.: "An Exploratory Study of Sources of Stereotypes of Old Age among Administrators". *Journal of Gerontology,* 32: 463–469, 1977.

Mc Tavish, D.G.: "Perceptions of Old People: A Review of Research Methodologies and Findings". *The Gerontologist,* 11: 90–101, 1971.

Nuessel, F.H.: "The Language of Agism". *The Gerontologist,* 22: 273–276, 1982.

Palmore, E.: *Agism: Negative and Positive.* New York: Springer, 1990.

Peacock, E.W. and Talley, W.M.: "Intergenerational Contact: A Way of Counter Agism". *Educational Gerontology,* 10: 13–24, 1984.

Richard, Kailash: "The New Ageism and the Failure Models: A Polemic". *The Gerontologist,* 19: 398, 1979.

Rodin, J. and Langer, E.: "Aging Labels: The Decline of Control and the Fall of Self-Esteem". *Journal of Social Issue,* 36(2): 12–29, 1980.

Schonfield, D.: "Who is Stereotyping Whom and Why?" *The Gerontologist,* 22: 267–272, 1982.

Sharma, K.L.: "A Study of Students' Stereotypes Towards Aging". *Indian Journal of Gerontology,* 2(1 and 2): 20–27, 1970.

Sharma, K.L.: "A Cross-cultural Comparison of Stereotypes Towards Older Persons". *Journal of Social Work,* 315–320, 1972.

Slater, J.A.: *A Catalogue of the Lygaeidae of the World.* Storrs: University of Connecticut xviii 1668: 353, 1964.

Tibbitts, C.: "Can We Invalidate Negative Stereotypes of Aging?" *The Gerontologist,* 19: 10–20, 1979.

Traxler, A.J.: Let's Get Gerontolosed: Developing a Sensitivity to Ageing-the Multipurpose Senior Centre Concept: A Training Manual for Practitioners Working with the Aging. Springfield, IL: Illinois Department of Aging, 1980.

Tuckman, J. and Lorge, I.: "Attitudes Towards Old People". *Journal of Social Psychology,* 327: 249–260, 1953.

CHAPTER **15**

A Comparative Study of Retired and Pre-Retired Elderly on Life Attitude Profile

Akbar Husain, Meena Arya and S.M. Ashrafimam

Retired and pre-retired elderly persons' attitude towards life influence many aspects of their lives. Attitude towards life changes in different stages of the family life cycle: (a) pre-retirement, (b) retirement and (c) late retirement years. It is clear that each of these stages present a different set of challenges and issues in later life and that significantly affect the quality of life. There are a number of factors throughout the life course that are essential in maintaining positive attitudes towards life and for the well-being of the individual. Recker and Peacock (1981) have noted seven factors – life purpose, existential vacuum, life control, death acceptance, will to meaning, goal seeking, future meaning to fulfil – which are vital for predicting the attitudes towards life. The attitudes towards life has been linked to existential psychology.

This study examined the retired and pre-retired elderly person's attitudes towards life. It was possible to compare how retired and pre-retired persons express attitudes towards life when they were in stages of retirement of pre-retirement years.

Method

Sample

The sample consisted of 63 retired and 82 pre-retired persons, aged 63 to 70 years and 56 to 60 years respectively. The individuals selected

IJG, 1998, Vol. 12, No. 3 and 4, pp. 102–105.

were identified by purposive sample procedure. Retired and pre-retired persons were the teachers of AMU, Aligarh. All persons who were in re-employment during the year 1993 were excluded from the sample.

Tool

The Life Attitude Profile (LAP) developed by Recker and Peacock (1981) was employed in the study. The LAP is a 44 items and 7-point Likert scale multidimensional test for measuring attitudes towards life. The LAP is designed to assess the degree of existential meaning and purpose in life and the strength of motivation to find meaning and purpose. The LAP, deals with seven factors, namely, life purpose, existential vacuum, life control, death acceptance, will to meaning, goal seeking and future meaning to fulfil.

Procedure

The data were collected individually from the respondents by the investigators either at their residence or in their respective departments.

Result and Discussion

Pre-retired subjects have scored significantly higher than the retired subjects on life purpose ($t=2.80$, $p<0.01$), existential vacuum ($t=6.95$, $p<0.01$), life control ($t=2.18$, $p<0.01$), death acceptance ($t=9.25$, $p<0.01$), will to meaning ($t=16.06$, $p<0.01$), goal seeking ($t=13.98$, $p<0.01$) and future meaning to fulfil ($t=16.3$, $p<0.01$), factors of life attitude profile.

For pre-retired subjects as compared to retired subjects, life seems more purposeful and prone to optimism and hope. The retired people over the age of sixty would wake up with feeling of sadness every morning because of uncertainty with the life. Lack of purpose in life is borne out from the lack of responsibility for coming to terms with life. A lack of purpose in life has been described as a general indication of depression. The pre-retired subjects' high attitude towards life purpose arises from the individual's unique experience of self, family, atmosphere and sociocultural factors.

Pr-retired subjects, in comparison to retired subjects express more about emptiness in their lives in such existential terms. These findings may be interpreted from Frankl's (1963) point of view. He claimed that existential conflicts do not necessarily indicate psychological disturbances. Since life has little meaning for the retired subjects, existential vacuum does not matter much in their case. The lack of purpose in life and the lower tendency of existential vacuum among retired subjects appears to be something of a victory over their conditions.

The mean score of pre-retired subjects was found to be significantly higher than the retired subject on 'life control'. This finding implies that the life control is the resource of the self for the pre-retired subjects in the face of positive attitudes towards life, will to meaning, and in the achievement of goal. Once the lack of life control is accepted by the retired subjects, their helplessness in the universe like life, comes to have little or no meaning.

Pre-retired subjects expressed higher tendency of death acceptance than the retired subjects. Existential vacuum reflects death acceptance as the necessary component of the human condition among pre-retired subjects. The acceptance of death exerts a powerful influence on personality functioning as an outer-reflection of an inner psychological process involving the fear of the loss of the self. Acceptance of death becomes the expression of insecurity and it lingers as an empty; despairing existence of "death in life". The lower tendency of acceptance of death, as expressed by retired subjects, either reflects the expression of a well developed integrated self or the empathic concern for others.

On 'will to meaning' factor of LAP, the pre-retired subjects scored significantly higher than the retired subjects. The pre-retired subjects were thought to be unique, responsible, courageous and transcendent. Perhaps, the feeling of depression and fear of individuation contributes little will to meaning among retired subjects. The lack of will to meaning among retired persons develop the feeling of insecurity, alienation from self and problems relating to self and to others. This finding may also be interpreted from the Frankl's (1963) point of view. According to Frankl, "the primary motivation in man consists of a 'will to meaning' which is more basic than the drive for pleasure or power. This meaning is unique and specific to each person."

Pre-retired as compared to retired subjects expressed a higher tendency of goal seeking. Attaining goals and in attempting to govern life chart a personal course of direction for finding the meaning of life. The emptiness of life of the retired subjects lies rooted in the failure to

Table 1

Differences between the mean scores of retired (N=63) and pre-retired (N=82) elderly on the factors of life attitude profile

Subjects	*Mean*	*SD*	*'t' value*
	Life Purpose		
Retired	42.55	6.11	
			2.80*
Pre-retired	45.47	6.42	
	Existential Vacuum		
Retired	24.19	3.27	
			6.95*
Pre-retired	28.83	4.00	
	Life Control		
Retired	21.92	2.52	
			2.18*
Pre-retired	29.23	4.08	
	Death Acceptance		
Retired	23.76	2.74	
			9.25*
Pre-retired	28.57	3.45	
	Will to meaning		
Retired	21.80	2.46	
			16.06*
Pre-retired	29.35	3.18	
	Goal Seeking		
Retired	22.05	3.18	
			13.98*
Pre-retired	29.74	3.48	
	Future Meaning to Fulfil		
Retired	21.08	3.12	
			16.32*
Pre-retired	30.06	3.55	

*Significant at the level of 0.05%.

finding meaning in life and a goal seeking behaviour. To the retired persons, if the challenge of life is not necessarily met, than life becomes goalless or with nothingness. In other words, anxiety or frustration over a lack of purpose may easily mask goal seeking. Striving towards goal thus continues to be responsible for behaviour and opens up to experience through choices.

The tendency of 'future meaning to fulfil' was found to be significantly higher among pre-retired than the retired persons. The family pressure, possessiveness, and competition all contributes to future meaning to fulfil among pre-retired persons. On the contrary, lack of purpose in life, lower level of life control, will to meaning and goal seeking transcend the existential dilemma that leads to future meaning to fulfil among retired persons.

References

Frankl, V.E. (1963): *Man's Search for Meaning.* New York: Pocket Books.

Recker, G.T. and Peacock, E.J. (1981): "The Life Attitude Profile (LAP): A Multidimensional Instrument for Assessing Attitudes Toward Life." *Canadian Journal of Behavioural Sciences,* 13, 264–273.

CHAPTER 16

Attitudes Towards Helping Elderly People

An Indian Study

Indira Jai Prakash

A variety of studies have demonstrated the examples of negative attitudes towards the elderly. Agism (Butler, 1969), vulnerability to agism, stereotypes attached to old age (Leland, 1977), negative evaluations of older subjects (Levin, 1988) are widely discussed topics in social gerontology. The current state of the art, literature, mass media and even humor is said to reflect in anti-age attitude (Palmore, 1990; Northcott, 1975). However, there is an awareness that cultural, subcultural variations should be acknowledged before generalizing from studies based on particular sociocultural settings. In a replication of Levin's study (1988), it was found that Indian subjects held less negative attitudes towards older subjects than American subjects (Sabitha and Prakash, 1991). Old people were perceived as benevolent, nurturant and wise by a majority of subjects in another study (Rajagopalan and Prakash, 1990).

MacLean and Chown (1988) developed and used a questionnaire with British and Canadian students to determine attitudes held towards the elderly people. The items on their questionnaire (ATE) assessed people's tendency to attribute blame to the old for their poor health and low income, tendency to dismiss needs of the elderly and the extent to which people would be willing to help to keep the elderly in their own homes at public expense. In their study, 71 psychology students from England and 124 social work students from Canada were compared on ATE and the Just World Belief scale. Majority of the

IJG, 1992, Vol. 6, No. 1 and 2, pp. 44–50.

subjects were female in the age range of 18 to 25 years. The Canadian sample was more likely to attribute blame to elderly than the British sample. Both the groups did not dismiss the needs of the elderly and approved government support to help the old stay in their own homes. The pattern of interrelations between the attitudes differed for the two groups.

An attempt was made here to study the attitudes of Indian subjects, as compared to British and Canadians, towards the elderly. Since the original sample was small and mostly consisted of female students of a narrow age range, in the present study ATE was used with male and female subjects from different age group and different backgrounds.

Method

Sample

In order to get a more representative view of ATE, three age groups were selected. Subjects in the age range of 20 to 30 years were designated as Young (Y); 40 to 50 years old subjects were called Middle aged (Ma); and subjects who were 60 and above were grouped as Old (O). There were 189 male and 169 female subjects (Total N=358). Sample included students (S), working persons (W), housewives (Hw), retire people (R), Hindu (H), Muslims (M), and Christians (C). Subjects were from different areas of Bangalore city. There was no special sampling procedure. Table 1 gives details of the sample.

Table 1
Showing sample characteristics

Variable	*n*	*Variable*	*n*
Male (M)	189	Hindu (H)	264
Female (F)	169	Muslim (Mu)	30
		Christian (C)	64
Total	358		
Young (Y)	169	Working (W)	149
Middle aged (Ma)	152	Nonworking (N)	160
Old (O)	87	Retired (R)	49

Assessment of ATE

The questionnaire about Attitudes towards the Elderly People (ATE) consists of nine items (MacLean and Chown, 1988) which are scaled on a Liker scale using five degrees of agreement. Three items relate to views on the extent of old people's own responsibility for their poor health and low income. A score of 9 or more on these three-item index (AB) indicated lack of attribution of blame to the elderly. Another three items (DN) measured the extent to which subjects tended to dismiss the needs of the elderly rather then help them keep active in society. Less than 9 on this scale indicated a tendency to brush aside the needs of elderly for the convenience of the society. The final three items (PH) measured the extent to which subjects were willing to help keep the elderly in their own homes at public expense. A score of less than 9 suggested that the respondents were in favour of provision of government supported home help for elderly.

A few modifications, mainly in the language of the questionnaire, were made to make it more understandable to Indian respondent. This modified version was administered individually to 358 subjects and the responses were scored. Three indexes were derived separately for Attribution of blame (AB), Denial of need for help (DN), and Providing home help (PH). The scores on these scales are analysed separately for different groups and also for cross-cultural differences.

Results

A sample of 358 subjects giving a fair representation of different religions, work status, and age groups was assessed using ATE. Tables 2 and 3 gives the mean scores on the three scales for the groups.

The mean scores obtained by subjects in the present study for the three scales is compared with those reported for British and Canadian subjects. The significance of differences between the means is reported in Table 4.

The responses of 358 subjects to the ATE was subjected to Factor Analysis in order to determine the factor structure of the questionnaire. The method used was Principal Component method and the matrix was subjected to varimax rotation. The rotated factor matrix yielded four factors accounting for 59.3 per cent of variance. Details of the factor loadings is given in Table 5.

Table 2
Scores on ATE for the sample

Groups	*AB*		*DN*		*PH*	
	Mean	*SD*	*Mean*	*SD*	*Mean*	*SD*
Male	6.34	2.31	9.90	2.60	8.03	2.62
Female	6.49	2.23	10.76	2.41	7.11	2.47
Hindu	6.24	2.18	10.19	2.54	7.73	2.42
Christian	7.13	2.35	10.86	2.58	7.53	2.42
Muslim	6.40	2.61	10.23	2.49	6.50	2.19
Young	6.73	2.09	10.48	2.53	7.96	2.40
M. aged	6.26	2.21	10.28	2.59	7.74	2.69
Old	6.06	2.58	10.06	2.53	7.13	2.69
Wkg	6.15	2.08	10.09	2.63	7.58	2.65
Nwkg	6.84	2.28	10.63	2.43	7.71	2.49
Rtd	5.78	2.56	9.94	2.57	7.27	2.72

Table 3
't' Values between groups

Group	*AB*	*DN*	*PH*
M and F	0.63	3.01**	3.42**
Y and Ma	1.79	0.64	1.56
Y and O	2.06	1.35	2.37*
Ma and O	0.29	0.61	0.87
H and C	2.76**	1.87	0.58
H and Mu	0.32	0.08	2.85**
C and Mu	1.30	1.12	2.05*
W and Nw	2.79**	1.87	0.44
W and R	0.91	0.74	0.69
NW and R	2.61**	1.12	1.01

* $P < 0.05$; ** $P < 0.01$.

Table 4
Cross-cultural differences

Groups	*n*	*AB*		*DN*		*PH*	
		Mean	*SD*	*Mean*	*SD*	*Mean*	*SD*
Indian (I)	358	6.41	2.27	10.31	3.29	7.59	2.59
British (B)#	71	10.44	1.93	11.92	3.29	4.77	2.08
Canadian (C)#	124	9.67	2.41	12.51	2.08	5.18	2.46
't' between							
I and B		15.5**			3.90**		10.00**
I and C		13.17**			8.00**		9.25**
B and C		2.35*			0.65		1.22

values as reported by MacLean and Chown (1988).
* P < 0.05, ** P <0.01.

Table 5
Rotated factor matrix for ATE responses

Variable	*Factor-1*	*Factor-2*	*Factor-3*	*Factor-4*
Item-1	0.71355*	0.08610	0.11188	0.13975
Item-2	0.76397*	–0.12346	0.02957	0.11705
Item-3	0.09825	0.71332*	0.13689	0.04977
Item-4	0.05523	0.72253*	–0.00005	0.03471
Item-5	0.26676	0.31775	0.55824*	0.25530
Item-6	0.37747	0.35446	–0.61925*	0.06158
Item-7	0.26871	–0.8141	–0.46886	0.63842*
Item-8	0.15079	0.06111	0.14083	0.86883*
Item-9	0.19062	0.12886	0.58131*	–0.05451

*Items with high loadings.

Discussion

In this study a larger sample, more representative in terms of age, sex, work status and religions was assessed using the ATE to get a comprehensive picture of attitudes held towards the old people. Even a superficial analysis reveals several differences in the attitudes held by Indian subjects when compared to the British and Canadian subjects studied by MacLean and Chown. Indian subjects were found to attributed blame to the elderly significantly more than the other two groups. Indian subjects held the older people responsible for their ill health and their financial problems in old age. Canadian subjects had higher blame scores than British students on this scale which the author attributed to certain socio-economic differences between the two groups. Within the present sample, male subjects attribute blame to a significantly greater degree than female, young more than old and working people more than non-working and the retired. It appears as if it is the young male who is in the workforce who has the most negative attitude towards the elderly in terms of attributing blame to them for their less than favourable condition in later life. In the absence of well planned and uniformly implemented welfare schemes for elderly in India, the responsibility of caring for oneself in old age seems to rest squarely on the shoulders of the elderly themselves.

Coming to the second scale, denial of needs of the elderly, Indian subjects are willing to consider the needs of the elderly and not dismiss them for their own convenience. The score on this scale is still considerably lower than British and Canadian scores. Yet, like the other two groups, the present sample does not push aside the concerns of the elderly when it clashes with the interests of the community. Probably the cultural prescriptions that the old have to be cared for (though it is their fault if they are needy and ill) are responsible for this tendency. Storm and Strike Schurman (1985) reporting on beliefs held in a small Canadian town regarding obligations for elderly care, note that children are perceived to have a strong obligation to assist the elders. This obligation was substantially reduced by circumstances such as geographical distance and financial exigency. The obligation of the government was also strong for all but psychological needs. It was also reported that old people were more likely to stress the responsibility of the old for his or her own welfare. The youngest group was more unrealistic and absolute about children's obligations. In this study, however, older subjects are more sympathetic to cause of the elderly. There are sex differences in attitudes, with women being more considerate of the needs of the elderly than men.

Indian subjects agree with their British-Canadian counterparts that help should be provided to old people to allow them to stay in their own homes. The issue of governmental support for home help is new in India and not many are aware either of such schemes or their implications. Yet, in theory, most agree that home help should be provided to the elderly. Age and religion make a difference to scores on this scale; old being more favourable and Muslims the most favourable. Among Christians in India, institutionalization is much more acceptable than in other communities. But, when compared to British and Canadian students, the present sample has significantly higher scores on this scale.

Cross-cultural differences are evident in this study with Indians blaming the elderly to a greater extent, being less likely to consider the needs of the elderly, and less eager to support governmental schemes for home help to elderly.

ATE had been pilot tested by the author on a convenience sample of 35 subjects to determine if the questions were understandable to a variety of people. In the present study, the responses of 358 subjects were factor analysed to determine their factor structure. Because there is no empirical evidence to support the division of the ATE into three scales. As can be seen from Table 5, four factors emerged accounting for nearly 60 per cent of the variance. The first two items contributing to factor I seemed similar to the first scale, Attribution of blame. Items 3 and 4 of factor 2 were similar to Denial of needs scale of the original. Factor 3 is relatively more difficult to interpret. It contains items (5, 6 and 9) that imply that the elderly need not be treated as a special group. Factor 4 has two items that deal with the issue of government support for the cause of the elderly. In general, however, the items deal with significant attitudes that people may have toward helping the elderly people. In summary cross cultural differences do exist in attitudes toward the elderly. Indian subjects hold attitudes that could be described as less favourable, humanitarian or welfare oriented when compared to British and Canadian subjects. Age, sex, work status and religion play a role in determining the attitudes.

References

Butler, R.N. (1969): "Agism: Another Form of Bigotry". *Gerontologist,* 9: 243–246.

Leland, J.D. (1977): "Attitudes Toward Old Age and Aging as Shown by Humor". *Gerontology,* 17 (3): 220–226.

Levin, W.C. (1988): "Age Stereotyping: College Students' Evaluations". *Research Aging*. 10(1): 134–147.

MacLean, J.M. and Chown, S.M. (1988): "Just World Beliefs and Attitudes Towards Helping Elderly People: A Comparison of British and Canadian University Students". *Intl. J. Aging and Human Development*. 26 (4): 249–260.

Northcott, H. (1975): "Too Young – Too Old: Age in the Worldwide Television". *The Gerontologist*. 3 (3): 181–188.

Palmore, E. (1990): *Ageism: Negative and Positive*, New York, Springer.

Rajagopalan, I. and Prakash, I.J. (1990): "A Study of Intergenerational Attitudes on the SAT". *Ind. J. Applied Psychol.* 27 (1): 15–19.

Sabitha, K. and Prakash, I.J. (1991): "Age Stereotyping: Replication of Levin's Study". *In Quality Aging*. I.J. Prakash (Ed.), Association of Gerontology (India), Varanasi, 135–140.

Storm, C., Storm, T. and Strike Schurman, J. (1985): "Obligation for Care: Beliefs in a Small Canadian Town". *Canadian J. on Aging 4(2): 75–85.*

Section D

Problems of the Elderly

Ageing, which is an inescapable reality of the human existence on the planet earth, plays a crucial role in the global demographic transition. According to projections by the UN Population Division, there will be two elderly persons for every child in the world by 2050. This implies that the aged 60 and above, which currently constitute less than 20 per cent of the population will account for 32 per cent of the population by 2050.

Another disturbing revelation made by the UN agency is that future fertility levels in the most developing countries is expected to fall below 2.1 children per woman, the level needed to ensure the long-term replacement of the population at some point in the 21st century. As for the developed countries such as Japan and Germany, rapid graying of the population could result in an acute manpower shortage, requiring the services of the "guest workers" to run the engines of economy in these industrialized countries.

Clearly, the changing balance between the age groups would make the aged more of a burden on society, as large proportion of the resources meant for developmental activities would need to be diverted to take care of the needs of the elderly population groups. Significantly, for countries like India and Thailand, it will take only 25 years for their aged population to get doubled.

As things stand, the rapid spread of modernization, growing urbanization and crumbling of joint family system have conspired to increase insecurity and loneliness among the geriatric population. However, India has not yet come out with an appropriate policy framework to provide social security for the elders. Lack of family support, poor financial status, physical and mental disorders and guilt of being dependent on others are some of the problems nagging the elderly population in India, and other countries around the world.

In fact, an in-depth study by the New Delhi-based All India Institute of Medial Sciences (AIIMS) says that elderly women are affected more by dementia, depression and psychosomatic disorders than their male counterparts. According to this study, the population structure of the elderly is dominated by poorly educated women, economically dependent on children without any tangible authority or status in the family.

Of course, an ageing society will give rise to special problems from health, family and social angels. For instance, there will be an increasing demand for geriatricians with knowledge and expertise required to handle and treat the elderly population. From the family side, the elderly population looks forward to emotional support, love and affection. But unfortunately, the concept of a welfare state where many of the needs of the ageing population are taken care of by the state is being criticized by agencies, such as the World Bank, which are keen that governments provide only minimum levels of social security to the elderly population groups.

As sociologists point out, the biggest enemies of the geriatric population include solitude, loneliness, isolation, neglect and a sense of not being wanted. In order to combat loneliness, the elderly population should interact with their friends, families and neighbours. Regular exercise and intake of a balanced diet will go a long way towards helping the elderly population maintain its physical fitness and mental poise.

Giving up alcohol, quitting smoking, avoiding stress and indulging in rest and relaxation are some of the other vital steps to turn the old age into a veritable blessing. In fact, in recent years, there has emerged a new professional group of geriatric animators who are well equipped to deal with the special problems of the senior citizens.

In addition to shelter, medicare and nutritional problems, the elderly population in India is also buffeted by a multidimensional socio-psychological pressure. Sometime back, the UN Secretary General Kofi Annan, while referring to the ageing population had observed: "Trees grow stronger over the years, river wider and like with the age, human beings gain immeasurable depth and breadth of experience and wisdom. That is why older persons should not only be respected and revered but they should be utilized as the rich resource to society that they are".

Unfortunately, very little attention has been focused on the pitiable plight of the elderly population in rural areas of the country. Field studies pertaining to the problems of the aged in rural India reveal that deteriorating health and economic insecurity are the most pressing problems facing the elderly population in the villages.

As pointed out by a sociologist, in spite of their poor physical and mental health, the aged males are forced to work to eke out a living. Similarly, in the absence of financial support from family and old-age pension schemes of the state governments, the plight of ageing population in the rural backyards of the country has assumed serious dimensions. In the ultimate analysis, what matters for the elderly is that whether they would be able to spend the last days of their life with support in terms of shelter and nutrition either from family or society.

On another front, an increasing number of older persons are falling prey to geriatric diseases such as rheumatism, arthritis, osteoporosis, dementia, cardiac complications and mental depression. A paper on the mental health of the ageing population by Dr Vikram Patel and Martin Prince, points out that in the developing world, including India, the aged with psychological problems do not get the required medical attention. In particular, the study found that while dementia is considered a normal process of ageing that a doctor cannot help much depression is rarely diagnosed or treated. Programme for the aged should deal with their physical, psychological and emotional needs. For loneliness and a sense of guilt on being dependent on the family continues to haunt them with sustained vigour. As such sociologists suggest that the aged should be made to involve themselves in creative and developmental programmes.

Summary of the Papers

The empirical studies included in this section deal with the various aspects of problems of senior citizens. Vidya Raghani and N.K. Singhi surveyed the problems of retired persons. Retirement brings two sets of consequences: (1) it offers freedom from one's long time career activity, relief from the stress of jobs and opportunity to develop new interests and activities and (2) retirement (generally) results in loss of routine with regard to utilization of one's working hours, reduction of income, reduced challenges to one's physiological performance-potential, loss of status as a contributor to economy and broken contacts with customary associations. In other words retired persons have to face loss of status, control, loneliness and alienation from the family and society.

The major problems felt by these respondents were: shortage of money, problem of passing time, widowhood, feeling of being physically weak, fear of death, mental tensions, feeling of social neglect, feeling of neglect by family and neglect by friends. In other words these problems may broadly be classified as health related problems, economic problems, financial, psychological, interpersonal relationship and proper use of time (leisure time activities).

World Health Organisation has defined health as a " state of complete physical, mental, social and spiritual well-being and not merely the absence of disease or infirmity". Health is obviously an important factor in the lives of the aged. Health status is a factor that has a bearing in almost every single aspect of our lives. It can determine what activities or tasks we can (not) engage in. Health can also effect the way we perceive ourselves.

Saroj Rathore in her paper entitled " A Comparative Study of Emotional Problems in Old and Middle-aged Men" compared two groups of respondents (30 old men over 60 years and middle-aged men age ranging 35–45 years) on different measures of emotional problems through Karolinksa Scale of Personality (KSP). She found that the old men have scored significantly higher on somatic anxiety, psychic anxiety, muscular tension, suspicion, inhibition of aggression and psychasthenia as compared to their middle-aged male counterparts. Old men's scores were significantly lower on socialization than the middle-aged ones. No significant differences in these two groups were found on the measures such as guilt, indirect aggression, verbal aggression, detachment, social desirability and irritability.

Abuse is a most frustrating thing in the lives of the elderly. In India we proclaim reverence for the elderly but its presence could be felt even in India. There are several types of elder abuse like assault, deprivation of food and deprivation of medical care and non-supply of prescribed drugs, emotional abuse, involuntary confinement and isolation, financial abuse, legal abuse etc. The prolonged abuse causes lots of psychological disorders like hysteria, phobia, compulsive and hypochondriac behaviour in elderly persons. S. Ushasree and S. Azmal Basha in their paper, "Domestic Abuse Among Elderly" studied 75 rural elderly of both the sexes residing in homes for aged. They identified the types of abuse the elderly were exposed. Results showed gender differences and ability differences in the percentages of physical, psychological, material and legal abuse which the subjects were exposed to.

The family serves as a fundamental structure for living together intimately and sharing economic, social and emotional responsibilities. The problems (such as financial, health and psycho-social problems of adjustment) faced by elderly are managed by the family, which is the primary care giver for its aged members. The belief, that the elderly face lesser problems in India due to the respect for elderly in the family and society than in West, is changing slowly. Because the traditional joint family system has wilted to be replaced by nuclear families with no room for old parents on the last phase of their lives. In the paper "Family Relations of the Elderly after Retirement and Widowhood" by Renu Malhotra and N.K. Chadha, have attempted to understand the impact of family support on the retired pensioners and non-pensioners and also the impact of widowhood on the status of the one hundred middle class elderly persons. The results indicate the changes in family relations, decision making, more closeness with some family member, topics of conversations, dependency and preference to live independently or willingness to stay in old age homes etc.

Overall economic condition and family responsibilities of elderly persons' have greater impact on the future life of the pensioners. The occupational career of an individual enabled him to fulfill his family obligations such as children's education, their marriage, housing problems and other social responsibilities. The pension amount will not be sufficient for those who have to fulfill certain family responsibilities and social obligations. A.L. Srivastava studied 400 retired persons. Almost 50 per cent respondents were of the view that the pension amount is sufficient for them. About 89.50 per cent wanted enhancement of pension amount. Some respondents complained about the behaviour of pension authorities, delay in the payment of pension etc.

Each development stage has its own uniqueness and tasks which are to be mastered and roles to be played by the individual. In the present phase of human history, life has become more charged with stresses and strains, despite tremendous technological advancements. R.K. Gunthey and Sarita Mathur administered JMPI (three broad areas – psychosis, psychoneurosis and psycho-somatic disorders) on 270 subjects of different age groups. The results indicate that a cluster of psychiatric problems have a continuous acceleration across the age. The physiological, psychological as well as the socio-economic changes with age may be the cause of greater severity of mental health problems in later period of life.

Priya Kumar and N.K. Chadha in their paper "Retirement and Aging: Leisure Activities and Health Ailments" tried to find out: (1) actual health status which comprises of the individual's physical state and (2) perceived health status, which is the individual's own perception about his health with respect to the others of his age. They have enlisted 17 common health complaints suffered by the aged. They also studied the leisure activities pursued by them and their effect on the well-being.

CHAPTER **17**

A Survey of the Problems of Retired Persons

Vidya Raghani and Narendra K. Singhi

A number of empirical studies have been conducted to explore the factors associated with successful adjustment in old age. The studies of Morgan (1937), Landis (1942), Cavan et al. (1949), Burgess (1954) have concluded that the satisfying health, family relationships and friendships, participation in leisuretime and other activities, feeling of permanent security, social status equal to that held previously, plans for the future participation of religious activities and beliefs in life after, are the principle factors which are positively related with good adjustment of old people.

Kunter (1955) found that significance of the factors associated with adjustment of the older people varied among different cultural settings. In other words, a variable positively related to adjustment for one socio-economic group might be negatively related to another group.

Supporting Kuhlen's conclusion regarding the validity of instrument used in previous studies and lack of external criteria of good and poor adjustment, it can be further concluded that emphasis should be given to the effects of retirement upon the individual and the determinants of good and poor adjustment after separation from work (retirement) another than establishing characteristics of the well adjusted old persons.

According to Friedman and Havighurst (1954) retirement brings two sets of consequences. (1) It offers freedom from one's long time

IJG, 1970, Vol. 2, No. 1 and 2, pp. 34–37.

career activity, relief from the stresses of jobs and opportunity to develop new interests and activities. (2) Retirement (generally) results in loss of routine with regard to utilization of one's working hours, reduction of income, reduced challenges to one's physiological performance potential, loss of status as a contribute to economy and broken contacts with customary associations. In other words, retired persons have to face loss of status, control, loneliness and alienation from the family and society. The purpose of the present study was to survey the problems faced by retired persons, their loneliness, the behaviour of family members towards retired persons, the opinion of these respondents towards the age of retirement was also studied.

Method

A questionnaire comprising items on various sets of problems of aged people was used to collect the data.

100 unselected retired persons: 50 gazetted officers and 50 non-gazetted (subordinates) retired servants of Rajasthan state government, of age ranging from 60 to 84 years were the subjects of this study.

Results and Discussion

Loneliness

A number of studies have been devoted to the loneliness of the aged persons. Marywood (1953), Tunstall (1966), Stren (1963) and others have attributed the alienation of the aged to the reduction of modes and opportunities for spontaneous and restricted social participation, retirement, widowhood and deprivation.

Lack of companionship, creative activity and employment of leisure in socially useful manner are some of the most important factors in alienation and feelings of isolation of the aged. The table below shows the number of persons feeling lonely after retirement.

Table 1

Percentage of persons feeling lonely after retirement

	Very much	*Much*	*Less*	*Least*	*Never*	*Norm*
Gazetted	2 (4%)	7 (14%)	7 (14%)	6 (12%)	28 (56%)	50
Non-gazetted	10 (20%)	11 (22%)	6 (12%)	2 (4%)	21 (42%)	50
Total	12 (12%)	18 (18%)	1 (13%)	8 (8%)	49 (49%)	100

When asked about the causes of the loneliness the following order of the causes was found: (i) No children, (ii) Fear of death, (iii) Shortage of money, (iv) Absence of wife, (v) Loss of income, (vi) No work to do, (vii) No hobbies, (viii) Loss of status and (ix) Constant sickness.

The behaviour of the family members towards the aged

It is a common complaint of the old people that the behaviour of family members with them has deteriorated after their retirement. The response to such question as "has there been any change after retirement in the behaviour of the family members towards you?", were obtained from the respondents. The Table 2 shows the reactions of the aged.

Although family and kinship ties still persist, but they are no longer central and vital. The result is that the older persons feel dethroned and devalued in the realm of family relations where they once reigned supreme. According to Burgess (1960) the old has lost his role of dominance and has not yet found a new one. The maladjustment with the changed role on the part of the aged and the perception of the aged by members of the family may probably be accounted for the bad behaviour towards the aged and its perception as such by the aged.

Table 2

Behaviour of the family members towards respondents after retirement

	Bad behaviour	*Good behaviour*	*Norm*
Gazetted	26 (52%)	24 (48%)	50
Non-gazetted	37 (74%)	13 (26%)	50
Total	63 (63%)	37 (37%)	100

Chi-square=5.19 Significant at 0.05 level.

Problems After Retirement

Retired persons were asked to rank in order of the major problems they face after retirement. The order of the major problems felt was:

(1) Shortage of money, (2) Problems of passing time, (3) Widowhood, (4) Feeling of being physically weak, (5) Fear of

death, (6) Mental tensions, (7) Feeling of social neglect, (8) Feeling of neglect by family and (9) Neglect by friends.

Attitudes Towards the Age of Retirement

Responses of the aged in the three areas mentioned above suggest that economic insecurity, loss of income and monetary problems are important in the adjustment of the retired persons. As these problems are related to retirement, it is obvious that these will influence the attitudes of the retired persons towards the age of retirement. The table shows the frequency of persons expressing their views about the age which they consider appropriate for retirement.

Table 3

	Age in years (Years)					
	50	*55*	*58*	*60*	*65*	*Total*
Gazetted	1(2%)	3(6%)	18(36%)	23 (46%)	5(10%)	50
Non-gazetted	1(2%)	9(18%)	16(32%)	18(36%)	6(12%)	50
Total	2(2%)	12(12%)	34(36%)	41(41%)	11(11%)	100

Presently the retirement age for Rajasthan government servants is 55 years. The table shows that 86 per cent respondents want an upward shift in the age of retirement. This is a clear indication of the importance which income plays in the life of the aged persons.

References

Burgess, E.W. (1954): "Social Relations Activities and Personal Adjustment". *Am. J. Sociology*, 59, 352–60.

Burgess, E.W. (1960): *Aging in Western Society*. Chicago: The University of Chicago Press, 290.

Cavan et al., (1949): *Personal Adjustment in Old Age*. Chicago: Science Research Associates.

Friedmann, E.A. and Havighurst, R.J. (1954): *The Meaning of Work and Retirement*. Chicago: The University of Chicago Press.

Kuhlen, R.G. (1959): "Aging and Life Adjustment" in *Hand Book of Aging and the Individual*. James Birren (Ed.). Chicago: The University of Chicago Press.

Kunter B. et al., (1955): *Five Hundred Over Sixty: A Community Survey on Aging*. New York: Russell Saga Foundation.

Landis, J.T. (1942): "Social Psychological Factors of Aging". *Social Forces*, 20: 468–70.

Marywood, M. (1953): *Pathology of Loneliness*. New York: Columbia University Press.

Morgan, Christine M. (1937): "The Attitude and Adjustments of Recipients of Old Age Assistance in Upstate and Metropolitian New York". *Arch. Psychol.* No. 214.

Stren, M. (1963): *In Encyclopedia of Mental Health*. Franklin Watts Inc.

Tunstall, J. (1966): *Old and Alone*. Routledge and Kegan Paul.

CHAPTER 18

A Comparative Study of Emotional Problems in Old and Middle-Aged Men

Saroj Rathore

It is widely believed that old age is a period of cumulative stress, deprivation and loss and, therefore, old people must be among the most unhappy of all groups. Emotional problems in old people have been studied from psychiatric point of view. The precise figures of the aged in the community needing psychiatric care is not easy to ascertain. Williamson et al. (1964) indicated that the general practitioners were unaware of 60 per cent of cases of neurosis, 76 per cent of depression and 87 per cent of the moderately demented in their practices. Kay et al. (1964) have reported that "medical services deal only with the visible point of the iceberg of medical disorders". A Danish study (Juel Nielson, 1965) showed within a year, two per cent of the population aged 60 and over contacted the medical institution for mental illness but only 0.5 per cent of these got in touch with any psychiatric institution.

Epidemiological studies in the West have revealed a total prevalence rate of psychiatric morbidity in old age ranging from 20 per cent to 45 per cent. Post (1959) held that 11 per cent of the aged population is in need of some care. The prevalence rate of all types of psychosis in old people seems to vary from 6 per cent to 8 per cent and about one per cent of these needs admission into psychiatric institution.

IJG, 1991, Vol. 5, No. 3 and 4, pp. 92–101.

In general, survey studies of the prevalence of mental disorders in India, reveal the rate for old people range from 22.34 (Dube, 1970) to 333 (Nandi et al., 1975) and 350 per one thousand (Ramachandran et al., 1979). Based on hospital attendances in Madurai, Venkoba Rao et al. (1972) reported that those over 50 contributed to 9.5 per cent and those above 60 to 2.3 per cent of the total attendance. This is in conformity with the report of Lin (1953) and also WHO communication (1959). A similar trend is noticeable from a Bangalore study (Anantharaman, 1975). Table 1 depicts the number of aged patients attending Venkoba Rao's Geropsychiatric clinic (Venkoba Rao, 1981).

Number of aged patients attending geropsychiatric clinic

Year	*Total*	*Aged 60 and above*	*Percentage*
1976	1915	32	1.60
1977	1985	49	2.45
1978	2625	67	2.30
1979	2907	79	2.60

This shows rising trend of aged attending psychiatric consultations. But most of these aged are considered to be cases of organic brain syndromes (OBS). That is why, Sethi, (1982) is of the view that dementia forms the major group of mental illnesses in old age (80%), functional psychoses are no less common. However, the rate of affective disorders and OBS in Venkoba Rao's (1983) Geropsychiatric clinic and field study offers a striking contrast as shown in the table below:

Diagnosis	*Geropsychiatric*	*Field study*
OBS	34.39%	9.8%
Affective Disorders	42.78%	67.07%

It clearly shows that problems of psychogenic origin is seen more in aged in field studies than hospital or clinic settings.

Venkoba Rao and Madhavan (1982) have also demonstrated that the risk of psychiatric illness including depression increases with advancing age. It is clear from the data provided by them as follows:

Prevalence of psychiatric illness at higher age group

Age Group	*All illness*	*Depression*
Over 60	89	60
60–70	71.5	50
70–80	124	80
80 and above	155	88

Ramchandran et al. (1982) also surveyed 400 persons aged over 50 to estimate rate of psychiatric problems in this age group. According to their results, 264 were found to be normal, 86 were diagnosed as suffering from depressive neurosis and 12 from endogenous depression. O.B.S. were seen in 13 cases, schizophrenia in 3 cases and personality disorders (other than depression) in 28 subjects. They reported prevalence rate as follows:

Prevalence rate of psychiatric disorders in aged over 50

	O.B.S.	*N (N=406)*	*Rate per 1000*
1.	O.B.S.	13	32
2.	Schizophrenia	3	7
3.	Depression	98	241
4.	Personality Disorders	28	69
	Total	142	349

Thus depression is the commonest clinical presentation in aged in our country as well. However, depression in Indian community is invisible in old people due to the factors like community tolerance, mistaking the withdrawal features of the old person to the process of aging itself, failure to perceive the depression as an illness by the family members and the society.

These observation from Indian studies erode the myth that depression in old age is much less in India than in the West. Among others, one of the factors which was found to be associated with depression in old age in India is the family structure and living alone. In rural parts of India, the joint family system, caste system and the family profession continue. However, due to industrialization, the joint family system is breaking up. Venkoba Rao et al. (1972) observed that 80 per cent of those in nuclear family preferred joint family for economic and emotional reasons. The old people are often widowed, unemployed and suffer from physical disabilities. When their emotional and financial needs are not adequately met by their family they come to suffer from emotional distress.

Retirement from job, demise of spouse, reduced income, considerable increase in leisure, changing attitude of younger generation (generation gap) etc., may be responsible for emotional problems (including depression) in old people.

Western studies by Jacoby, (1986); Kay et al. (1964); Bergmann, (1971); Shepherd et al. (1966); Williamson et al. (1964) have also amply demonstrated that old people entertain neurotic presentations including depression and suicide. Thus, emotional life of old is not believed to be happy.

It is expected that we would be less happy if we had poorer health, lower status, less money and fewer friends. Since all these – together with decline in sexual vigour, loss of physical beauty and the imminence of death – are linked with old age, most of us regard the approach of old age with attitudes ranging from resignation to gloom, to desperation. Surely old people must be among the most unhappy and would be entertaining very poor subjective well-being of all groups. Even Aristotle described aged as persons having little left to them (cited by Birren, 1959).

Some investigators namely, Butler, (1978); Leon et al. (1979); Lawton et al. (1980) have reported that older persons are prone to hypochondriasis. It is true that sickness and disability among older persons entail frustrations for the physician, an economic burden for society and an unappealing prospect for younger men and women contemplating their own futures. All these suggest likely possibility of old people entertaining poor quality of life as well as subjective well-being. Indian studies are conspicuous by their absence in this area.

Yet, studies done in the West have come to different conclusions. Studies carried out by Andrews and Withey, (1976), Campbell et al. (1976) have demonstrated that old people may be more satisfied with life than are younger men and women. Thus, the findings of these researchers' subscribe to the view which is against the negative stereotypes of aging. Costa and his associates have reported data from the Augmented Baltimore Longitudinal Study of Aging (ABLSA), a well-educated, generally healthy community – dwelling group of volunteers who cover the full adult range and have been studied for as much as 25 years. These groups of researchers (Costa and McCrae, 1980; 1981; 1984; Costa et al., 1984) have provided another look at old age – which present aged as satisfied persons. They hold that retirement, once thought to be enforced idleness, is enjoyed by many persons as a time for leisure and as much or little productive activity as they care for. They further add that old age may be happiest time of life depending on past history of the person and their personality make up. Costa and McCrae, (1987) also found that ageing individuals are not hypochondriacs. Similarly Larson, (1978) observed that well-being does not decline with age.

Studies reviewed above are instructive in pointing out the debate on quality of life (QOL) or emotional life in old age. Studies carried out from psychiatric point of view present negative stereotypes of ageing. On the other hand, studies considering role of personality and social support system variables come to positive perception of QOL of aged. Absence of Indian studies and controversies on quality of life in old age underline the importance of taking up such a research project. Therefore, the present study was carried out to fill up this research gap.

Major aim of the present study was to compare the emotional problems in old age and middle-aged men. More specifically, the research was designed to make comparative study of emotional problems such as somatic anxiety, psychic anxiety, muscular tension, social desirability, impulsiveness, monotony avoidance, detachment, psychasthenia, guilt, inhibition of aggression in old and middle-aged men.

Methodology

Sample

The sample of the present study was selected from the residents of Tilak Nagar Colony, Near University of Rajasthan, Jaipur.

Thirty old persons were selected with the following criteria of omission and inclusion:

(a) All the subjects must be males.
(b) Age must be above 60.
(c) All the subjects must be at least graduate by their education.

(d) They must have retired from government jobs.

(e) Persons retired from medical services must not be included in sample.

(f) After retirement they must not be in job taking re-employment.

Most of these persons were retired from administrative, accounts and teaching services. Their age range was 62 to 75 with mean age of 64.57 years.

A matched control of 30 subjects were taken from the same colony. Most of them were also in administrative, accounts and teaching services. All were males with minimum education of graduation. Their age range was 35 to 45 years with mean age of 40.43 years. This matched control group of 30 subjects belonged to middle-age group.

Tools

These subjects (older persons, N=30 and middle-aged persons N=30; were administered Karolinkska Scale of Personality (KSP). KSP was developed by Schalling and co-workers, (1978). The KSP contains 15 sub-scales viz., somatic anxiety, psychic anxiety, muscular tension, impulsiveness, monotony avoidance, detachment, social desirability, socialisation, suspension, guilt, indirect aggression, verbal aggression, irritability, inhibition of aggression and psychasthenia. Each item of KSP has 4 response alternatives. The scores are summed up in above mentioned 15 measures.

Procedure

The KSP, was administered individually to subjects of both the groups. After giving required instructions to each subject individually, the scale was handed over to the subject to be filled by him. The data were classified into 15 categories. Means and standard deviations were computed for each category for both the groups separately. To see the difference between the two groups of subjects, 't' values for each category was found out.

Results

The data obtained on various measures of emotional problems for aged and middle-aged (control group) through KSP, was summed up in four tables comprising total 15 measures. To see the significance of difference between the two groups of subjects 't' test was computed for each measure. For detailed information see Table 1 to Table 4.

Table 1

Comparison between aged and middle-aged on the three measures of KSP concerning anxiety proneness

Measures	*Aged group (N=30)*		*Middle-aged group (N=30)*		*t*	*p*
	X	*SD*	*X*	*SD*		
Somatic anxiety (SA)	20.37	8.36	15.27	4.78	2.89	<0.01
Psychic anxiety (PA)	25.57	6.30	10.10	5.11	4.37	<0.001
Muscular tension (MT)	18.87	7.02	14.47	4.12	2.97	<0.01

It is clear from the above Table 1 that the aged scored significantly more than their middle-aged counterparts on all the three indices of anxiety proneness. The difference between the means of these two groups is highly significant on SA; PS as well as on MT. Thus it can be easily inferred that old persons entertain high level of anxieties.

Table 2

Comparison between aged and middle-aged on the KSP related to extroversion

Measures	*Aged group (N=30)*		*Middle-aged group (N=30)*		*t*	*p*
	X	*SD*	*X*	*SD*		
Impulsiveness (I)	25.13	3.99	22.17	3.47	2.25	<0.05
Monotony avoidance (MA)	22.60	2.71	24.97	4.57	2.44	<0.05
Detachment (De)	22.47	4.52	21.80	3.39	0.65	n.s.

The Table 2 given above depicts that the mean scores of aged and middle-aged groups significantly differ on I and MA at 0.05 level. However, no significant mean difference was observed on De in these groups. Thus, it can be interpreted that aged are significantly high on impulsivity and low on monotony avoidance when compared to the sample of middle-aged one. However, both the groups are more or less similar on detachment.

Table 3

Comparison between aged and middle-aged on measures of desirability and socialization of KSP

Measures	Aged group (N=30)		Middle-aged Group (N=30)		t.	p
	X	SD	X	SD		
Social desirability (SD)	32.03	5.09	30.73	5.39	0.95	n.s.
Socialization (So)	58.93	8.34	63.40	7.25	2.21	<0.05

It is explicit from the means and standard deviations given in the above Table 3 that and middle-aged subjects did not differ significantly on social desirability, although on socialization (So) measure their scores have significant difference.

Middle-aged subjects had greater socialization scores than the aged ones. It can thus be inferred that old people do not keep the company of others to the extent done by middle-aged ones.

Table 4

Comparison between aged and middle-aged on seven measures of KSP

Measures	Aged group (N=30)		Middle-aged group (N=30)		t	p
	X	SD	X	SD		
Suspicion (S)	12.97	2.43	11.77	1.81	2.21	<0.05
Guilt (G)	12.47	2.76	11.53	1.70	1.59	n.s.
Indirect aggression (A)	9.60	3.31	10.00	2.68	0.52	n.s.
Verbal aggression (VA)	11.07	3.00	11.87	2.70	1.14	n.s.
Irritability (Irr)	11.23	3.21	10.77	3.54	0.54	n.s.
Inhibition of Aggression (Inh Ab)	24.47	4.73	21.67	4.15	2.46	<0.025
Psychassthenia (Ps)	25.23	5.21	21.77	3.08	3.14	<0.01

On examining Table 4 it becomes clear that there is significant difference between the means of aged and middle-aged persons only on suspicion (S), inhibition of aggression (Inh Ag) and psychasthenia (Ps). Old persons had scored significantly higher than the middle-aged ones on these three measures. Thus, it can be inferred that old persons are more suspicious; entertain greater inhibition of aggression and high on psychasthenia than the middle-aged persons. However, no significant mean difference in the two groups were found on the measures of G; IA; VA and Irr.

Discussion

The present study was aimed at exploring emotional life in old age. The sample of the study was very restricted and selective. Thirty men over 60 years of age and retired from government service with minimum education of graduation were compared with 30 matched group of middle-aged men in service 35 years to 45 years, on selected measures of emotional problems.

Of the emotional problems, specific variables relevant to old age (such as anxiety proneness; impulsiveness, monotony avoidance; detachment; aggression; hostility etc.) were chosen so as to understand psychological aspects of ageing. Fortunately enough, most of these measures could be covered in KSP scale, unfamiliar to most of the researches in our country. Items sample of this study had no problem in taking the test in English as all of them were highly educated.

The major finding of great significance emerged from this study is that old men are characterized by several negative characteristics as higher levels of somatic anxiety, psychic anxiety, muscular tension, suspicion, inhibition of aggression, psychasthenia, and lower socialization in comparison with middle-aged men on KSP by and large, hypotheses set are accepted. These observations of the study are in agreement with popular view that old age as a time of depression and dejection. It is further believed that old age symbolizes with health worries and old people show failure to cope with health threats. Realization of existential anxiety in terms of being and not being in the world may be more pronounced during the old age. Emotional problems of anxiety proneness in old age in terms of somatic anxiety, psychic anxiety and muscular tension may be the result of experience of existential anxiety in later years of life. According to a study by Tuckman and Lorge (1952), mental health professionals believe many negative stereotypes about the aged and 24 per cent of them agree with the statement: "The aged are a burden on society". In 1950s, most of the writers attributed emotional problems or functional maladjustment in old age mainly to impotence and inadequacy, using the middle age model as the base line criterion.

Findings of the present study on negative attributes and emotional problems to old people get support from other studies as well. Jacoby and Bergmann, (1986) for example, reported that 12 per cent of elderly people resident in the community show at least moderately severe psychiatric morbidity of a neurotic type. Similarly, Kay et al. (1964) disclosed at least 5 per cent of the studied sample of old people with such neurotic ailments with a history of less than five years duration. Bergmann, (1971) also indicated that in more than half of the sample, the neurosis had first appeared after the age of 60. Shepherd and his associates, (1966) suggested that conspicuous psychiatric morbidity of neurotic type does not decline with increasing age. Furthermore, Williamson et al. (1964) found that 65 per cent of all elderly subjects with neurotic disorder in their survey of general practice in Edinburgh were unknown to their own family doctor.

Emotional problems of neurotic nature in old men than middle-aged men of this study are also comparable with Indian researches. Dube (1970), Sethi et al. (1972) Verghese et al. (1975) studied the prevalence of psychiatric disorders in the Indian community. In their studies all age groups were studied and hence it was not possible to determine the family structure in particular of old age subjects and its association to emotional disorders. A study of elderly subject was, however, done on a hospital population by Venkoba Rao et al. (1972). They observed that affective disorders formed 21 per cent of the whole series.

There is a wide spread belief that emotional problems, particularly depression in old age are infrequent in our country as compared to the West. Joint family system or other cultural practices which provide satisfaction and security to the old man account for this. However, this notion does not hold true. Ramchandran et al. (1982) reported, for example that the psychiatric disorders in the aged in our country are infrequent appears to be a myth ! Their study found that about 33 per cent of subjects aged over 60 years in the community were found to exhibit manifestations of mental illness. They (Ramchandran et al., 1982) conducted another epidemiological survey of 406 subjects aged over 50. Depression was the commonest diagnosis made with 24.1 per cent. Venkoba Rao and Madhavan (1982) also surveyed 686 subjects aged 60 and above in South to explore the magnitude of emotional problems in aged. The prevalence of psychiatric morbidity was estimated at 89/1000. In India, the trend that figures is at present half of the Western rate.

It is clear from the observations made from Western as well as Indian studies, that emotional problems of affective disorders, depression, suicide etc., are not uncommon in old persons and hence higher scores on anxiety proneness, suspicion and inhibition of aggression, in old men than middle-aged men of this study are not starting.

References

Anantharaman, R.N. (1975): Psychology of Aging: A Study of Adjustment. Ph. D. Thesis, Bangalore University, India.

Andrews, F.M. and Withey, S.B. (1976): *Social Indicators of Well-being: Americans' Perceptions of Life Quality*. New York: Plenum.

Bergmann, K. (1971): "The Neuroses in Old Age". In D.W.K. Kay and A. Walk (Eds.): Recent Development in Psychogeriatrics. *British Journal of Psychiatry*. Special Publication, 6: 39–50.

Birren, J.E. (Ed.) (1959): *Handbook of Aging and the Individual*. Chicago: The University of Chicago Press.

Butler, R.N. (1978): "The Doctor and the Aged Patient". In W. Reichel (Ed.). *The Geriatric Patient*. New York: H.P. Publishing.

Campbell, A., Converse, P.E. and Rodgers, W.L. (1976): *The Quality of American Life: Perceptions, Evaluations, and Satisfactions*. New York: Russell Sage Foundation.

Costa, P.T. Jr. and McCrae, R.R. (1984): "Personality as a Life Long Determinant of Well Being". In C. Malatesta and C. Izard (Eds.), *Affective Processes in Adult Development and Aging*. Beverley Hills, C.A.: Sage.

Costa, P.T. Jr. and McCrae, R.R. (1985): "Hypochondriasis, Neuroticism and Aging. When Are Somatic Complaints Unfounded?". *American Psychologist, 40: 19–28.*

Costa, P.T. Jr., McCrae, R.R. and Norris, A.H. (1981): "Personal Adjustment to Aging: Longitudinal Prediction from Neuroticism and Extraversion". *Journal of Gerontology,* 36: 78–85.

Costa, P.T. Jr., Zonderman, A.B., McCrae, R.R., Cornoni-Huntiley,J., Locke, B.Z. and Barhano, H.E. (1987): "Longitudinal Analyses of Psychological Well-being in a National Sample: Stability of Mean Levels". *Journal of Gerontology,* 42: 50–55.

Costa, P.T., Jr. and McCrae, R.R. (1980): "Influence of Extra Version and Neuroticism on Subjective Well-being: Happy and Unhappy People". *Journal of Personality and Social Psychology,* 38: 668–678.

Dube, K.C. (1970): "A Study of Prevalence and Biosocial Variation in Mental Illness in a Rural and Urban Community in U.P. India". *Acta. Psychiat. Scand.*48: 18.

Jacoby, R. and Bergmann, K. (1986): "The Psychiatry of Old Age". In, *Essential of Postgraduate Psychiatry.* London: Grume & Stratton, Bergmann, 495.

Juel Nielson, N. (1965): Some results and experiences from recent epidemiological investigation. Oldon, *Denmark Report on the Symposium held by the Royal College of Physicians.*

Kay, D.W.K., Beamish, P. and Roth, M. (1964): "Old Agemental Disorders in New Castle Upon Tyne: Part-I, A Study of Prevalence". *British Journal of Psychiatry,*110: 146–154.

Larson, R. (1978): "Thirty Years of Research on the Subjective Well-being of Older Americans". *Journal of Gerontology,* 33: 109–125.

Lawton, M.P., Whelihan, W.M. and Belsky, J.K. (1980): "Personality Tests and their Uses with Older Adults". In J. Birren and R.B. Sloane (Eds.), *Handbook of Mental Health and Aging.* New York: Prentice-Hall, 537–553.

Leon, R.R., Gillum B., Gillum, R.,and Gouze, M. (1979): "Personality Stability and Change Over a 30 Years Period Middle Age to Old Age". *Journal of Consulting and Clinical Psychology,* 23: 245–259.

Lin, T.Y. (1953): "A Study of The Incidence of Mental Disorder in Chinese and Other Cultures". *Psychiatry* (Washington), 16: 313.

Nandi, D.N., Ajmani, S., Ganguli, A., Banerji, G., Boral, G.C., Ghose, A. and Shankar S. (1975): "Psychiatric Disorders in a Village Community in West Bengal". *Indian Journal of Psychiatry.* 17: 87.

Post, F. (1959): "Mental Health in Old Age". *Public Health.* (London), 73: 412.

Ramchandran, V., Sharda Menon, M. and Ramamurti, B. (1979): "Psychiatric Disorders in Subjects Aged Over Fifty". *Indian Journal of Psychiatry.* 22: 193.

Ramchandran. V., Sharda Menon, M., Arunagiri, S. (1982): "Socio-Cultural Factors in the Late Onset of Depression". *Indian Journal of Psychiatry.* 24: 268–273.

Schalling, D. (1978): "Psychopathy-related Personality Variables and Psychophysiology of Socialisation". In R.D. Hare, and D. Schalling (Eds.), *Psychopathic Behaviour: Approaches to Research.* Chichestler: Wiley.

Sethi, B.B. (1982): Editorial Geriatric Psychiatry: An Upcoming Challenge. *Indian Journal of Psychiatry*. 24: 195.

Sethi, B.B., Gupta, S.C., Kumar, R. and Kumari, P. (1972): "A Psychiatric Survey of 500 Rural Families". *Indian Journal of Psychiatry*. 14: 183.

Shepherd, M., Cooper, B., Brown, A.C., and Kalton, G.W. (1966): *Psychiatric Illness in General Practice*. Oxford University Press.

Tuckman, J. and Lqrge, I. (1952): Attitude Toward the Aged. *Science*, 115: 685–687.

Venkoba Rao, A. and Madhavan, T. (1982): "A Gerophychiatric Morbidity Survey in a Semiurban Area Near Madurai". *Indian Journal of Psychiatry*. 24: 258–267.

Venkoba Rao, A., and Madhavan, T. (1983): Depression and Suicide Behaviour in the Aged, *Indian Journal of Psychiatry*, 25: 251–259.

Venkoba Rao, A. (1981): "Mental Health and Aging in India". *Indian Journal of Psychiatry*. 23: 11–20.

Venkoba Rao, A.,Virudhugirinathan, B.S. and Malthi, R. (1972): "Mental Illness in Patients Aged Fifty and Over: A Psychiatric, Psychological and Sociological Study". *Indian Journal of Psychiatry*. 14: 319.

Verghese, A., Beign, A., Seneman, L.A., Sunder Rao, S.S. and Benjamain, V. (1975): "A Social Psychiatric Study on a Representative Group of Families in Vellore Town". *Indian Journal of Medical Research*, 61: 508.

Williamson, J., Stokoe, I.H., Gray, S., Fish, Mi. Smith, A. McGhee, A. and Stephenson, F. (1964): "Old People at Home". *Lancent*. 1: 1117.

World Health Organization (1959): Mental Health Problems of Ageing and the Aged. Technical Reports Series No. 171, Geneva.

CHAPTER 19

Domestic Abuse Among the Elderly

S. Ushasree and S. Azmal Basha

The phenomenon of elder abuse, though it is age old, attained the attention of academicians and those in the service of the aged only recently. Its presence could be felt even in India where we proclaim reverence for the elderly and believed it as an ingrained characteristic of most of the traditional Indians.

Though child abuse was recognized in 1960's itself, till recently elder abuse was a hidden problem. Later investigations found that couples who behaved aggressively towards children and spouses were also found to behave similarly with the elderly (Strauss, Gelles and Steinmetz, 1980). Most often the onus that is attached to elder abuse interferes with the exploration of its prevalence. Sometimes the abused deny the existence of physical abuse and neglect but still, stated explicitly or not, abuse is the most frustrating thing in the lives of the elderly.

Review of related literature shows the evidence of several types of elder abuse like assault, deprivation of food and prescribed drugs, emotional abuse, involuntary confinement or isolation, financial abuse, legal abuse etc. According to public information report issued by British Geriatric Society (1985) most of the victims were found to be over 75, females, role less within the family, functionally impaired, lonely, fearful, living at home with an adult child and in some cases immobile and incontinent. Several theories like dependency theory,

IJG, 1999, Vol. 13, Nos. 3 and 4, pp. 99–104.

stressed caregiver's theory and exchange theory were postulated to explain the causation of elder abuse. Supporting the carer's stress theory, the study of Mildenberger and Wessman (1986) found that the perpetrator of elder abuse most often was a relative of the victim and had taken care of that person for number of years. The caretaker was burdened with stresses which include financial demands, changes in lifestyle and social isolation.

Beyond the reasons of its causation abuse is distressing. Conduct disorders and neurotic disorders like hysteria, phobia, compulsive and hypochondriac behaviour and psychotic conditions among some were also identified among the elderly exposed to prolonged abuse (Filinson and Ingman, 1989; Gorbach et al., 1988).

Elder abuse appears to cut across all social classes as well as racial, ethnic and religious groups (Block and Sinnott, 1979). However, it may be expected that elder abuse is less in eastern societies where the elder status is not traditionally tied to economic status or health and elder care formed part of the filial piety. But as societies become more and more industrialized and urbanized, the social change might result in increased cases of elder abuse.

In this context, it was hoped that an examination of behaviour variables affecting domestic abuse among the elderly would throw more light on the experiences of the Indian aged. It was found in many cases that elder abuse is the result of failure to provide a comprehensive continuum of care for the elderly. It may be inferred from such situation that less disabled aged persons causing less dependence on others physically or functionally may get exempted or differentiated from those with more disabilities in their source and types of abuse. Against this backdrop, the present study was planned to study the behaviour variables affecting domestic abuse also among the more and less disabled elderly.

Method

Sample

The sample of the study comprised 35 men and 40 women ranging in age from 65–86 years, residents of aged homes in and around Tirupati, Andhra Pradesh. These homes are situated in sub-urban areas and almost all the residents were from the nearby villages. They were all illiterates excepting eight men who attended elementary school. They were all small farmers and some were agricultural labour while they were younger.

Tools

A structured interview guide was used in collecting data. It had two parts. The first part had some items from the disability in daily activities and sensory and cognitive disability borrowed from sections of the old Age Disability Scale developed by Ramamurti and Jamuna (1990). The second part consisted of questions dealing with the type of abuse, the person has experienced. There were also some prove questions meant to explore the identity of perpetrator and the nature of abuse and the perceived cause of the abused of the abuser behind the act.

Procedure

All the residents of the selected homes for the aged were contacted personally and only those who volunteered to participate in the study could be involved. In a very informal atmosphere each subject was interviewed in privacy after assuring them of confidentiality of their data. Each interview session lasted for a period of 30–45 minutes.

Results and Discussion

Data obtained for the second part of the interview guide was processed for identifying abuse viz., neglect of prescribed drugs, neglect of food, financial exploitation (material abuse) deprivation of attention (neglect of physical needs), deprivation of affection (emotional needs), derogatory verbal remarks, confinement (physical isolation), physical violence, loud talking (threatening voice) and legal abuse. The percentages of abuse reported under each head and their ranks are given in Table 1 for the entire sample and also genderwise separately.

Results in the Table 1 suggest that the elderly had been neglected of proper medical care and food and they also appear to be exploited financially to a greater extent (ranking 1, 2, 3). Much of the grievances expressed by subjects under these categories might be understood to some extent as the inability of the family to cater to the needs of the elderly owing to the involvement of finances in these matters. Apart from this, data also show considerable percentage of abuse experienced by subjects in the form of lack of attention, lack of

Table 1

Percentages and ranks of variables involved in elder abuse

Variables	*No. of occurrence (N=75)*	*Response (%)*	*Rank*	*Response(%)*	*Men (N=35) rank*	*Women (N=40) response %*	*Rank*
Neglect of medical	59	78	1	86	1	72	2
Neglect of food	57	75	2	77	2	75	1
Financial abuse	50	66	3	69	5	65	3
Lack of attention	45	60	4	74	3	47	5
Lack of affection	43	57	5	63	6	52	4
Derogatory comments	39	52	6	71	4	35	7
Confinement	33	44	7	51	9	37	6
violence	32	43	8	60	7	27	8
Loud talking	31	41	9	54	8	30	9
Legal abuse	26	34	10	51	9	20	10

Table 2
Percentages and ranks of variables in the abuse of disabled elderly

Variables	*More disabled*		*Less disabled*	
	Response (%)	*Rank*	*Response (%)*	*Rank*
Neglect of food	93	1	56	1
Neglect of medical care	75	2	56	1
Lack of affection	75	2	18	9
Lack of attention	75	2	25	6
Financial abuse	68	5	43	3
Violence	56	6	18	9
Confinement	50	8	38	4
Loud talking	50	8	25	6
Derogatory comments	53	7	25	6
Legal abuse	31	10	31	5

affection, derogatory comments, physical confinement, violence, loud talking and legal abuse in that order. These results bear close comparability with those obtained by Peretti and Majecen (1991) on a sample of American elderly.

Comparison made between elderly men and women in this regard showed some differences in the occurrence of each type of abuse. While neglect of medical care and food alternate ranks 1 and 2, legal abuse occupies the last rank in both men and women's cases. Differential socialization practices could be seen affecting them mostly when the variable reported lack of attention is concerned. As far as life in the domestic setting is concerned men are given to be helped by women in the house where as women are expected to help themselves unless dire necessity exists. The difference between men and women in this aspect perhaps reflects differential treatment of their carers as well as their own perceptual differences (Most of their carers were their daughters-in-law). Similarly, compared to women it appears to be not that each to exploit elderly men financially and also to impose physical confinement on them. More elderly men than their counterparts in the sample appear to be abused by women at home in the form of derogatory comments and also experiencing violence from the male member in the family. Percentage of violence reported by elderly women is comparatively less. This may support the view that female carers choose to react verbally to frustration and males to some extent withstand their physical aggressive acts as far as elderly women are concerned. Differences in the reported legal abuse, though in smaller percentages, also speak of gender differences favouring women.

Next, examination of data for the differences in the ranks obtained by the more and the less disabled (Table 2) show that both the groups were similarly abused as far as food and medical care were concerned. However, glaring differences could be seen between the two groups in almost all the variables. The more disabled were found to be severely feeling abused for lack of affection and lack of attention from their carers whereas the less disabled seemed to be exploited more financially and were exposed to perhaps owing to their comparatively better capacity to resist exploitation of others. Relatively less occurrences of abuse in the form of violence, derogatory comments, loud talking and lack of affection among the less disabled might also be because of the threat of retaliation they could pose to their carers in a better manner than the more disabled.

One speculation related to the underlying causes of elder abuse is ageism and another readily available explanation is the burden of care giving. It is the consequence of failure to provide comprehensive long-term care. Constant long-term care without respite is really stressful. In some cases, more particularly with marginal families due to the cost of maintaining frail parents or grandparents while raising children and family might force the adult children into a moral conflict due to competing responsibilities (Sykes, 1996). As the subjects of the study belong to the rural areas, non-availability of proper medical care in the community is an added disadvantage to the caregivers for taking the frail elderly to doctors in the urban areas for treatment as it involves considerable monetary commitment too. Thus, with few or limited resources the pressure to support their young and the elderly might lead to elder abuse in the domestic situation. Another important dimension that needs to be highlighted at this juncture is one of the drawbacks in the patriarchal system in the society which commends its womenfolk to live with their in-law's family. And worldwide majorly the women are the caregivers in the homefront. In such case, the quality of caring that these women tender depends on several things like anticipation regarding the properties that they would inherit from their in-law, the facilities available at home to aid in their caring and the history of family relations and power/love equation that they had with their parents-in-law ever since they were married. Of the three aforementioned, since the present behaviour is mostly a repetition of longstanding relation patterns, the last one appears to be more powerful in determining the quality of caring and making the cared abused more or less or not at all.

Thus results of the study imply to a large extent the carers 'attitude towards the elderly. It reflects carers' failure. Punishing the caregivers or making them guilty for the abuse is not the solution. Every citizen has got a basic human right to live with dignity. Therefore the government should also shoulder the responsibility. It can provide alternative arrangements for the frail elderly at risk situations. Caregivers need to be trained and supported for providing free or paid respite care. Respite care can also be catered by establishing day care centres both at rich and poor localities either by the state or by voluntary organizations. The media can also help reduce elder abuse by exposing its nature, prevalence and solutions to the issues. Public education in this regard helps the elderly immensely.

References

Block, M.R. and Sinott J.D. (1979): *The Battered Elder Synodrome: An Exploratory Study,* College Park: University of Marryland, Centre for Aging.

Filinson, R. and Ingman, S. (1989): *Elder Abuse-practice and Policy.* New York: Human Sciences.

Gorbach, P., Neill, J.I. and Williams, J. (1988): *A Need for Care?* Vermont, Gower.

Mildenberger, C. and Wessman, H. (1986): "Abuse and Neglect of Elderly Persons by Family: A Special Communication". *Physical Therapy.* 66: 537–539.

Peretti, P.O. and Mauecen, K.G. (1991): "Emotional Abuse among the Elderly: Affecting Behaviour Variables". *Social Behaviour and Personality.* 19 (4): 255–261.

Ramamurti, P.V. and Jamuna, D. (1990): "The Old Age Disability Scale". *The Journal of Psychology,* 3(1).

Strauss, M.A., Gelles, R.J. and Steinmetz, S.K. (1980): Behind Closed Doors: Violence in the American Family. *Garden City,* New York: Anchor.

Sykes, J.T. (1996): "Elder Abuse: Progress among Societies". *Psychology International.* 7(2).

CHAPTER 20

Family Relations of the Elderly after Retirement and Widowhood

Renu Malhotra and N.K. Chadha

Human existence is a continuum with conception at one end and death at the other, and that the later years, even the terminal days, need to be seen as part of this continuum. The belief, that the elderly face lesser problems in India than in the west, is changing slowly.

Though the nature of problems that the elderly face may differ after retirement, but financial, health and psycho-social problems of adjustment have been the major problems of the aged. These problems are managed by the family, which is the primary caregiver for its aged members. But disrupted family system is the major contributor to the severity of problems of the aged.

The family serves as a fundamental structure for living together intimately and sharing economic, social and emotional responsibilities. Indian family system takes up the role of an insurance cover for the individual. Care of the aged is an inbuilt norm in our traditional family. But today elderly persons in India, spend the evening of their lives in isolation, penury and frailty.

The traditional joint family system has wilted to be replaced by nuclear families with no room for old parents on the last leg of their life. Resentment towards the elderly at times leads to exploitation of their position and intergenerational conflict. Gangrade (1989), also

IJG, 1996, Vol. 10, Nos. 1–4, pp. 39–50.

found that due to intergenerational conflict, young people prefer nuclear families while a majority of parents still prefer joint families.

After retirement, there is erosion of authority of the elderly due to transition from the role of provider to dependent, and this rules in lack of respect for the elderly as well as neglect too (Alfred de Souza, 1982).

Slowly, It is being realized that continued reliance on family support, as the social agent to support older persons, is a weak reed on which well-being of elderly is planned. There is no doubt that instead of going through bitter exchanges day in and day out, the elders too prefer to stay separately while the children look after them only monetarily.

Today, elderly are treated as a burden, an unfortunate byproduct of medical advances and are at times mentioned in the same breath with the mentally ill, the handicapped and the dying. To devalue the aged in this way is to deny that we are ageing and will someday to become old, loose our youthfulness or face the inevitability of our deaths.

Methodology

Objectives

(i) To find differences if any, between pensioners and non-pensioners; as well as married and widower respondents on changes in relations with family after retirement, decision making in family affairs, agreement of family to their views, elderly people's adjustment with young generation and respect given to elderly.

(ii) To find out with whom the elderly converse the most, their topics of conversation, change in behaviour of family after service, dependency on family and living preferences. In case of both pensioners and non-pensioners as well as married and widower elderly.

Tools

The present study used the following tools for investigatory purposes:

(i) *Present Information Schedule:* A personal data form was used to procure demographic and biographical information from the subjects.

(ii) *Family Support Schedule:* This comprised of eleven questions relating to relationships between family members during the ageing process, support and participation given to elderly in society, family's role in bringing security and meaning to older persons' life and choice of living arrangement among the elderly.

Sample

The sample consisted of 100 subjects chosen from three residential areas of West Delhi:

(i) Rajouri Garden, (ii) Subhash Nagar, (iii) Ajay Enclave

The sample was divided in four group

Group A	Pensioners male (married)	N=25
Group B	Pensioners male (widowers)	N=25
Group C	Non-pensioner male (married)	N=25
Group D	Non-pensioner male (widowers)	N=25

Most of the respondents included in the sample were members of Rajouri Garden Retired People's Association. The investigator wanted to study the retired people from all walks of life. But persons who voluntarily retire from active life may not have to face many problems as compared to people who are forced to retire at a certain age. So, as a group, self-employed persons like doctors, lawyers or businessmen were eliminated. Elderly people from middle income group were taken. In order, to make a comparison between pensioner's and non-pensioner's, retired persons from private organizations and also from government and semi-government organizations were taken.

Table 1

Description of the characteristics of the sample

Characteristics	*Pensioners*		*Non-pensioners*	
Age range	58–80	59–83	59–82	59–92
Sex	MA	WD	MA	WD
Socio-economic status	MIG	MIG	MIG	MIG
Retd. from govt. orgzn.	—	1	10	16
Retd. from private orgzn.	25	23	11	5
Retd. from semi-govt. orgzn.	—	1	4	4

Collection of Data

Initially the questionnaires were given to a few subjects (in each of the group) known to the investigator. These subjects were then asked to name other elderly known to them. This chain procedure was continued till the required number of subjects in each group had been obtained.

In our country people are not forthcoming in discussing their problems. Thus, the interview was taken by asking one question in several ways. The investigator emphasized the plight of retired people and that the Government of India might consider the usefulness of the study and something helpful (to them) might come out of it. Though there were a few cases of outright refusals, some respondents showed interest and encouraged the investigation.

Scoring

The responses of the subjects under all the four categories were converted into frequencies and frequency per cent scores for each question.

Results

The large number of non-pensioners as compared to pensioners reported change in relations with family after retirement. Also 18 per cent of widowers report changes in family relations than 12 per cent married respondents (see Table 2).

Table 2 also shows that more percentage of non-pensioners' report taking decisions themselves (48%) or jointly (34%); while 16 per cent of pensioners' reported to take decisions with wife; by wife alone (6%), by son alone (14%) and by son, self and daughter in consultation with each other (6%).

Large number of widowers' maintained that they take decision themselves or that decision is made by son or in consultation with son and daughter. While married respondents state that major decisions are taken by self and wife, wife alone and jointly.

Large percentage of pensioners feel that their family always or sometimes agrees to their views. While 22 per cent non-pensioners' state that their family never agrees to their views.

Widower respondents stated that their family agreed to their views sometimes; while majority of married respondents stated that their views are never agreed to. Equal number of both married and widowers feel their views meet frequent approval.

Pensioners felt that young people did not pose any problem for them. While a majority of non-pensioners found it difficult to adjust with them, 40 per cent of married respondents find it difficult to deal with younger family members. While 26 per cent of widowers said that they adjust accordingly. About 56 per cent of pensioners reported that they have not experienced any sort of disrespect and 22 per cent said that they are respected as usual. Only 20 per cent of non-pensioners say that they are respected more after retirement; 2 per cent pensioners and 4 per cent non-pensioners felt that they were not given due respect after the death of their wives.

While 60 per cent married respondents reported that they had not experienced any sort of disrespect. Widowers maintained that they are disrespected more after the death of their wives.

Results in Table 2 show that non-pensioner respondents frequently converse with their sons, friends and grandchildren while pensioners report conversing a lot with wife, daughters and relatives.

Widowers obtained high percentage scores on conversation with sons, daughters, grandchildren and friends, while married subjects obtained high percentage scores on conversation with wife.

Pensioner respondents conversed mainly on family matters, politics/social affairs, religion, health and mutual welfare; while non-pensioners obtained high percentage scores on topics like financial problems.

Married reportedly conversed mainly on family matters, religion, health and mutual welfare. Widowers obtained high scores on politics/social affairs, financial problems, general topics like career of children, literary interests, scientific discoveries and poetry.

Results in Table 5 show that, more number of non-pensioners report changes in behaviour of wife, sons, daughters and relatives. Also though a large number of both pensioners and non-pensioners stated no change in relations, more number of pensioners reported this.

About 36 per cent married subjects reported change in relations, 9 per cent stated change in behaviour of wife and relatives (12%) while widowers reported change in behaviour of sons and daughters.

Table 6 shows that while a majority of both pensioners and non-pensioners say that they are not dependent on anyone; the percentage of pensioners is relatively more (80%). They also state that they are dependent on sons (52%), and daughters (52%). Non-pensioners obtained high scores on dependency on wife (48%) and others (4%) like servant etc. in old age.

Widowers (64%) state they are not dependent on anyone, dependent on son (32%), daughters (28%) and friends and relatives (4%), while married subjects reported being dependant on wife (48%).

Results in Table 7 show that non-pensioners wanted to stay with children. About 10 per cent of pensioners stated already living independently, while 28 per cent of them preferred to live independently.

Larger number of widowers wanted to stay with children, and equal number of both married and widowers preferred to live independently.

While a majority of both pensioners and non-pensioners were not willing to stay in old age homes. Around 18 per cent of pensioners preferred to stay in old age homes and 16 per cent non-pensioners stated that their family would like them to stay in old age homes.

Equal number of married subjects and widowers showed their preference for as well as unwillingness to stay in old age colonies. But 16 per cent of widowers felt that their family would appreciate it if they shifted to an old age colony.

Discussion

Ageing and family relationships, have been central forces shaping individual lives throughout history. While family may in some senses be a 'safe heaven' from harsh realities of life, Studies have found that close personal bonds can also serve to express and apply ageism (Butler and Dowd, 1980).

Family Relations of Pensioners and Non-Pensioners

When a person is in service, he may be the head of the family and all the important decisions are usually taken after consultation with him. But after retirement, he may have to be satisfied with a secondary position. And at times he may only be nominally informed about some of the important family matters.

In the present investigation also, more number of non-pensioners as compared to pensioners stated that there has been a change in family relations towards them after retirement. Also while

48 per cent non-pensioners take decisions themselves, 34 per cent of subjects say they take decisions jointly. Also 14 per cent of pensioners say that decision making is done by son, or reduction in the position of the elderly in family after retirement. Majumdar (1985), stated that there is loss of status accompanied by a sense of alienation and hopelessness among the elderly after retirement caused by economic dependence, physical weakness and domestic event. Elderly people staying with other younger members may have to face problems of adjustment too. This is because as they have been habituated to dictate terms, they may not be able to do so now because of their changed status. A number of non-pensioner respondents in the study felt that it was difficult for them to adjust with younger generation.

Usually, the opinion of the head of the family prevails. But after retirement, other family members who did not care to voice their disagreement may become bold. 20 per cent of pensioners stated that their family never agrees to their views and 76 per cent non-pensioners reported that their family agrees to them only sometimes.

About 14 per cent of both pensioners and non-pensioners felt that they are disrespected after retirement as they are no longer earning and are of no use to family. These are the respondents who have lost their status in family and other members have a dominant position. Dube (1955) said that parents dominate the family till their middle age (40–45), but with approaching old age they recede to the background.

Conversations with family members is one indicator of interrelationship between various family members. Family is commonly defined as a network of relations, related by descent or marriage. Large number of non-pensioners frequently converse with their sons, friends, grandchildren on financial problems, scientific discoveries and career of children etc. But most pensioners converse with wife, daughters and relatives on family matters, general topics, religion etc. Johnson (1992), also states that subjects with children are more active with all relatives, as children link them to grand children and relatives by marriage.

With change in economic status, it is conceivable that the behaviour of other members towards elderly people may also change. While 68.3 per cent pensioners felt that there has not been any change in relations with family. More numbers of non-pensioners subjects felt that there has been a change in the attitude of their sons,

Table 2

Frequency of Responses

Variables	*Pensioners*				*Non-Pensioners*			
	MA (N=25)		*WD (N=25)*		*MA (N=25)*		*WD (N=25)*	
	F	*%*	*F*	*%*	*F*	*%*	*F*	*%*
Family Relationship								
Change in relations	2	8	3	12	4	16	6	24
No Change in relation	23	92	22	88	21	84	19	76
Decision Making								
Self	9	36	14	56	8	32	16	64
Self and wife	8	32	14	56	8	32	16	64
Wife alone	3	12	0	0	2	8	0	0
Self + Son + Daughter	0	0	3	12	0	0	2	8
Son alone	1	4	6	24	2	8	1	4
Jointly	4	16	2	8	11	44	6	24

Cont'd...

Cont'd...

Agreement In Views								
Always	10	40	3	12	0	0	7	28
Sometimes	5	60	21	84	15	60	17	68
Never	0	0	1	4	10	40	1	4
Adjustability With Young								
No difficulty	11	44	14	56	10	40	11	44
Difficult to get along	9	36	5	20	11	44	7	28
True, get adjusted	5	20	6	24	4	16	7	28
Respect								
No experienced disrespect	17	68	11	44	13	52	13	52
Respected as usual	5	20	6	24	5	20	0	0
Respected more after retirement	1	4	2	8	5	20	5	20
Disrespected after retirement	2	8	5	20	2	8	5	20
Disrespected after death of wife	0	0	1	4	0	0	2	

Table 3

Frequency and frequency percentage scores for pensioners and non-pensioners on 'with whom the elderly converse the most'

Response	Pensioners						Non-Pensioners					
	MA(N=25)			WD(N=25)			MA(N=25)			WD(N=25)		
	F	%	Ranks	F	%	Ranks	F	%	Ranks	F	%	Ranks
None	0			0			0			0		
Wife	25	100	1	0			22	88	1	0		
Son	12	48	2	18	72	1	13	52	2	16	64	1
Daughter	7	28	3	16	64	2	7	28	3	10	40	2
Grandchildren	0	0		2	8	4.5	1	4	5.5	2	8	4
Friends	0	0		4	16	3	3	12	4	5	20	3
Other relatives	1	4	4	2	4	4.5	1	4	55	1	4	5
		N=45			N=42			N=47			N=36	

Table 4

Frequency and frequency percentage scores for pensioners and non-pensioners on 'topics on conversation'

Topics	Pensioners						Non-Pensioners					
	MA(N=25)			WD(N=25)			MA(N=25)			WD(N=25)		
	F	%	Ranks	F	%	Ranks	F	%	Ranks	F	%	Ranks
General	6	24	2	12	48	1	9	36	2	10	40	2
Family affairs	19	76	1	9	36	2	15	60	1	15	60	1
Politics/Social affairs	5	20	3.5	7	28	3	5	20	3.5	7	28	3
Financial problems	1	4	6	1	4	7	2	8	5.5	4	16	5
Religion	5	20	3.5	3	12	5	2	8	5.5	4	16	5
Health/mutual welfare	2	8%	5	2	8	6	1	4	7	0		
Other topics	0			5	20	4	5	20	3.5	4	16	5
		N=38			N=39			N=39			N=44	

Table 5

Frequency and frequency percentage scores for pensioners and non pensioners on 'change in behaviour of family members after retirement'

Observations	*Pensioners*						*Non-Pensioners*					
	MA (N=25)			*WD(N=25)*			*MA(N=25)*			*WD(N=25)*		
	F	*%*	*Ranks*	*F*	*%*	*Ranks*	*F*	*%*	*Ranks*	*F*	*%*	*Ranks*
No change observed	21	84	1	20	80	1	19	76	1	18	72	1
Wife has changed	1	4	5	0	0	0	2	8	4.5	0	0	
Sons have changed	2	8	4	3	12	3.5	3	12	3	7	28	2
Daughters have changed	3	12	2.5	3	12	3.5	2	8	4.5	5	20	3
Relatives have changed	3	12	2.5	4	16	2	5	20	2	3	12	4
		N=30			N=30			N=31			N=33	

Table 6

Frequency and frequency percentage scores for pensioners and non-pensioners on their 'dependency on family in old age'

Dependency	*Pensioners*						*Non-Pensioners*					
	MA (N=25)			*WD(N=25)*			*MA(N=25)*			*WD(N=25)*		
	F	*%*	*Ranks*	*F*	*%*	*Ranks*	*F*	*%*	*Ranks*	*F*	*%*	*Ranks*
Dependent on wife	6	24	2.5	0	0	0	12	48	1	0	0	0
Dependent on son	6	24	2.5	9	36	2.5	4	16	3	8	32	2
Dependent on daughter	5	20	4	9	36	2.5	1	4	4	7	28	3
Dependent on others	0	0	0	0	0	0	0	0	0	1	4	4
Independent	19	76	1	16	64	1	10	40	2	16	64	1
		N=36			N=34			N=27			N=32	

Table 7

Frequency and frequency percentage scores for pensioners and non-pensioners on their 'preferences to live independently'

Living Reference	*Pensioners*				*Non-Pensioners*			
	MA (N=25)		*WD(N=25)*		*MA(N=25)*		*WD(N=25)*	
	F	*%*	*F*	*%*	*F*	*%*	*F*	*%*
Already living independently	3	12	2	8	0	0	0	0
Prefer to live independently	7	28	7	28	6	24	6	24
Live with children	12	48	16	44	18	72	18	72
Live either way	3	12	0	0	1	4	1	4

Table 8

Frequency and frequency percentage scores for pensioners and non-pensioners on their 'willingness to stay in old age colonies and their families' views regarding it

Responses	*Pensioners*				*Non-Pensioners*			
	MA (N=25)		*WD(N=25)*		*MA(N=25)*		*WD(N=25)*	
	F	*%*	*F*	*%*	*F*	*%*	*F*	*%*
Yes	3	12	4	16	5	20	4	16
No	22	88	21	84	20	80	21	84
Approval								
Yes	1	4	4	16	4	17.4	4	16.7
No	24	96	21	84	19	82.6	20	83.3

daughters and relatives. This is because the children who were dependent on him for financial support may have become earners themselves and may not respect the respondents to that extent.

In old age a person may also have to depend on other individuals for assistance. While pensioners state that they depend on their sons and daughters; non-pensioners feel that they are more dependent on their wives and other people like servants etc.

In our country we are emotionally committed to joint family. Almost 72 per cent of non-pensioners subjects wanted to stay with children and 28 per cent of pensioners reported that they would prefer to live independently.

People enter special living settings because these arrangements allow them to satisfy basic needs more economically and efficiently than is otherwise possible. Almost equal number (83%) of both pensioners and non-pensioners, were not willing to stay in old homes and only 18 per cent of non-pensioners, preferred to stay in old age colonies. Research studies indicate that though the elderly respondents may prefer to stay away from their family, but, various physical and financial limitations may force an individual to turn to their family for support. Majority of respondents, both pensioners and non-pensioners felt their family would not approve their stay in old age colonies, though 17 per cent of non-pensioners felt that this arrangement would suit their family.

Family Relations of Married and Widowers

Belief in the family as the prime source of care can stem from, the needs and values of the children to take care of their elderly relatives. However, the ability and willingness of the family to take care of the elderly is often reducing. Widower respondents reported that the attitude of family towards them has changed after retirement. Majumdar (1985), also found that after retirement there is a feeling among the aged that everyone's attitude towards them has changed.

In respect of power, control and decision making at home and in work place, age grading has been very important. 60 per cent widowers stated that they take decisions themselves, 14 per cent say sons take decisions, 32 per cent married subjects reported that they take decisions in consultation with wife and 10 per cent say, that their wives alone take decisions. Hence, older people in some families still yield considerable influence in decision making at home.

After retirement, respondents may become conscious of the fact that, their words do not carry that sort of respect. While a large number of married subjects as compared to widowers feel that their views are never adhered to; widower Subjects state that their family agrees to their suggestions sometimes.

At times due to differing values and needs, tensions may arise between older and younger generations. While 50 per cent widowers did not have any adjustment problems with younger generation, 26 per cent of them also stated that they adjust according to situation. Almost 40 per cent of married subjects, found it difficult to deal with younger family members. Doeroa (1980), found that advancement in age result in insecurity and more of adjustment problems.

To reach the latter stages of one's life and find that no one accept you as you are, can be very threatening. While a majority of married subjects as disrespected and 6 per cent of them said they are disrespected after death of wife. Hence widowers who have lost their wives, have lost the one person most likely to re-assure them of their worth.

Close family relationship involve high levels of attachment and affection built up over the entire life. But the small marital unit in old age can be rendered vulnerable by low levels of resources, skills and knowledge. While a majority of married subjects reported that there has not been any change in behaviour of family, a few of them observed a change in behaviour of their wife and relatives. On the other hand widowers had observed a change in attitude of their sons and daughters.

About 64 per cent widowers and 76 per cent of married subjects maintained that they were not dependent on any one. A small number of married subjects however, stated that they are dependent on their wife and a small number of widower respondents also stated that they were dependent on their sons, daughters, friends and relatives.

Immediate impact of widowhood is on living arrangement as it forces a person to learn to live a single life. About 68 per cent of widowers preferred to stay with their children, while only 6 per cent of married subjects stated that they are already living independently.

For quite a few people cherished dream of old age is a house full of children and grandchildren. But due to feelings of dejection by children, many elderly people are seeking institutional care. About 84 per cent of both married and widower subjects stated that they do not want to stay in old age homes while 8 per cent of them preferred to be institutionalized. More number of widower subjects also felt that their family would appreciate it if they are shifted to an old age colony. This is because, when the spouse dies, living arrangements inevitably change and diverge according to the situation of the surviving partner.

In the end, it can be said that family support is the best shield for the aged, and it should be enhanced rather than discarded in the garb of modernity. Homes for the aged are not for those living in a joint family but for those individuals who have no one to look after them so that they do not feel miserable or depressed.

References

Bhowmick, Bula (1993): "Old-age-home-'Sandhya' Costly Stay, Uncertain Future". *The Hindustan Times*. May 8, New Delhi.

Birren, J.E. (1964): *The Psychology of Aging*. Prentice Hall, Englewood Cliffs, New Jersey.

David, R.P. (1990): "Aging in East and South-East Asia". A Division of Holder and Stoughton, London.

de Souza, Alfred (1982): *The Social Organisation of Aging among the Urban Poor*. Indian Social Institute, New Delhi.

Desai, K.G. and Naik, R.D. (1968): *Problems of Retired People in Greater Bombay*. Tata Institute of Social Sciences, Bombay.

Doeora, M.G. (1980): "Adjustment and Life Satisfaction in Old Age". *Journal of Gerontology*. Vol 40(2): 82–88.

Dowd, Butler (1980): In "Aging and Families: A Support Network Perspective" by H.L. Kending (1986). Allen & Unwin, Sydney.

Dube, S.C. (1955): *Indian Village*. Routledge and Kegan Paul, London.

Gangrade, K.D. (1978): "Intergenerational Conflict: A Sociological Study of Indian Youth". *A SCNA Survey*. Vol. 5, 10: 924–936.

Gangrade, K.D. (1989): "Emerging Conception of Aging in India: A Socio-cultural Perspective". *The Eastern Anthropologist*. Vol. 42: 2.

Gujral, Sheela (1993): "Retiring with Grace". *The Hindustan Times*. Saturday Magazine, January 16, New Delhi.

Johnson, C.L. et al. (1992): "Family Functioning in Late Life". *Journal of Gerontology*. Vol. 47 (2): 866–872.

Kending, H.L. (1986): *Ageing and Families: A Support Network Perspective*. Allen & Unwin, Sydney.

Luthra, P.N. (1994): "In Favour of the Family". *The Hindustan Times*. Saturday Magazine, Jan. 29, New Delhi.

Machinery, G. (1987): "Status of Retired in Family after Retirement". *Journal of Psychological Researches*. Vol. 31(3): 135.

Majumdar, C. (1985): "The End of the Road". *The Hindustan Times.* Saturday Magazine, October 06, New Delhi.

Mangala, A.P. and Chadha, N.K. (1991): "Social Network Approach to Old Age". *The Eastern Anthropologist.* Vol. 44(4).

Singh, Mahinder (1993): "Homes Away from Homes". *The Hindustan Times.* Saturday Magazine, July 03, New Delhi.

CHAPTER 21

Economic Condition of the Old Aged Persons and their Pension Holding Status

A.L. Srivastava

This paper deals with the overall economic condition of the old aged persons. The broad contours of the occupational mobility of the old aged persons along with the accumulation of movable and immovable assets have been discussed. The aim of the exploration is to find out how the occupational career of the respondents have enabled them to fulfil major obligations vis-à-vis children's education, marriage, land purchase, house construction etc.

The data regarding the pension holding status of the old aged persons, problems being faced in the fixation and disbursement of pension amount, sufficiency of pension amount etc., have been analysed. The aim is to find out the current economic status of the respondents and what satisfaction or dissatisfaction they have with the pension amount.

Method of the Study

The universe of the present study consists of the old aged persons living in the city of Varanasi. For the purpose of the present study, persons between the age of 56 years to 85 years have been treated as old aged persons. As there was no readily available list of such old aged persons, therefore the exact number of old aged persons is difficult to be ascertained. Moreover the information regarding the

IJG, 1996, Vol. 10, No. 1–4, pp. 51–60.

retired persons drawing pensions belonging to various work organization was also very scanty and scattered. Therefore, attempts were made to collect and collate information regarding old aged persons were from various agencies and departments and information regarding their age, status, occupation, residence etc., were ascertained.

The sample technique adopted for the present study has been snowball technique. In the first instance, a retired person was located and then he was asked to inform about two or more retired persons. This process was replicated till the desired number of respondents i.e., 400 old aged persons were contacted and interviewed for the study.

For the purpose of present study both primary and secondary data have been used. The primary data have been collected mainly through the use of structured interview schedule. Apart from this interview schedule, primary data have been collected through informal talks with the respondents and field observation. The secondary data of the study have been collected from government records, published reports and research materials.

The data have been analysed descriptively.

Interpretation of Data

Occupational Mobility of the Respondents

Occupational mobility may be discussed by examining both the mobility of the occupations themselves and individual movement from one occupation to another. Mobility may involve change in locus, function, income, prestige, power, independence or other occupational attributes.

Old age person's occupational profile is a long one which may register lots of changes both inter-occupational mobility and intra-occupational mobility. A study of occupational shift thus provides a clue to the understanding of the occupational status and economic problems of the old aged persons. In the present study there are 60 per cent respondents who have no occupational shift in their life. Their first occupation is the last occupation. However 40 per cent respondents have registered occupational shifts in their career. Among these 22.25 per cent respondents have one change in their occupational career, 8.25 per cent have two changes; 6.75 per cent have three changes and 2.75 per cent respondents have four changes in their occupational career. These changes are related to shift from one job position to another job position or from one type of business/occupation to another type of business/occupation.

Table 1

Occupational mobility of the respondents

Occupational Mobility	*Frequency*	*Percentage*
No change of occupation	240	60.00
One change	89	22.25
Two changes	33	08.25
Three changes	27	06.75
Four changes	11	02.75
Total	400	100.00

Resources for Change of Occupation

Our exploration into the reasons for the occupational shift indicate that job security and economic prosperity are the two dominant factors which have compelled the respondents to go for new occupation because of better economic prospects of the new occupation; 11 per cent respondents have changed occupation to gain security and permanency in the new job; 8.25 per cent have changed occupation as previous occupation was less paying; 4.25 respondents have changed on account of more prestige in the new occupation and 3.25 per cent respondent report insecurity in previous occupation as a reason for the change of occupation.

Setbacks/Problems in Occupational Career

In order to understand the occupational profile of the old aged persons under study, the respondents have been asked to mention the setbacks/problems in their occupational career. It has been found that as large as 75 per cent respondents have had no serious problem in their occupational career. Among those who have faced problems, 6 per cent of them reported frequent and 13.25 per cent reported obstruction in the way of promotion as the major hurdle in their occupational career. There are 4 per cent respondents who have stated serious loss in business and 1.75 per cent respondents have stated taxation problem as the most complicated problem in their occupational career.

Table 2
Reason for change of occupation

Reasons	*Frequency*	*Percentage*
Previous occupation less paying	33	8.25
Insecurity in previous occupation	13	3.25
New occupation had better economic prospects	53	13.25
New occupation more prestigious	17	4.25
Security and permanency in the new job	44	11.00
Not applicable/no response	240	60.00
Total	400	100.00

The respondents have been asked to describe the level of satisfaction with their occupational career. There are 11.25 per cent respondents who have described their occupational career as extremely satisfactory. For 54 per cent respondents it has been satisfactory. There are 26.25 per cent respondents who considered their occupational career neither satisfactory nor unsatisfactory but so-so. There are only 8.50 per cent respondents who have not been satisfied with their occupational career. Out of these 6.75 per cent termed it as unsatisfactory whereas for 7 respondents (1.75%) their occupational career has been extremely unsatisfactory. Therefore, it can be concluded that the majority of the respondents consider their occupational career as satisfactory. They have further stated that in terms of salary, promotion, placement and interpersonal relationship within the work organization they were by and large satisfied.

Sufficiency of Income in Providing Support to Children's Education

The respondents have been asked whether their income was sufficient to provide satisfactory education to their children/dependents. Majority of respondents (80.50%) asserted that their income was sufficient to provide good education to their children/dependents whereas 18.50 per cent respondents stated that it was not sufficient to provide good education. Though majority of respondents stated that financial position was sufficient enough to provide adequate education to their progeny yet a number of them have felt the pinch of their low income in providing better education facilities to their children.

Table 3

Reason for change of occupation

Setback/Problems in the occupational career	*Frequency*	*Percentage*
Frequent transfer	24	6.00
Promotion throttled	53	13.25
Serious loss in business	16	4.00
Sales Tax/ Income Tax difficulties	07	1.75
No difficulty	300	75.00
Total	400	100.00

Table 4

Satisfaction with occupational career

Satisfaction with occupational career	*Frequency*	*Percentage*
Extremely satisfactory	45	11.25
Satisfactory	216	54.00
So-so	105	26.25
Unsatisfactory	27	6.75
Extremely unsatisfactory	07	1.75
Total	400	100.00

Table 5

Sufficiency of income in providing support for children's education

Educational and financial position	*Frequency*	*Percentage*
Sufficient	322	80.50
Insufficient	74	18.50
No response	04	01.00
Total	400	100.00

Sufficiency of Financial Position in the Solemnization of Children's Marriage

Marriage has become a costly affair. Huge investment in the form of 'Tilak', jewellery, dowery and entertainment of guests etc., are needed to help solemnize the marriage. In case where dowery is very high, one finds it very difficult to meet out the heavy marriage expenditure through his own income. Family assets, the relatives and friends' financial help or else borrowing from other sources are needed to cover the marital expenses. The respondents of the present study have been asked to state whether the income from their occupation was helpful in solemnizing the marriage of their children/dependents. It may be seen that only 44.50 per cent respondents have stated that they fulfilled the marital obligations through their own income very satisfactorily but 49.50 per cent respondents have stated that this was partially helpful in solemnising the marriages of their children. They have to fall back to the assets of the family as a whole or else they took loan/help from the relatives, friends and others. There are 6 per cent respondents who have not given any explicit answer to this query.

Table 6

Sufficiency of financial positions in the solemnization of children's marriage

Marriage and financial position	*Frequency*	*Percentage*
Very helpful	178	44.50
Partially helpful	198	49.50
No response	24	6.00
Total	400	100.00

Accumulation of Asset by the Respondents

Life long persuasion of an occupation may lead to accumulation of substantial assets. Life saving may be invested in numerous ways. It may be in the form of simple bank deposit to enable one to fulfil one's responsibility or it may help in sickness, accident and other calamities. The savings may be invested in the purchase of land or construction of house or else in the purchase of valuable items such as jewellery, consumer goods etc. Thus life saving is a form of social security and social defence as well as a symbol of status. For the old aged persons life saving provide him an adage in the form of power and influence in the family.

Enquiring into this dimension, it has been found that 5 per cent respondents have utilized their life saving in the form of land purchase; 8.75 per cent respondents have constructed their residential houses; 46.25 per cent respondents have simple bank deposit only; 6.50 per cent have bank deposit along with costly jewellery; 13.75 per cent respondents have bank deposit alongwith residential house and 9.50 per cent respondents whose life saving was rather meagre and they were not successful in accumulating any substantial asset. Thus it is clear that the saving have been mainly cash deposit to cover contingencies in old age or to purchase land/house/jewellery to provide better conditions of life for their family.

Table 7
Accumulation of asset

Accumulation of asset	*Frequency*	*Percentage*
Land purchase	20	05.00
House construction	35	08.75
Bank deposit	185	46.25
Jewellery purchase and bank deposit	26	06.50
House and bank deposit	55	13.75
Land and bank deposit	38	09.50
No significant assets	41	10.25
Total	400	100.00

Position Holding Status of the Respondents

One of the major problems faced in old age is that of income for maintenance. Retired employees of the government and organized sector of industry are comparatively better off as regard to old age benefits. In government services retired employees are eligible for pension, gratuity, leave encashment and provident fund.

The system of payment of pension to government employees dates back to more than a hundred years over since the enactment of the Pension Act 1871. From time to time, the retirement benefits have been liberalized including payment of pension to family in the event of death of the employee in service, and relief to neutralize price increases. Some of these measures, introduced recently, reflect the governments' concern towards the well-being of its retired employees.

For old aged persons regular pension is a source of livelihood and also psychic gratification which contribute to the continuity of life. Better pension status and regular timely payment of pension are great source of relief to the old aged persons. If it is not so then the miseries of old life get compounded.

Our enquiry into the pension holding status of the respondents has revealed that as large as 68.75 per cent respondents are receiving pension. Most of the respondents have been government employees where pension forms an integral part of the occupational career. However, a few of them who have worked in private organizations do not enjoy pension benefits. There are 31.25 per cent respondents who are not pensionholders as they have engaged themselves in business, shopkeeper in self-employed occupations.

Table 8
Pension holding status of the respondents

Pension holding status of the respondents	*Frequency*	*Percentage*
Yes	275	68.75
No	125	31.25
Total	400	100.00

Difficulties in Obtaining the Pension

Retired employees have to face considerable difficulties in the fixation and payment of pension amount. These difficulties in old age with falling health and paucity of resources lead to agony and frustrations, apart from financial difficulties. Enquiring into these aspects, it has been found that 12.75 per cent respondents had to face difficulties with regard to the fixation of pension amount. There are 10.25 per cent respondents who have reported apathy of officials towards pensionholders as the major source of discontentment. There are 30.75 per cent respondents who have not faced any significant difficulties in the fixation and release of pension. Thus it is clear that in the present study, most of the pensionholders have to face some sort of difficulties in the award of receipt of the pension.

Table 9
Difficulties in obtaining the pension

Nature of difficulties	*Frequency*	*Percentage*
Considerable time lag	51	12.75
Apathy of officials	41	10.25
Problem in fixation	60	15.00
No problem	123	30.75
Not applicable/no response	125	31.25
Total	400	100.00

Delay in Release of Pension

One of the major problems a retired person has to face, is the release of first pension amount. After a lot of paper work, administrative formalities and 'pairavi' the first pension amount gets released. Greater the delay greater is the hardships for a newly retired person who has lost his job and has no other source of income. As regards the respondents of the present study, it has been found that 15.75 per cent respondents received their first pension in less than 6 months of their retirement; 37 per cent of them between 6 and 12 months and 16.00 per cent of them between 12 and 18 months. Thus, it is clear that a considerable time lag has occurred in the receipt of first pension after the retirement. This would have definitely contributed to the economic hardship of a newly retired person.

Table 10
Delay in release of pension

Time gap	*Frequency*	*Percentage*
Less than six months	63	15.75
6–12 months	148	37.00
12–18 months	64	16.00
Not applicable	125	31.25
Total	400	100.00

Mode of Pension Payment

The respondents have been asked to state the mode of the payment of the pension. It has been found that the respondents receive the amount of the pension through money order; or treasury or banks. There are 9.25 per cent respondents who have reported that they receive their pension through money order. Receiving the amount through treasury has been reported by 40.5 per cent respondents. There are 19.25 per cent respondents who have stated that they receive payment through banks. Thus it is clear that in most of the cases, pension is paid through treasury which is rather more secure and convenient method of pension payment. However, the very old pensionholders do confront difficulties in reaching treasury each month.

Table 11
Mode of pension payment

Nature of mode	*Frequency*	*Percentage*
Through money order	37	09.25
Through treasury	161	40.25
Through bank	77	19.25
Not applicable/no response	125	31.25
Total	400	100.00

Behaviour of Pension Authority

The respondents have been asked to express their opinion regarding the behaviour of pension sanctioning/disbursing authorities towards the pensionholders. It may be seen that only 16.25 per cent respondents have stated that the pension sanctioning authorities are sympathetic and considerate towards them. There are 37 per cent respondents who have stated that the pension authorities behave as per routine. There are 11 per cent respondents who have stated that the pension sanctioning authorities are unsympathetic and apathetic towards them. There are 4 per cent respondents who have not expressed any concrete opinion in this regard. Thus it is clear that retired pensionholders, who expect highly considerate behaviour on the part of their pension authorities, are often disappointed and find the pension authorities as routine and inconsiderate persons.

Sufficiency of Pension Amount

The respondents have been further inquired about the sufficiency of the pension amount i.e., whether it is sufficient for their personal requirement and immediate liability. There are only 19.50 per cent respondents who have stated that their pension is sufficient for their personal requirement and for the fulfilment of immediate liability whereas 49.25 per cent said that it is not sufficient to cover their heavy liabilities. By and large the pensionholders included in the present study have enumerated soaring prices as the main reason for insufficiency of pension amount.

Table 12
Behaviour of pension authorities

Behaviour pattern	*Frequency*	*Percentage*
Sympathetic	65	16
Routine	148	37
Unsympathetic	46	11
I cannot say	16	04
Not applicable	125	31
Total	400	100

Table 13
Sufficiency of pension amount

Sufficiency of pension amount	*Frequency*	*Percentage*
Yes	78	50
No	197	49
Not applicable	125	31
Total	400	100

Enhancement of Pension Amount

Exploration made to ascertain the respondents desire for enhancement in their pension amount has been explored. It has been found that most of the respondents (56.50%) have preferred enhancement in their pension amount. There are only 4.50 per cent respondents who stated that they do not require any enhancement in their pension amount whereas 7.75 per cent respondents could not give a clear answer to this query. The respondents have further stated that enhancement of pension amount should be in tune with the price index and it should be periodically reviewed and revised.

Table 14
Enhancement of pension amount

Enhancement of pension amount	*Frequency*	*Percentage*
Yes	226	89
No	18	04
I cannot say	31	07
Not applicable	125	31
Total	400	100

Conclusion

In this paper the broad features of the occupational career of the respondents have been analysed. It has been found that most of the respondents (60%) stuck to their original occupation while 40 per cent respondents had changed their occupation more than once. The reason for change had been search for better economic opportunities and security. Most of the respondents considered their occupational career either satisfactory (54%) or extremely satisfactory (11.25%). A few respondents considered their occupational career as unsatisfactory (6.75%) and extremely unsatisfactory (1.75%). Most of the respondents had expressed that their income status was sufficient enough to support their children's education (80.50%). However, they found their income status not so helpful in fulfilling the marital obligations of their children/dependents. Most of the respondents had accumulated bank deposit, purchased land and constructed house through life saving. But such accumulation of asset in most of the cases was of marginal level.

In the sample 68.75 per cent respondents were pensionholders. These respondents in most of the cases had to face difficulties in pension fixation and disbursement after a considerable time lag or apathetic attitude of the pension authorities. Some of the respondents had to wait for more than one year to receive their first pension. The major mode of payment of pension amount was through treasury in cash. However, some of the respondents' pension amount was being credited to their bank account or remitted to them through money order. The respondents felt that the pension amount was to meet the daily requirement of their life. The pension amount was meagre in the context of high price rise. Most of the respondents (56.50%) preferred enhancement of pension amount in a manner that they could fulfil the obligations of their personal and familial life.

CHAPTER **22**

Influence of Age on Mental Stress

R.K. Gunthey and Sarita Mathur

At each developmental stage different tasks are to be mastered and roles played effectively. Each developmental stage has its own unique demands to be met by the person. In the present phase of human history, life has become more and more charged with stresses and strains, despite tremendous advancements. Psychologically, physical distance has shrunked and the human system has not yet evolved to any significant level vis-à-vis the technological revolutions and consequent changes in man's ecosystem. However, man with his versatile capacity for homeostasis, does try to restore effective adjustment with his environment.

The influence of age on MMPI responses has been investigated by Meehl (1951). It was found that older subjects obtained more peak scores on MMPI scales than younger subjects. Gerner (1979) and Zury (1980) in a major review article on depression in the elderly, emphasize the multiple losses that older persons are likely to encounter. They noted that this age group is more likely to suffer loss of family members, friends, health and physical attractiveness. Life satisfaction might be considered as a vulnerability or resistance factor with regard to stress related disorders (Baruffol et al., 1995). Generalized anxiety disorders in the elderly is associated with elevated anxiety, worry, social fears and depression and there is negative relationship between age and subjective level of stress (Beck et al.,

IJG, 1997, Vol. 11, No. 1 and 2, pp. 36–39.

1996; Nussbaum et al., 1995). Therefore, to study the influence of age on mental stress the present investigation attempted to find out the patterns of mental stress from early adulthood to old age males.

Method

Sample

Using the incidental-cum-purposive sampling technique, a sample of 270 males was selected. The sample was classified in three age levels: early adulthood (25 years to 30 years, N=100), middle age group (40 years to 45 years, N=90) and old age group (55 years and above, N=68).

Tools

Sort form-A of Jodhpur Multiphasic Personality Inventory (JMPI) was used in data collection (Joshi and Malik, 1981).

Procedure

In the present study, age level was used as independent variable and mental stress as dependent variable. Inter-group comparisons were used as control in the present study, e.g., mental stress of 'early adulthood' was compared with mental stress of old and middle age groups and 'middle age' group was compared with the 'old age' and 'early adulthood' groups of subjects. All the subjects were educated (passed secondary examination) and belonged to the same socio-economic status.

Results and Discussion

A cluster of psychiatric problems is obtained from the above results, which has a continuous acceleration across the ages for the male subjects. The cluster has the psychotic problems like manic depression, hebephrenia, schizophrenia (simple), psychotic depression and schizophrenic paranoid. Psychoneurotic problems like conversion and schizophrenic paranoid. Psychoneurotic problems like conversion-reaction, phobia, depression and neurasthenia. On psychoses part of the JMPI the old age people scored comparatively higher mean for scales like – manic-depression Hebephrenia, Schizophrenia (simple), psychotic – depression and schizophrenic paranoid than the other groups. Problems like manic-depression, hebephrenia,

Table 1

Showing mean, SD and significance of difference at different age levels on psychotic part of JMPI

Groups		*MD*	*HEB*	*SC(S)*	*PD*	*SCPA*	*PA*
25 years to 30 years (Male, N=100)	M	27.52	5.55	29.48	5.92	3.54	12.83
	SD	7.77	2.83	13.21	2.79	2.58	5.85
40 years to 45 years (Male, N=92)	M	26.22	6.47	33.91	6.30	4.71	15.18
	SD	9.31	3.57	13.86	3.31	3.56	8.0
55 years and above (Male, N=78)	M	36.17	7.60	35.04	7.82	5.87	13.46
	SD	10.17	3.23	9.12	3.84	3.40	6.44
't' values							
25 years to 30 years v/s 40 years to 45 years		1.04NS	1.98*	2.26*	0.85NS	2.59	2.31*
25 years to 30 years v/s 55 years and above		6.22**	4.42**	3.32**	3.70**	4.97**	0.67NS
40 years to 45 years v/s		6.62**	2.16*	0.64NS	2.74**	2.16*	1.56NS

*P<.05, **P<.01, NS - Not significant
MD - Manic Depression; HEB - Hebphrenia; SC (S) - Schizophrenia (simple); PD - Psychotic Depression; SCPA - Schizophrenia Paranoid; PA - Paranoia.

Table 2

Showing mean, SD and Significance of difference at different age levels on psychotic part of JMPI

Groups		*An*	*OC*	*CR*	*Hy (D)*	*Ph*	*D*	*Ne*	*SI*
25 years to 30 years (Male, N=100)	M	14.95	13.83	8.41	3.35	3.09	13.75	6.88	19.42
	SD	7.75	7.31	5.38	2.10	2.37	6.89	2.99	5.14
40 years to 45 years (Male, N=92)	M	15.25	15.09	9.66	36.76	4.16	14.29	7.78	19.72
	SD	7.22	8.55	4.99	2.92	2.64	6.25	1.17	6.58
55 years and above (Male, N=78)	M	16.19	15.21	11.40	3.62	3.99	17.01	11.73	21.17
	SD	4.59	4.98	4.64	2.75	2.38	5.05	4.08	4.77
't' values									
25 years to 30 years v/s 40 years to 45 years		0.28NS	1.09NS	1.66NS	11.20**	2.90**	0.57NS	1.73NS	0.35NS
25 years to 30 years v/s 55 years and above		1.32NS	1.50NS	3.95**	0.72NS	2.50*	3.64**	8.92**	2.36*
40 years to 45 years v/s 55 years and above		1.03NS	0.11NS	2.35*	0.32NS	0.44NS	3.14**	6.27**	1.66NS

*P<.05, **P<.01, NS - Not significant

An – Anxiety; OC - Obsessive Compulsive; CR - Conversion Reaction; Hy (D) - Hysteria Dissociative; pH - Phobia; D - Depression; Ne - Neurasthenia; SI - Social Introversion

Table 3

Showing mean, SD and significance of difference at different age levels on psychotic part of JMPI

Groups		*PU*	*ANR*	*UC*	*Hy.T.*	*Br.A.*
25 years to 30 years (Male, N=100)	M	19.78	12.33	27.33	18.95	31.4
	SD	8.17	6.56	7.72	7.14	8.66
40 years to 45 years (Male, N=92)	M	19.66	14.27	28.12	20.75	30.88
	SD	6.43	6.51	8.16	7.01	8.18
55 years and above (Male, N=78)	M	22.33	16.96	29.27	25.01	31.87
	SD	6.33	6.57	5.78	5.97	6.40
't' values						
25 years to 30 years v/s 40 years to 45 years		0.11NS	2.05*	0.69NS	1.77NS	0.13NS
25 years to 30 years v/s 55 years and above		2.25**	4.67**	1.92NS	6.16**	0.74NS
40 years to 45 years v/s 55 years and above		2.61**	2.68**	1.07NS	4.27**	0.89NS

*P<.05, **P<.01, NS - Not significant
PU - Peptic Ulcer; ANR - Anorexia Nervosa; UC - Ulcerative Colitus; Hy.T - Hypertension;
Br.A - Bronchial Asthma.

schizophrenia (simple) and schizophrenia paranoid also have severity in middle-age people as compared to early adult subjects. Problems like anxiety, obsessive compulsive, conversion reaction, hysterical dissociate, phobia, depression and neurasthania aged group has significantly higher mean than the other groups. While middle age groups have burden of psychoneurotic problems like conversion reaction, phobia, neurosthenia and depression as compared to early adult males. Older people consistently showed moderate elevations on depression and hypochondrisis scale. Elderly period of life is more prone to mania, depression, anxiety, schizophrenia and personality disorders (Beckman, 1995). Anxiety disorders are less common in the elderly than in younger adults. Generalized anxiety disorders and phobias account for most anxiety in late life (Flint, 1994).

The physiological, psychological as well as the socio-economic changes with age may be the cause of greater severity of mental health problems in later period of life. An older person faces numerous very real fears and insecurities that may not be the characteristic of earlier life periods, like that produced by retirement. Many people depend greatly on their work for status, for self-identity, for satisfying inter-personal relationship and for the meaning of their lives. Retirement often does not meet those needs and may lead to irreversible mental strain. Retirement usually also leads to severe stress like reduction in income which further augments the older person's adjustive burden. As the individual grows older, he is faced with the inevitable loss of loved ones, friend and contemporaries. The death of the mate with whom one may have shared many years of close companionship often poses certain particularly difficult adjustment problems. Defiance by sons dependability of them, decline in influence over family members, change or disturbances in sleep and lack of control over emotions may also be the causes of mental health problems in old age people.

References

Baruffol, Eric, Gisle, L. and Corten, P. (1995): "Life Satisfaction as a Mediator between Distressing Events and Neurotic Impairment in a General Population". *Acta Psychiatrica Scandinavica.* Vol. 92(1): 56–62.

Beck, J., Gayle, Stanley, Melinda, A. and Zebb, Barbara J. (1996): "A Descriptive Study". *Behaviour Research and Therapy*. Vol. 34 (3): 225–234.

Beckman, Artjan T.F., Deg, Dorly J.H., Van Tilburg, Theo' Smith and Jan Hetal (1995): "Major and Minor Depression in Later Life: A Study of Prevalence and Risk Factors". *Journal of Affective Disorders*. 36 (1–2): 65–75.

Flint, A. (1994): "Epidemiology in Comorbidity of Anxiety Disorders in the Elderly". *American Journal of Psychiatry*. Vol. 151(5): 640–649.

Gerner, R.H. (1979): "Depression in the Elderly" in O.J. Kaplan (Ed.) *Psychology of Aging*. New York: Academic Press.

Joshi, M.C. and Malik, A.K. (1981): *Manual of Jodhpur Multiphasic Personality Inventory*. Varanasi, Rupa Psychological Association, 1981.

Meehl, B.A. (1951): *Principles of Psychopathology: An Experimental Approach*. New York: McGraw Hill.

Nussbaum, Paul D. and Goreczny, Anthony J. (1995): "Self-appraisal of Stress Level and Related Psychopathology". *Journal of Anxiety Disorders*. Vol. 9(6): 463–472.

Zury, W.W.K.(1980): "Affective Disorders" in E.W. Busse and D.G. Blazer (Eds.), *Handbook of Geriatric Psychiatry*. New York: Van Nostr and Reinhold.

CHAPTER 23

Retirement and Ageing

Leisure Activities and Health Ailments

Priya Kanwar and N.K. Chadha

"Age is a thing of mind over matter. If you don't mind. It doesn't matter". These words have been rightly said by Mark Twain, however in today's contemporary world, 'old' is a strong word confirming myriad negative images. We make many decisions or have them made for us based upon assumptions about age. Although one ages from the moment of conception to the moment of death. Children are considered to be growing and developing while adults are thought of as 'ageing'.

Old age is a crucial stage in one's life. One is lucky enough if have a smooth sailing from middle age into old age and is not confronted with a variety of bewildering problems. But in case of people who lead an active life in service, the change is drastic. From an active life one is thrown suddenly into inactive life of retirement.

Retirement is a major turning point in adult development since it is the social milestone marking the shift from the middle years to the later years of life. According to Carp (1960) "Retirement is a relatively new phase in human development. In the past, retirement often suggested disability. Most adults worked until they died, a retirement from life not work."

Retirement as a mass phenomenon is a modern industrial creation. The impact of retirement is tremendous as it results in loss of role, status, power and an occupational identity. Therefore, at this stage a major reorganization of one's life activities is required. There can be considerable degree of social isolation if new activities are not

IJG, 1997, Vol. 11, No. 1 and 2, pp. 28–35.

found to replace work related activities. The implication that the individual is no longer able to carry out the work role is especially problematic. Retirement can lead to low morale, decreased level of satisfaction, depression and feelings of loneliness and helplessness.

Retirement is non-employment rather than unemployment. Unemployed adults are seeking work while non-employed adults have stopped working. Retirement has numerous dimensions and consequently can be defined in several ways. The most inclusive definition of a retired person is "an individual who is not fully time annually and who receives some kind of retirement pension from previous years of job service" (Epstein and Murray, 1968).

(i) *Retirement as an event,* where the retirement is an occasion that makes the transition from middle age to the later years of adulthood. For some individuals, it may also mark the end of period of work and the beginning of a period of relative leisure.

(ii) *Retirement as a position,* where the individual moves into a relatively new social position with the accompanying expectations and roles. There is major characteristic decline in the standard of living and a reduction in the number of roles played.

(iii) *Retirement as a process,* which involves working through the conflicts and concerns inherent in a major transition. These concerns have to work with factors such as the individuals' health, whether retirement is mandatory or voluntary and the meaning the individual personally attributes to retirement.

A popular opinion is that emergence of problems after retirement is due to ambiguity and non-availability of roles for old persons. Our socialization process does not adequately prepare even fully mature adults for the trauma of retirement. It ultimately leads to problems of ill health, psychological maladjustment, economic hardship, disturbed relationship within family and improper utilization of leisure time. Cushing (1952) suggested four essentials of successfully meeting the problems of retirement:

(i) Financial security
(ii) A time consuming interest
(iii) A gradual tapering off work
(iv) Companionship of one's own co-peers.

Leisure Activities

Leisure has been the concern of man through the ages. In antiquity, it represented man's ultimate goal, a life of tranquility and contemplation. In modern days it seems to be wring into man's ultimate problem. How to cope with a life that has set man free from the daily struggle for survival; but has not taught him to be himself and take advantage of never before existing opportunities.

According to Neulinger (1974) "Leisure once meant a way of life, a state of being. Today, leisure is generally defined in position to work as time leftover, as a residue".

Leisure is also defined as personally expressive discretionary activity varying in intensity of involvement from relevation and diversion at the low end of the continuum, through personal development and creativity at higher levels upto sensual transcendence at the highest levels of cognitive, emotional and physical involvement.

Researchers generally group leisure activities into four categories:

(a) *Cultural*: Such as attendance at sporting events, church and religious meetings, clubs, going to the movies etc.

(b) *Physical*: Including camping, fishing, gardening, golf, hunting and jobs around home etc.

(c) *Social*: Such a playing cards, drinking with friends at a bar, visiting family relatives and friends, going to parties etc.

(d) *Solitary*: Including, reading religious textbooks, magazines, newspapers, listening to radio and watching television.

Research indicates that leisure activities vary according to age in period of life cycle and these activities are, at all points of the life cycle, related to a number of factors such as income level, personality, health, ability level, transportation, educational level etc. Each of these factors can play a significant role in the selection of and participation in leisure activities at all points along the life cycle and having someone to do something with and viewing leisure positively is also very important.

Health

Health is a complex term to define. What constitutes 'good' health for individuals in one life period may constitute poor health in a different life period. Also what constitutes 'good' health for some individuals may constitute 'poor' health for others. The reverse can also be true. People are willing to accept different physical states as 'normal' depending on past health and current demands and expectations. At best, the term 'health' is a subjective one.

The World Health Organisation has defined health as "a state of complete physical, mental and social well-being and not merely the absence of disease or infirmity" (WHO, 1946).

Health is obviously an important factor in the lives of the aged. Health status is a factor that has a bearing in almost every single aspect of our lives; it can determine what activities or tasks we can (not) engage in. Health can also effect the way we perceive ourselves. In essence, one of the most important aspects of old age is health.

'Health' consists of two aspects in the study of elderly:

1. Actual health status which comprises of the individual's physical state, and
2. Perceived health status, which is the individuals's own perception about his health with respect to others of his age.

Those in good health (or perceive their health as good) or with high activity levels, continue to perceive themselves as middle-aged. Often older people can identify a particular incident such as a fall, stroke, or heart attack which made them feel that they were growing older. However, health problems need not be acute to bring about a feeling of ageing.

Tiring easily or difficulties in driving or walking may be frequent small reminders to the person that they are not as young and fit as they once were.

Method

Objectives

1. To make a profile of leisure activities of pre-retirement and post-retirement group of elderlies.
2. To make a profile of common health problems faced by pre-retirement, retirement and post-retirement group of elderlies.

Sample

The sample for the present study was divided according to the three major groups as given in the following design:

(a) Retiring in 3–4 years : (N=45)
(b) Retiring within a year : (N=45)
(c) Retired for more than 2 years : (N=45)

The sample was a non-probability one. Most of the respondents were from following three residential areas of Delhi.

(i) Paschim Vihar
(ii) Sunder Vihar
(iii) Meera Bagh

Tools

The tools employed in the present study for investigating purposes comprised of questions which had been earlier used with elderly population. The following schedules were employed to obtain information.

1. Personal information schedule.
2. Leisure activities record: This record gives a list of 24 leisure activities which were compiled by John Van Willigen and Chadha (1987). The activities were classified under four major categories: cultural, physical, social and solitary activities.
3. Common ailments of old age checklist: Self constructed list of ailments associated with old age. The respondents tick mark against those applicable to them.

Results

Table 1 reveals that pre-retired differ significantly from retired at 0.05 level on their pursuit of leisure activities. A significant differences is not seen between the retired and post-retired groups.

Table 1

Comparison between different groups on their leisure time activities

Groups	*No.*	*Mean*	*SD*	*'t' value*
Pre-retirement	45	9.9	3.4	Pre-ret vs ret.=2.03
Retirement	45	11.6	4.0	Ret. vs. Post-ret=0.08*
Post-retirement	45	11.5	4.1	Pre-ret. vs. Post-ret.=1.96*

Table 2 reveals that retired and post-retired differ significantly at 0.01 level. Pre-retired and post-retired also differ at 0.01 level of significance on their actual physical health.

Table 3 indicates that the pre-retired, retired and post-retired often engage themselves in activities like reading books and magazines, listening to radio and watch TV among other activities. The three groups also like to attend movies and watch video, and like to do household chores and odd jobs at home.

Table 4 reveals that the post-retired group face maximum member of health problems, followed by the retired group and then the pre-retired group.

Table 2

Comparison between different groups on their health problems

Groups	*No.*	*Mean*	*SD*	*'t' value*
Pre-retirement	45	1.5	1.0	Pre-ret vs ret.=0.85
Retirement	45	1.7	1.0	Ret. vs Post-ret=5.34**
Post-retirement	45	3.5	2.3	Pre-ret. vs Post-ret.=5.21**

** Significant at 0.01 level.

Table 3

Percentage of persons pursuing different leisure activities

	Leisure activities	*Pre-ret*	*Ret*	*Post-ret*
1.	Attend movies or watch video	60.5	65.5	55.5
2.	Visit places of worship	45	53.0	48
3.	Morning and evening walks	35.5	70.5	55.5
4.	Read religious books	32.5	30.5	41
5.	Read other books, magazines etc.	85.5	85.5	83
6.	Play cards	23	21	26
7.	Listen to radio, watch TV	100	91	98
8.	Look after children, grandchildren	31	45.5	48
9.	Write letters	38	61	48
10.	Household jobs, odd chores	70.5	71	63
11.	Gardening	38	53	63
12.	Exercise and play games	33	61	38
13.	Visit friends, relatives	60.5	65.5	56
14.	Speak on phone	55.5	58	48
15.	Gossip with family friends	28	36	40.5
16.	Visit the local mess or club	25.5	28	23
17.	Listen to music	33	48	61
18.	Nap or rest during the day	33	43	55.5
19.	Outing with family members	50.0	46	51
20.	Entertain friends	40.5	61	53
21.	Attendance at community events	28	31	41
22.	Perform voluntary acts to help others	23	45.5	48
23.	Doing nothing	2.5	0	10.5

Table 4

Percentage of responses on common health problem faced by pre-retired and post-retired

	Leisure activities	*Pre-ret*	*Ret*	*Post-ret*
1.	Impairment of vision	32.5	33	50.5
2.	Impairment of hearing	7.5	3	21
3.	Blood pressure	22.5	23	51
4.	Bowel irregularities	10	11	18
5.	Backache	17.5	16	21
6.	Arthritis	15	16	25
7.	Chest pain	2.5	3	8
8.	Forgetfulness	10	16	33
9.	Diabetes	10	10	18
10.	Heart disease	5	11	26
11.	Acute cough	2.5	5	3
12.	Giddiness	2.5	0	8
13.	Weakness	5	16	43
14.	Prostats	0	1	8
15.	Uterus cancer	0	3	0
16.	Sleeplessness	0	10	20
17.	Any other complaint (S)	7.5	5	11

Discussion

The Psychology of ageing has a long history as other areas of psychology, but the impetus to research and organization of information did not come until recent years. According to Bromley (1960) "We spend about one-quarter of our lives growing-up and three-quarters growing old. It is strange, therefore, that psychologists and others concerned have devoted most of their efforts to the study of childhood and adolescence than old age". The present study is a geropsychological approach to the various psychological, physical and social variables revolving around retirement and also involving due to retirement in an already retired and about to retire elderly in the Indian context.

Leisure Activities

As life expectancy increases the number of individuals who take early retirement increases and leisure activities and their development are becoming of greater importance. Leisure activities are in which an individual engages in during his free time. In the present study various leisure activities were grouped under two broad categories, i.e., solitary and physical activities, and social and cultural activities. Leisure activities that are solitary in nature include reading newspapers, listening to radio, viewing TV, attending movies and reading religious books, while physical activities are household chores, hobbies like – gardening, social service, morning and evening walks etc. Cultural activities are visiting religious places etc., and various social activities are visiting friends, looking after grand-children, visiting relatives, playing cards and helping others.

Results indicate a significant difference in the mean number of leisure activities between the pre-retirement and retirement groups as well as between pre-retirement and post-retirement groups of elderlies at 0.05 level of significance. The low mean score of pre-retirement group in comparison to the retirement and post-retirement could be due to the availability of free time to pursue the various leisure activities since this group of people are still in service.

Atchely (1971) points out that leisure activities can serve as a bridge between pre- and post-retirement life. The percentage profile of leisure activities pursued by the three criterion groups of elderlies in the groups, that is pre-retirement, retirement and post-retirement engage in solitary activities like reading books, magazines, newspapers etc., listening to radio and watching TV. The other common highly indulged activity is physical in nature, that a high percentage of retiring group engaged in morning and evening walks but a very low number of pre-retirement, which could be due to a very hectic life routine of the pre-retirement group. The same reason could be attributed to another physical activity of gardening on which the post-retired are high.

The retirement group have the feeling of new found freedom and are quite relaxed. So they indulge in a number of activities apart from the one mentioned above. These are solitary activities like attending movies or watching videos, writing letters, cultural activity like visiting places of worship, physical activities like gardening and exercise. Playing games to keep fit, and social activities like visiting friends, relatives, speaking on the phone and entertaining friends.

The pre-treatment score average on social activities like visiting friends, relatives, speaking on the phone and outings with family members. Average number of post-retired also indulge in solitary activities like attending movies or watching video, listening to radio, watching TV having a nap or resting during the day, physical activity like visiting friends, relatives, outings with family members and entertaining friends.

Kelly (1987) says that leisure activities vary according to age or period of the life cycle and major factors affecting leisure behaviour are: income level, personality interests, health conditions, ability level, transportation, and other social characteristics.

It has been noted that indulgence in leisure activities has led to less loneliness and more life satisfaction among the pre-retired and retired groups.

Kaur and Kaur (1987) found that many aged spent time usually in gossiping, playing cards, reading and religious activities.

Chadha (1991); Sharma (1969) found that after retirement, a large majority of the aged are involved in solitary or family-based activities. This is evident in the present study as well. This is due to the fact that different occupational background influence the type of leisure time pursuits.

In a study by Garcia (1982) it was concluded that the increase of leisure time, following retirement is potentially problematic for the elderly and can result in such adversities as depression, loneliness and boredom and sometime to drinking. It is also concluded that there is a need to better prepare individuals for the use of leisure time and that each community must ensure that leisure time resources exist and the elderly are not excluded from them.

Health

"For whatsoever a man soweth, that he shall also reap" (Gal. 6:7). This biblical quotation when applied to health of the older people may also mean that what you did yesterday affects your health tomorrow. The health of elderly is partly a result of their health practices throughout their lives. Health of many individuals becomes problematic in old age. Individuals who have never been risk in their lives begin to show signs of declining health. The physical stamina of the individual also show a decline in old age. A retired individual may then pose the problem of his health for himself and his family members.

The results obtained in the percentage profile of common health problems faced by pre-retirement, retirement and post-retirement groups indicated that the pre-retirement group is faced mainly by blood pressure and backache. The retired group is faced by impairment of vision and blood pressure. The post-retirement group is also faced by impairment of vision, blood pressure and weakness.

Kaplan (1988) stated that self-rating of health are important psycho-social parameters in the evaluation of health status in determining the prognosis of an elderly person and in analysing survival.

Apart from uterus cancer, all the other fifteen ailments are prevalent in the post-retirement group has rated itself highly on all common health ailments as compared to the pre-retirement and retirement groups. The second to score high are the retirement group followed by the pre-retirement group.

References

Atchley, R.C.T. (1971): *Sociology of Retirement.* Cambridge, Mass-Schenrman.

Bromely, D.G. (1960): *The Psychology of Human Aging,* Penguin, Baltimore.

Carp, F.M. (1966): *Adult Psychology.* Harper and Raw, New York.

Chadha, N.K. (1991): “Leisure Time Activities among the Aged: A Comparative Study”, *Social Sciences International,* 7. No. 2: 12–34.

Cushing, J.G.N. (1952): “Problems of Retirement”. *Mental Hygiene.* New York. Vol. 36: 449–455.

Epstein and Murray (1968): In Turner and Helons. *Life Span Development.* W.B. Saunders Co. 1968.

Garcia, A. (1982): *Life After Work: On Retirement and Leisure,* Praeger Publishers. Inc. US.

Kaplan, G., Barell, V. and Lusky, A. (1988): “Subjective State of Health and Survival in Elderly Adults”. *Gerontology and Geriatrics.* Section 20,Volume 32, Issue I, 43/4: S 114–120.

Kaur, S. and Kaur, M. (1987): “Psychological Problems of the Aged”. Sharma and Bak (Eds.), *Aging in India: Challenge to the Society.*

Kelly, J. (1987): *A New Sociology of Leisure,* MacMillan, New York.

Neulinger (1974): *The Psychology of Leisure: Research Approaches to the Study of Leisure,* Springfield, Illinois; Charles C. Thomas.

Sharma, K.L. (1969): "Leisure Time Activities of Retired Persons", *Indian Journal of Gerontology,* Vol. 1, No. 1, pp. 31–37.

Van, Willigen and Chadha, N.K. (1987): "Techniques for Collecting Social Network Data for Studies of Social Aging". *Indian Journal of Social Work.* 21 (4): 612–615.

WHO, (1946), The Preamble to the Constitution of WHO.

Section E
Social Status and Social Support

The social support and physical health are two very important factors which help the overall well-being of the individual. A general theory, that has been drawn from many researches over the past few decades postulates that social support essentially predicts the outcome of physical and mental health for everyone. There are six criteria that researchers use to measure the level of overall social support available for the specific person or situation (Cutrona, Russell and Rose, 1986). First, the amount of attachment provided by a lover or spouse. Second, measure the level of social integration that the individuals are involved with. It usually comes from a group of people or friends. Third, assurance of worth from others such as positive reinforcement that could inspire and boost the self-esteem. The fourth criterion is the reliable alliance support that is provided by others, which means that the individual knows that he can depend on receiving support from family members whenever it was needed. Fifth, the guidance of assurances of support given to the individual from a higher figure person such as a teacher or parent. The last criterion is the opportunity for nurturance. It means the person would get some social enhancement by having children of his/her own and providing a nurturing experience.

Health

Many studies indicate that an individual who has high social support tends to have less chance of getting depression and anxiety disorders. In contrast, only a handful of studies show that there is no relationship between social support and lowering of the blood pressure. The level of social support also has been found to be related to a lower rate of early death. The familial support is a psychological enhancement to help the individual to reduce his/her stress. These findings are somewhat weak and further studies need to be done to gather more specific information about the influence of social support on physical health (Uchino et al., 1996).

There is a significant relation between emotions and health. Anyone who has positive emotion and beliefs is likely to enhance his/her physical health. As expected, being in a good mood refreshes mind and relieves of the stress. Laughing is said to have a good deal of influence on reducing or forgetting the hassles of daily life. Strong social support is necessary to help succeed in achieving these traits of overall physical well-being (Salovey, Detweiler, Steward and Rothman, 2000).

Personality Type

There are some aggressive adults living in society. Such adults are diagnosed with Type A personality. Anger, aggressiveness, and hostility are the common characteristics of this type of personality. These are unhealthy personality traits, which could adversely affect the general health of such adults. Eventually, the research finds that there is some direct link between Type A personality and coronary heart diseases (Friedmann and Booth-Kewley, 1987). There is no scientific evidence yet, but researchers have suggested a general hypothesis that low social support may create Type A personality. The researchers also revealed a strong relationship between social support and the absence of coronary heart diseases. More social support would soothe the individuals with Type A personality, leading to better physical health, thus reducing the risk of developing coronary heart diseases. Environmental stress is likely to increase the chance of getting physical illness (Maddi, Bartone and Puccett, 1987).

Socio-economic Status

One's socio-economic status also is a major factor in whether or not an individual gets enough social support. The socio-economic status is the measurement of level of income each person has determining his/her level of economic status in society. For example, if the specified person's income is low, compared to national average, would be considered having low socio-economic status. As expected, anyone who comes from a lower socio-economic class would be more likely to receive less social support. Such persons do not have enough resources available to back social support. They also tend to have less self-control. Consequently, they become more sensitive to stressors in their environment and are less able to control their reactions and become frustrated. Unfortunately, the social strain, which is common in their daily lives, increases the risk for lower social class individuals to develop some kinds of physical and mental illness or a lower sense of well-being. It is surprising that adults who have higher socio-economic status tend to receive more social support (Gallo, Bogart, Vranceanu and Matthews, 2005).

Corey M. Clark's paper, "Relations Between Social Support and Physical Health," discussed the implication of social support and people's physical health. He discussed the three age groups, adolescences, middle-aged adults, and older adults. He stated the six criteria of social support as mentioned above.

Clark went into depth about how older people had to rely on other people for social support and he provided examples of how they could to that. The fifth criteria was omitted from this age group, because there is no higher figure to look for support when one is the mellow age of 80. But Clark does not mention a major area of social interaction for older people, that is, the communities, which are obviously geared towards providing a social environment for similar individuals.

The physical health of an individual can be greatly affected by his or her social support system and level of social support. The most elemental factor by which this effect of socialization works is a basic and sometimes overlooked reason for the success of psychotherapy. Sometimes just knowing that there is someone to talk to and confide in can help people overcomes their problems just as much as any treatment. Those with a greater social support system, whether family or friends, have a greater chance of resolving problems which they face. The process of coping can be improved simply because someone is there to talk with about problems to give unconditional love and support or provide a resolution

Later in life, when individuals reach the point at which they are unable to care for themselves or others, a decision must be made whether they will take up residence in a retirement home or hospital. There seems to be a much higher rate of happiness if individuals decide for themselves that they are to move. Being forced into a care residence can cause negative feelings and sometimes depression because of feelings of uselessness. However, if the person willingly and openly decides to take up residence in a care facility, the advantages are great. In addition to providing physical care, the social system of the facility can provide the residences with ample amounts of peer interactions, due mainly to proximity. Because of more active social life, residents in care facilities have a more positive outlook on life and tend to be happier than those living by themselves (Field, Orrell and Walker, 2002).

Summary of the Papers

The present section contains four papers. A comprehensive study "A Study of Aged 60 Years and Above in Social Profile" was conducted by C.K. Purohit and R. Sharma. One-third of the subjects were engaged in agricultural activities and majority of aged persons were dependents. Dependency increased with age. Majority of persons were living with their spouses and children and very few were living with relatives and friends and living alone. Loss of family leadership was very higher. The hobbies and interests were mainly confined to religious activities. Young persons have started believing elderly socio-economic burden. A case study "Changing Status of Elderlies in Rural India" conducted by A.P. Mangla aims to analyse findings related to Jat elderly residing in Galibpur village (Haryana). He found that Jat elderly still enjoy high social status, authority, and respect and security in spite of industrialization, urbanization, occupational mobility, education and changing individualistic philosophy of life. The roles of the elderly of this community are well defined. The reasons for this situation may be attributed to the longing for traditional values, strong joint family system, kinship bonds and dependence on traditional occupations. In a study "Elderly Women of Kachhi Basti: A Socio-Psychological Profile" – K.L. Sharma found that most of their activities were limited to purely to the fulfillment of their biological needs. Apart from some common problems, a significant difference was noticed in responses of widows and married women. Due to the struggle for survival the elderly widow women forgot the year and day of the deaths of their husbands and engrossed themselves in meeting the difficulties of life. Husband is a great support in old age. For widow's economic dependence, lack of proper and sufficient food and clothes, fear of future, progressive decline in health and lack of caring in sickness are the common factors which are the causes in creating difficulties in their coping with ageing problems.

"Scenario of Segregated Seniors" paper written by Saraswati Mishra have described the state of the inmates of 'old age homes' with special reference to their happiness, in the context of their social integration and segregation. The study suggests that most of the residents showed dissatisfaction with their segregated life in old age homes.

References

Cutrona, C., Russell, D. and Rose, J. (1986): "Social Support and Adaptation to Stress by the Elderly". *Psychology and Aging. 1,* 47–54.

Field, E.M., Walter, H.M. and Orrell, M.W. (2002): "The Social Networks and Health of Older People Living in Sheltered Housing". *Aging and Mental Health.* 6: 372–386.

Friedman, H.S. and Booth-Kewley, S. (1987): "Personality, Type A Behaviour, and Coronary Heart Disease: The Role of Emotional Expression". *Journal of Personality and Social Psychology.* 53: 783–792.

Gallo, L.C., Bogart, L.M., Vranceanu, A. and Matthews, K.A. (2005): "Socioeconomic Status, Resources, Psychological Experiences, and Emotional Responses: A Test of the Reserve Capacity Model". *Journal of Personality and Social Psychology.* 88: 386–399.

Maddi, S.R., Bartone, P.T. and Puccetti, M.C. (1987): "Stressful Events are Indeed a Factor in Physical Illness Reply". *Journal of Personality and Social Psychology.* 52: 833–843.

Salovey, P., Detweiler, J.B., Steward, W.T. and Rothman, A.J. (2000): "Emotional States and Physical Health". *American Psychologist.* 55: 110–121.

Uchino, B.N., Cacioppo, J.T. and Kiecolt-Glaser, J.K. (1996): "The Relationship between Social Support and Physiological Processes: A Review with Emphasis on Underlying Mechanisms and Implications for Health". *Psychological Bulletin.* 119: 488–531.

CHAPTER 24

A Study of Aged 60 Years and Above in Social Profile

C.K. Purohit and Rameshwar Sharma

Population structure of a community depends upon (1) the past trends in fertility, mortality and migration behaviour of couples; (2) health conditions and (3) cultural and social factors. In India over the past fifty years, the proportion of elderly persons, 65 years and over, has increased from 2.4 per cent in 1911 to 3.2 per cent in 1956, and in 1971 it is expected to be 3.4 per cent. In spite of increase in life expectations at birth, decline in mortality and slight decline in high birth rate, population in aged group has increased. The nationwide crash programme of family planning is attempting to bring down high birth rate to 25 per 1000 by 1975–76. The population of aged persons 60 years and above would increase from 27.7 millions (5%) in 1966 to 46.5 millions (6.1%) in 1986 (Chandrashekheran, 1965). In comparison, in the USA 15.6 million persons (8.5%) over 65 years of age are likely to become 20 millions (10.0%) by 1975 (Leake, 1961); whereas in the UK there were 5.4 million aged persons (11.8%) in this age group in the year 1961 (Richardson, 1964).

Although in India the proportion of aged persons is relatively low only in percentage, but higher than developed countries due to high total population. The gerontological problems will increase in trend of unitary family formation with increase in industrialization and urbanization (Raj and Prasad, 1971). The present study of aged persons

IJG, 1972, Vol. 4, No. 3 and 4, pp. 71–83.

living in rural areas, has been conducted to explore the social problems of the aged persons in rural setting.

Materials and Methods

The study of aged (persons was carried out between 18th Feb. 1970 to 31st May, 1970) in 29 (50%) randomly selected villages of the area covered by the Rural Health Training Centre, Naila. The centre is working under the Department of Preventive and Social Medicine, S.M.S. Medical College, Jaipur.

Present study recorded 521 (5.04%) aged persons in a population of 10,325. There were 290 (5.2%) males and 231 (4.36%) females. Only 374 (71.78%) aged were interrogated, while 147 (28.22%) could not be included because of their repeated non-availability at the time of survey. The information was collected on pre-planned, pre-tested case schedules by interview method, followed by on the spot clinical examination. For the purpose of this study, persons 60 years and above were regarded as aged persons.

Observations

Family Information

Out of 429 families, 320 (74.59%) families were studied. The average size of the family observed was 5.46. One hundred sixty five (51.56%) families were small sized families (1–5 members); 127 (32.69%) were medium sized families (6–9 members) and 28 (8.75%) were large sized families (10 and more members). There were 19 (5.93%) families were joint or multiple families (260 or 81.25%) as compared to single families (6) or 18.75 per cent.

In the present study, 319 (99.7%) families were Hindu and one family was Muslim. Majority of them belonged to lower castes, i.e., Scheduled Tribes (26.25%); whereas 121 (37.81%) families belonged to higher castes i.e., Brahmins (21.56%); Rajputs (8.75%) and Mahajans (7.5%), only 3 families could not state their caste.

Information regarding economic status of the families has its limitations in absence of exact information about their income and expenditure. Using Prasad's (1970) social class classification, 99 (87.18%) families were classified in social classes IV and V; while only 29 (9.06%) families belonged to social classes I to III; remaining 12 (3.76%) families did not state their income. To evaluate the general sanitary conditions and living conditions, an arbitrary scoring method was employed. Living conditions of most of the families were far from satisfactory. It was poor to very poor in 299 families (93.4%), 18 families (STI) fall in average and good in only three families (0.9%). The main factors contributing to poor living conditions were absence of latrines, ill-ventilated houses, absence of separate kitchen and inadequate floor area.

Aged Persons

Age and Sex Distribution

Age and sex distribution of aged persons have been shown in Table 1. It was observed that in the age groups 65 years and above males predominated over females whereas in the age group 60–64, females predominated over males. This is because of wide age difference between spouses. Percentage of aged persons declined in both sexes with increase in age.

Table 1

Age and sex distribution of aged persons

Age group	*Male*		*Female*		*Total*	*%age*
	No.	*%*	*No.*	*%*		
60–64	74	35.75	91	54.49	165	44.14
65–69	51	24.64	21	12.57	72	19.25
70–74	43	20.70	38	22.76	81	21.66
75–79	17	8.21	7	4.19	24	6.41
80–84	18	8.69	8	4.79	26	6.94
84 +	4	1.94	2	1.20	6	1.60
Total	207	100.00	167	100.00	374	100.00

Marital Status

Amongst male group, 151 (72.95%) aged were married; 47 (27.71%) were widowers and only 9 (4.34%) aged persons never married for unknown reasons. Majority of them, 111 (66.45%) were widows and only 56 (33.54%) were married. In the group of widow(er)s, 60

(37.97%) aged persons could adjust well and continued their normal life. However, 98 (62.03%) aged persons could not adjust (50%) or were indifferent (12.03%). Large percentage of widows (69.37%) could not adjust well than their counterparts (4.25%). Intra-family relationship was good in all married aged persons and 37.02 per cent widow(er)s. In majority of the widow(er)s 62.98 per cent, intra-family relationship was either bad (49.35%) or indifferent (13.63%).Bad intra-family relationship was encountered more in the widow group (67.26%) as compared to widowers (4.5%).

Educational Status

All the 167 women were illiterate. Amongst aged males, none was educated more than primary (3.38%) and those who could read or write were considered as just literate.

Economic Status

Majority of the aged persons were from social classes IV and V (88.50%); whereas 7.75 per cent were from social classes I to III. Remaining 14 (9.74%) aged persons did not state their income.

Dependency Status

At the time of survey, 73 (19.51%) aged persons – 29.05 per cent men and 6.58 per cent women – were earners; 54 (14.43%) were earner dependants – 21.25 per cent men and 6.0 per cent women. A large proportion (247 or 66.04%) were dependants – 48.79 per cent men and 87.42 per cent women and dependency increased with age (Table 2). Even after 70 years of age, 33 (24.08%) aged persons were actively engaged in some occupation. Incapicitation and disabilities were the main causes of dependency.

Table 2

Dependency status of aged persons by age group

Age group	*No. examined*	*Earner*		*Earner dependents*		*Fully dependents*	
		No.	*%*	*No.*	*%*	*No.*	*%*
60–69	237	60	25.31	34	14.34	143	60.33
70–79	105	11	10.47	17	16.19	77	73.33
80 +	32	2	6.25	3	9.37	27	84.37
Total	374	73	19.51	54	14.45	247	66.4

Occupational Status

Occupational status of aged persons has been shown in Table 3.

Past Occupation

165 female reported to be looking after their household work and helping their malefolks in their respective occupation. Only two women reported to be begging for livelihood and one of them continued to do it even at the time of survey. Amongst males, principal occupations were agriculture (63.25%), crafts (18.08%); shopkeeping (8.68%) and service (6.28%). Service group included chowkidars, servants, barbers, washermen etc. Unclassified group of workers were engaged in religious activities of the community.

Table 3
Occupation of aged persons

Occupation	*Present occupation*		*Past occupation*	
	No.	*%*	*No.*	*%*
Administrative	1	0.78	—	—
Shopkeepers	10	7.87	18	4.82
Farmers	86	67.87	133	35.58
Quarryman	—	—	1	0.26
Craftsman	18	14.17	27	7.22
Service	5	3.96	13	3.47
Unclassified workers	6	4.73	8	2.14
Armed forces	—	—	5	1.33
Begger	1	0.78	4	1.06
Housewives	—	—	165	44.12
Total	127	100.00	374	100.00

Present Occupation

There were 127 (33.95%) aged persons – 126 men and 21 women – were actively engaged in some occupation at the time of survey. Amongst males principal occupations were farming (62.26%);

carpentry (16.98%); shopkeeping (9.40%) and service (4.71). Retired persons from the armed forces had changed over to farming. Amongst females, 20 were working in farms and one was beggar.

Living Unit

In the present study, 189 (50.54%) aged persons lived with their spouses and children; 152 (40.68%) lived with children; 18 (4.82%) lived with spouses; 10 (2.67%) lived alone and 5 (1.34%) lived with their distant relatives (Table 4). All the unmarried males either lived alone or with relatives. Amongst the group of widows, one woman lived alone and two lived with relatives. Majority of the widow(s) lived with their children. Of the 15 aged persons living alone or with relatives, four were abandoned by their children and relatives and two were abandoned by their children; such persons belonged to lower social classes (VI and V). The majority of the aged persons i.e., 27 (93.1%) belonging to social classes I to III, lived either with their spouses or spouses and children; only 2 (6.9%) lived alone. None of the aged persons of these social classes lived with relatives. On the other hand in social classes IV and V, 13 (3.92%) aged persons lived either with relatives or alone; majority (318 or 96.08%) however lived with their children and/or spouses (Table 5).

Table 4

Living unit of aged persons according to marital status and sex

Living units	*Marital status*						*Total*	*%*
	Men			*Women*				
	S	*M*	*W*	*S*	*M*	*W*		
Alone	6	—	3	—	—	1	10	2.67
With spouse	—	9	—	—	9	—	18	4.82
With children*	—	—	44	—	—	108	152	40.62
With spouse and children	—	142	—	—	47	—	189	50.54
With distant relatives	3	—	—	—	—	2	5	1.34
Total	9	151	47	—	56	111	374	100.00

*Children included dependant and/or supporting children.

Table 5

Living unit of aged persons according to social class

Living units	*No. examined*	*Social class*					
		I	*II*	*III*	*IV*	*V*	*N.S.*
Alone	10	—	—	2	3	5	—
With spouse	18	—	2	6	2	4	4
With children*	152	2	2	5	73	63	7
With spouse and children	189	—	2	8	90	86	3
With distant relatives	5	—	—	—	—	5	—
Total	374	2	6	21	168	163	14

*Children included dependant and/or supporting children.

Status of Head of the Family

A large proportion of aged persons (308 or 81.01%) enjoyed the status of head of the family, group included heads of 56 aged married women (15.51%) widow could not enjoy this status and her children or relatives enjoyed this status. There were 13 (3.48%) widow(er)s who could not be recognized as head of the family because of ill health, though they lived with their children. It was observed that loss of family leadership was twice higher in social classes IV and V (67 or 20.2%) as compared to social classes I to III (3 or 10.2%). (Table 6). The control over land and family property confers greater authority and respect to the rich aged persons of higher socio-economic status. The economic status, old age and death of spouses were the important factors in determining the prestige, authority and respect of the aged person in their own families.

Addictions

About 238 (63.63%) aged persons – 85.99 per cent men and 35.92 per cent women had addictions. Thirty-eight man had two addictions as compared to 140 man and 60 women, who had one addition. Addictions were due to tobacco (85.50%); alcohol (12.31%); Bhang

(1.08%); Naswar (0.72%) and Opium (0.36%). Tobacco-chewing and smoking was done by all socio-economic classes of people. Other addictions were more prevalent in social classes IV and V.

Table 6

Status of aged persons by head of the family and social class

Status as head of the family	*Social class*						*Total*	*%age*
	I	*II*	*III*	*IV*	*V*	*N.S.*		
Elderly male	1	4	18	112	113	10	258	68.93
Elderly female (widow)	1	1	1	21	18	3	45	12.03
Others (Elderly is widow)	—	1	2	27	27	1	58	15.51
Others (Elderly in ill-health)	—	—	—	8	5	—	13	3.48
Total	2	6	21	168	163	14	374	100.00

Happiness in Old Age

At the time of study, 187 (50%) aged persons were happy; however equal percentage of them were either unhappy (36.9%) or indifferent towards their life (13.1%), females were twice unhappy or indifferent as compared to males. All widows were unhappy or indifferent. Unhappiness increased with increase in age (Table 7). Unhappiness was more common in the lower socio-economic classes. Persons of upper socio-economic strata were either happy or indifferently disposed towards their life (Table 8). In accordance with the prevailing views and values attached to senescence, and 7 (24.1%) aged persons were indifferent towards life in upper and middle socio-economic group as compared to lower classes (39 or 11.7%). Depressed persons were more in poor and very poor classes as compared to upper and middle social classes. Causes of unhappiness were enquired from 138 aged persons. Principal causes of unhappiness were widowhood and loneliness (75.82%); loss of children (9.89%); loss of employment (2.74%) and indebtedness (11.53%). Ninety-four (68.11%) aged persons were having two or more causes of unhappiness.

Table 7
Happiness in aged persons by age group

Age group	*No. examined*	*Felt happy*		*Felt unhappy*	
		No.	*%*	*No.*	*%*
60–63	165	98	59.4	67	40.6
65–69	72	42	58.3	30	41.7
70–74	81	32	38.3	49	61.7
75–79	24	8	33.4	16	66.6
80–84	26	6	23.1	20	76.9
80 +	6	1	16.7	5	83.3
Total	474	187	50.0	187	50.0

Table 8
Happiness in aged persons by social class

Age group	*No. exami-ned*	*Felt happy*		*Indifferent*		*Felt unhappy*	
		No.	*%*	*No.*	*%*	*No.*	*%*
Not stated	14	5	35.71	3	21.42	6	42.85
I	2	—	—	1	50.00	1	50.00
II	6	4	66.66	1	16.66	1	16.66
III	21	12	57.14	5	23.80	4	19.04
IV	168	84	50.00	16	9.53	68	40.47
F	163	82	50.30	23	14.11	58	35.58
Total	374	187	50.00	49	13.10	138	36.90

Knowledge about Old Age Pension Benefit

Under the Rajasthan Old Age Pension Rules 1967, old age pension benefit is provided to the destitute aged persons 65 years and above. When enquired, 306 (81.81%) aged persons did not know about it, whereas only 43 males and 25 females knew about it. This group was married and lived with their spouses and children.

Hobbies and Interests

Only 181 (48.39%) aged persons had hobbies and interests. This group included 103 males and 78 females. Majority of them (157 or

86.74%) had one hobby and interest. These were due to religious activities (73.75%): community singing (13.06%); village politics (4.32%); cards and chess (1.44%); reading (0.96%) and others (9.61%). Women had more interest in religious activities.

Participation in Community Activities

Only 43 (11.49%) aged participated in community activities. Majority of them, both men and women participated in religious activities (62.55%). Other community activities like leadership, panchayat activities were pursued by men only.

Views of Aged Persons about Young Folks

Views of the aged persons about their present social set-up in relation to young members of the family was enquired from 363 respondents. Majority of the aged persons reported that they were cared for at the time of sickness (93.48%); respected (76.49%); felt secure in the family (49.14%) and were sought for advice in the family affairs (84.44%) (Table 9). Women were less cared for, respected, given security and called for advice as compared to men. Such problems were more complained about by widows.

Table 9

Views of aged persons about their young folks

Questions		Men		Women		Total	%
		No.	%	No.	%		
1. Is your advise sought in the family affairs?	Yes	171	86.36	113	72.90	284	84.44
	No	27	13.64	42	27.10	69	19.54
2. Do you feel secure in the family?	Yes	185	94.44	112	72.25	297	94.14
	No	13	5.56	43	27.75	56	15.86
3. How are you treated in the family?	Respected	166	83.83	104	67.13	270	76.49
	Neglected	15	7.57	30	19.35	45	12.75
	Indifferent	17	8.58	21	13.55	38	10.74
4. Does some one care when you are sick	Yes	190	96.01	140	90.33	330	93.48
	No	8	3.99	15	9.67	23	6.51

Views of Young Folks about their Elderly Persons

Views of young folks about their elderly persons was enquired from main earning members. Only 246 persons responded. It was observed that majority of them (24%) paid respect, looked after old persons and felt secure by the presence of elderly member in the family. However, about 66 per cent of them have started believing them as socio-economic burden (Table 10).

Table 10

Views of the young folks about their elderly persons

Questions	*Yes*		*No*	
	No.	*%*	*No.*	*%*
1. Do you respect old persons in the family?	233	94.71	13	5.29
2. Do you share his views for family affairs?	230	93.49	16	6.51
3. Do you feel protected by his presence?	225	91.42	21	8.58
4. Do you care him when he is sick?	233	94.71	13	5.29
5. Does he share responsibility with you?	184	74.75	62	25.24’
6. Do you believe he is not a socio-economic burden?	162	66.39	84	83.61

Diseases and Disabilities

All the aged persons were sick at the time of survey. Average sickness per person was found to be 4.07 and 3.85 in males and females, respectively. The cause of illness at the time of survey were chronic bronchitis (70.05%); anemia (65.24%); constipation (47.06%); cataract (39.83%); arthritis (25.40%); hypertension (12.56%); avitaminosrs (11.49%) and corneal capacity (10.69%). At the time of survey 85 (22.72%) aged persons were disabled. The causes of disabilities were recorded as difficulty in walking and standing (7.5%); partial blindness (5.34%); partial deafness (4.01%); abnormal involuntary movements (3.74%) and complete blindness (2.24%) (Purohit, 1971).

Discussion

Age brings status and prestige to men, both in the family and community in a primitive society, the older persons were respected, as they performed important functions. In developed society, the old people may be wise and experienced but much of their wisdom and experience is considered irrelevant and there is disregard for them, although tampered by a sense of obligation in respect of their maintenance and care (Slater, 1963). However, in the present study aged persons were respected and looked after by their young folks, though some of them believed them to be a socio-economic burden.

Changing thoughts of young persons of developed countries are responsible for increase in homes for aged and living alone. In New York city, 25 per cent of the aged persons lived alone and equal percentage lived with their spouses in 1960 (Reid, 1962). Similarly Meyrick and Cox (1969) reported that 22 per cent aged persons were living alone in 1968 as compared to 15 per cent in 1960–61.However very small percentage of aged persons lived alone (7.6%) in rural areas of Lucknow district (Raj and Prasad, 1971) and in the present study such persons required better care and help.

Burn (1959) is of the opinion that elderly persons living alone or with spouses have poor living conditions. Similarly, almost all persons could be said to live in poor living conditions in the present study.

Socio-economic status has its impact on living conditions, educational dependency, living unit, status in the family, happiness, diseases and disabilities, etc. In the present study, such impacts were visible.

Ageing has been characterized by inactive and unproductive life. Raj and Prasad, (1971) have reported that 14.7 per cent aged persons were not working. In the present study, however, more persons were found to be dependents (66.04%). Such observations were also made by Scmitt (1955) and Meyrick and Cox (1969).

Recognition as head of the family gives a great satisfaction to the elderly persons. In the present study larger proportion (303 or 81.01%) enjoyed this status. However in other studies 50.87 per cent of the aged persons have been reported to enjoy this status (Raj and Prasad, 1971). Similarly in the western countries also up to 66 per cent enjoy this status (Scmitt, 1955). By and large it can be said that in joint families elderly persons are still recognized as head of the family.

Townsend (1959) has reported increase in unhappiness with social insecurity, absence of relations and loss of occupation in old age. Causes of unhappiness in the study of Raj and Prasad (1971) were death of spouse (49.5%), death of children (14.5%) infirmity (24.3%); crop failure (6.8%) and indebtedness (4.8%). Similar factors have been also observed in the present study.

About 50 per cent of the aged persons had some hobbies or interest in the present study. Anderson and Cown (1956) have also made similar observations. This may be due to the fact that most of the people find themselves lonely and embraced in the modern set-up of the society and have hardly developed any hobby during their life time (Townsend,1959).

After widowhood relations have been found to worsen and this can be appreciated because in our society the right to become head of the family and financial benefits go to the eldest male child, therefore, daughter-in-law acquires prime position in presence of widow dependent.

Medical care is difficult to obtain when physical and social isolation is present and in the absence of children and relatives, they finally get themselves hospitalized (Taubenhaus and McCormick, 1969). This problem is a community problem and today in western countries most of the hospital beds are occupied by chronically sick aged persons. High sickness and disability in the lower require care and help in our country (Raj and Prasad, 1971; Raj, B., 1971). In the present study all persons were chronically ill; more being from poor socio-economic classes, and needed specialized care and help. About 39.83 per cent cataract cases needed cataract operations; 65.24 per cent anemic needed nutritional care and education; 38.23 per cent periodontal-disease cases required treatment and oral hygiene education; 47.06 per cent constipated cases needed education about bowel care, 22.22 per cent disabled needed rehabilitation. These were the important socio-medical problems prevalent amongst rural aged persons and needed remedical measures.

References

Anderson, W.E. and Cowon, N.R. (1956): "Work and Retirement". *Lancet*. 2: 1344–47.

Burn, J.L. (1959): *Recent Advances in Public Health*. London: Churchill.

Chandrasekhran, C. (1965): "Indian Demographic Trends with a Population Projections into Next 28 Years and their Significance for Social Welfare". *Indian Journal of Social Welfare*. 26: 120–123.

Idem (1971): "A Study of Rural Aged Persons in Social Profile". *Indian Journal of Social Work*. 32 (2).

Leake, D.C. (1961): "New Statistics on Longetivity". *Geriatrics*. 6: 166.

Meyrick, R.L. and Cox, A. (1969): "A Geriatric Survey Repeated". *Lancet*. 1: 1146–9.

Prasad, B.G. (1970): "Change Proposed in the Social Classification of Indian Families". *Journal Indian Med. Ass*. 56(6): 198–199.

Purohit, C.K. (1971): A Study of General Health Status of Persons Aged 60 Years and Above in the Rural Health Training Centre. Area, Naila. Thesis submitted to the University of Rajasthan for M.D. (PSM).

Raj, B. (1971): "A Medico-Social Study of Aged Persons in Certain Village. *Ind. Med. Gaz*. 10 (9): 25–31.

Raj, B. and Prasad, B.G. (1971): "Health Status of the Aged in India: A Study in Three Villages". *Geriatrics*. 25 (6): 142–85.

Reid, M. (1962): "Home Nursing Care of Aged in New York City". *Pub. Health. Reports*, 77: 421–5.

Richardson, I.M. (1964): *Age and Need* (1st ed.), Edinburgh and London: E. and S. Livingston Ltd. 10–18.

Semitt, R.C. (1955): "Old Age in Hawaii: A Study of the Older Population of Ohio". *Geriatrics*. 10: 89–42.

Slater, P.E. (1963): "Cultural Attitudes Towards the Aged". *Geriatrics*. 18: 308–314.

Taubenhaus, L.J. and McCormick, J.G. (1969): "The Use of Physical Services by the Aged". *Geriatrics*. 18: 122–32.

Townsend, P. (1959): "Social Surveys of Old Age in Great Britain, (1944–58)". *Bull*. WHO 21: 553–591.

CHAPTER 25

Changing Status of Elderlies in Rural India

A Case Study

A.P. Mangla

Subject of social gerontology is relatively new in India. It was only during the late seventies that the growing dimensions of ageing began to attract social scientists' attention due to increasing population of sixty-plus. Studies on various aspects of social gerontology conducted in India are mostly in the context of urban societies, whereas a larger segment of the Indian aged population lives in villages. Status of the aged in India and other countries differ. Similarly, the social conditions of urban and rural aged differ. Industrialization, urbanization, occupational mobility, education and growth of individualistic philosophy etc., have influenced the status of the rural elderlies, while traditional values, strong joint family system and kinship bond and dependence on traditional occupations still provide them authority, status and respect in rural India.

The present study deals with village elderlies of a north Indian village in general and the agriculturalist Jat elderlies of this region in particular. Focussing on a small area, this study has attempted to understand the impact of the phenomenon of rapid social change on the life and work style of the rural elderlies.

Methodology

Universe

The field investigations were conducted in Galibpur village, located about forty-three kilometers to the south-west Delhi on the

IJG, 1994, Vol. 8, No. 3 and 4, pp. 73–81.

Delhi-Haryana border. The village, by and large, is a culturally homogenous unit with traditionally agriculturist Jats as the dominant caste, both in respect of population and landholdings; the Nai (Barber), the Chamar (Cobler), the Chude and the Badi (a Muslim begger community) are the other castes inhabiting the village. Despite increasing urban influence, the area continues to maintain its rural identity.

Demographic Profile

Demographic profile of various castes in Galibpur is given in Table 1.

Table 1

Castewise and sexwise population of Galibpur

Caste	*No. of households*	*Males*	*Females*	*Total population*
Jat	92	315	284	599
Nai	8	26	20	46
Badi	9	26	24	50
Chamar	22	62	56	118
Chude	16	42	38	80

Technique Used

Data were collected mainly with the help of genealogical method, interviews and observation. Respondents, being elderlies, were asked small and simple questions with extra patience. Each respondent was explained clearly the purpose of the study. Also, interviewees' interest was maintained during the discussions. All the village elderlies, (N=48) were contacted personally.

Findings of the Study

While the patrilineal, patrilocal and patriarchal Jat community is still agriculture-oriented considerably, the members of other castes, in most of the cases, have shifted to non-traditional occupations.

Barring the five immigrant households, the entire Jat community of Galibpur belongs to 'Dabas Gotra' constituting a single 'khandan' (maximal lineage) with four identifiable and localized kinship groups. Peculiar to north Indian agriculturist communities, the pattern of settlement of the kin-oriented Jat community is based on patrilineage; agnatically related kins are clustered in terms of their residence and agriculture fields. The other castes are also clustered separately. Elderlies in Galibpur constitute only a small proportion of the village population as is evident from the following facts:

(i) The village elderlies (N=48) constitute only a small proportion of the total population (N=893; 5.4%).

(ii) Proportion of old population is much less than the proportion of child population (40.2%).

(iii) Elderly males (N=28) outnumber the elderly females (N=20), being 5.94 and 4.74 per cent respectively of the total village population.

(iv) The Jat community (N=599) shows a similar pattern; the proportion of elderlies (N=33) being only 5.5 per cent of the Jat population.

(v) Higher percentage of village elderly males (9.92% of adult males) is indicative of their larger life expectancy as compared to the female elderlies (7.49% of adult females). Likewise, among the Jats, the proportion of male elderlies is more than the female elderlies, being 6.3 per cent and 4.57 per cent respectively. In all, 9.17 per cent of adult Jats are the elderlies. However, the proportion of elderlies among the Jat adults is more (10.58%) as compared to female elderlies out of female adult Jats (7.60%). In other words, while there are 714 female elderlies per thousand male elderlies in the village, for 1000 Jat male elderies, the Jat female elderlies are only 650. The higher percentage of male elderlies is attributed to:
   - Lower life expectancy among the females; and
   - Wife is younger than her husband.

(vi) Out of 48 elderlies, 33 belong to the Jats-showing thereby that life expectancy is comparatively more among the Jats due to their improved socio-economic conditions in the past than that among the lower castes.

(vii) Widows (N=13) outnumber the widowers (N=8) due to the same reasons given above.

It was observed that the village elderlies possess either no formal education or only low level of education. However, in the patrilineal set-up of social structure, the males, including the elderlies, generally enjoy better status in most of the life ways, including residence, succession and inheritance.

Among the Jat agriculturists of the village, rule of inheritance of land (and other property) through the male-line has significantly influenced the pattern of residence and clustering of agricultural fields of patrilineal kinsmen. Since common vested interest in ancestral land has resulted in residential immobility, spatial distribution with limited geographical area has become an important factor contributing to cohesion among kinsmen. The clustering of patrilineal kinsmen in a single locality facilitates frequent contact between them. Thus, the friendship circle of the Jat elderlies, like in other village elderlies in such an atmosphere find in the kinship groups all that is meaningful in their relationships – their sociability, their security and their status. Unlike urban elderlies, therefore, loneliness is not an alarming problem for the Jat rural elderlies.

Since interpersonal communication is more among the individuals of similar relevant characteristics such as age, the elderlies generally are more communicative among themselves. Also, intensity of interaction decreases with the distance in the web of kinship ties – as we move from 'ghar' (household – to 'kunba' or major lineage) to 'khandan' (maximal lineage), the degree of communication among these elderly kinsmen decreases.

In leisure time, particularly in the evenings, the elderlies sit around a 'hookh' (hubble-bubble). They joke with each other, play cards, narrate their day-to-day experiences and discuss many things of common interest. The focus of discussion is generally an individual, his action and activities. Growth of individual 'baithaks' (main sitting room for the males), more among the Jats (85% Jat households possess 'baithaks'), have delimited inter-personal communication among the elderlies since they prefer to be visited in their own 'baithaks'. In fact changing rural society, dialogue between generations is comparatively less. Inter-personal communication the elderlies do not share their knowledge unless approached. It was observed that with increasing age, older persons become intrapunitive and ego-defencive.

Authority and Leadership of the Jat Elderlies

Generally, the eldest member of a patrilineal Jat kinship group, unless he becomes physically inactive, is considered as the head of that

Table 2

Showing sex, marital status and age distribution of the inhabitants of Galibpur village

	Males				*Females*				*Total*			
	S	*M*	*W*	*T*	*S*	*M*	*W*	*T*	*S*	*M*	*W*	*T*
Children upto 15 years	188	1	—	189	169	1	—	170	357	2	—	359
Adults	64	203	15	282	18	214	20	252	82	417	35	534
Total	252	204	15	471	187	215	20	422	439	419	35	893
Elderlies (60+)	—	20	8	28	—	7	13	20	—	27	21	48

S: stands for Single, M: stands for Married, W: stands for Widower, T: stands for Total.

Table 3

Showing sex, marital status and age distribution of Jat community Galibpur village

	Males				*Females*				*Total*			
	S	*M*	*W*	*T*	*S*	*M*	*W*	*T*	*S*	*M*	*W*	*T*
Children upto 15 years	126	—	—	126	133	—	—	133	239	—	—	239
Adults	42	135	12	189	11	148	12	171	53	283	24	360
Total	168	135	12	315	124	148	12	287	292	283	24	599
Elderlies (60+)	—	13	7	20	—	6	7	13	—	19	14	33

S: stands for Single, M: stands for Married, W: stands for Widower, T: stands for Total.

kinship group and his authority, as the head of that kinship group is respected by all the patrilineal kinsmen of the group. Four 'kunbas' (major lineages) and ten Jat 'sub-kunbas' in Galibpur have separate (elderly) heads. Old age also linked with political authority, each 'kunba' head decides which faction his kinsmen should join at the time of panchayat elections, etc. Decision about participation of a 'kunba' member in various functions like marriage etc., in a household belonging to other Jat 'kunba' is taken by the 'kunba' head and is obeyed by all. In matter of disputes, these elderly kinsmen are always requested for mediation. Thus, the elderlies, by and large, still enjoy power, authority, respect and security considerably.

Elderlies and their Household Roles

In the following description of household roles of the elderlies, broad outlines of actual behaviour are given within which some variations may occur.

Aged parents, because of traditional values, socio-economic conditions and sons' financial and otherwise dependence on them, continue to enjoy considerable authority and respect. Particularly the father, irrespective of his education and non-earning nature, commands, authoritative influence and he continues to have deciding role in respect of various household matters. Father's authoritative position acts as the strongest bond that keeps a household intact.

Among the pre-dominantly agricultural communities like the Jats of Galibpur, with clear emphasis on agnatic principle, father's role in the household assumes the greatest significance. Non-withstanding the importance of imparting training, experience and professional skill, sons' dependence on agriculture and ancestral land enhances father's authority over them. Although land is verbally allotted to the son as 'khets' (fields) within the lifetime of the father, the entire land remains in his name and is cultivated under his authority. Sons have joint ownership right of enjoyment of land but no right to demand a legal share in it. Thus, father-son relationship is based on an authoritative pattern. Also, father is more communicative to his sons, because working in the fields in the past had brought them closer. Father, even in his old age, therefore, is consulted in traditional occupational matters. However, an elderly man with adult children is rather a lonely person in his household whose sons keep a respectable distance from him and their wives even more so, despite holding authority.

As a mother, an elderly women is heard out patiently and respectfully. As Mandelbaum (1972) had noted, the pivotal, mediating role a mother often takes between her husband and her sons when they are adolescents, continues when they are mature men with children of their own. In all important matters like marriage, etc., final consent has to be obtained from the elderly parents.

In his role as husband, man, irrespective of his age has ever remained superior. In his old age also, he remains the initiator and the receiver of deference from his wife. As aged wife, on the other hand, shifts her interest to others in the household, while the growing husband becomes more dependant on his wife since he cannot readily be on familiar terms with younger people in the household (Madan, 1965).

In the absence of parents, the parental authority rests with the eldest brother. Especially when one brother is considerably older than the other, their relationship is less likely to become strained as the elder brother in that situation easily assumes the responsibilities and respect that father normally commands.

The grandparents, irrespective of their non-earning nature, are respected. The oldest male of the highest generation is supposed to receive the most respect and obedience and care (Orenstein, 1965). To grandchildren, the father's father is part of the parental authority as was pointed out by Mandelbaum, "In the joint families of high ranking landowner, however, the parental grandfather is often a figure of some consequence to his grandchildren. He is expected to exert his authority in instructing and disciplining the children and so should be strict with them" (ibid.). Notwithstanding their authority, the grandchildren enjoy joking relationship with their grandfather. Grandfather, too, enjoys authority in all household matters. However, the intergenerational gap is gradually increasing as a consequence of urbanization, spread of education and occupational and residential mobility.

It was observed that life expectancy was more among the high ranking (Jat) landlords. Out of 48 village elderlies, 33 (68.7%) are the Jats. As Mandelbaum (1972) has noted, relatively, a few economically weaker men survive long enough to be grandfathers for an considerable length of time. However, since the economic condition of the lower castes has improved considerably during the recent years mainly due to shift to non-traditional occupations, life expectancy is likely to be increased in future.

Daughter-in-law maintains relationship of avoidance by observing strict 'pardah' from her 'Sasur' (father-in-law). She is expected to talk to her father-in-law only in undertones. Mother-in-law, by virtue of her age and traditional higher position, holds the power. Traditionally, relationship of mother-in-law and daughter-in-law has been strained as the former imposes all sorts of constraints on her. Her authority prevails particularly because she is generally supported by her sons as has been argued by Kapadia (1966) that "in the traditional family man was expected to be closer to her mother rather than to his wife". However, filial bond becomes weaker after death of the father, birth of children and affecting mother-in-laws authority over her daughter-in-law.

Urban influence, better education and increase in age of spouses at marriage have undoubtedly influenced the authoritative position of the elderlies as in-laws. Nevertheless, because of arranged marriages, the consanguineal bond remains stronger than the conjugal bond and the elderly in-laws continue to enjoy considerable respect and authority.

Factors Responsible for the Changing Condition of the Elderlies

Obviously, with increasing urban influence one should expect changes in life pattern of the people, young and old, of a village like that of Galibpur. Various factors have contributed to the changes that are taking place in the lifestyle of the rural elderlies. Some of these are:

Growth of Simple Households

Extended household has ever provided the elderlies psychological satisfaction, authority, status and security. With strong kinship relationship between its members, they enjoyed respect and co-operation in an extended household. Generally, an elderly, belonging to a large extended household and having command over its members, is considered more authoritative and influential in the village community. Besides, traditional values are well maintained in such extended household. However, due to rapid social changes, extended household is giving way to simple household (out of 147 households, 86 are simple households in the village), adversely affecting the status of the elderlies.

Fragmentation of Agricultural Land

Among the Jat agricultural community in Galibpur, the father has ever enjoyed authority and respect of his sons because of their traditional dependence on ancestral land, residential and occupational immobility. However, continuous fragmentation of agricultural land has resulted in smaller landholdings (average Jat landholding in Galibpur being 24 bighas and 17 biswas) and increase in number of landless households (17 or 18.5%). Consequently, sons do not generally find much prospects in small-sized ancestral land and, therefore, they are much less dependent on their father. Gradual erosion of father's authority over his sons is reflected in the growing disorganizing tendencies among the brothers in an extended household. While in the past, for instance, the sons separated only after the death of the father, the strongest bond of linkage between the patrilineal kinsmen in a household, there are many instances where sons, eroding father's authority, have separated during his lifetime.

Spread of Education

Irrespective of the nature of traditional occupations, the villagers generally do not find much prospects in them for the youngsters. Consequently, there is growing concern about children's education which is evident from the fact that the number of school-going children in age group 5–15 years is significant (80.3%). Since the children now devote more time in their studies, their fields of interest and orientation have remarkably changed. Increasing involvement in education has reduced the degree of interpersonal communication, thereby widening the generational gap.

With spread of education, individuals in the household tend to be caught between tradition and modernity often leading to ambivalence in attitude towards the use of the knowledge and experience of the past in solving problems of the present. When this happens, it tends to make the elderlies less valued.

Occupational Mobility

Those shifted to non-traditional occupations no longer have direct interest in their traditional occupational activities which, otherwise, often provide matters for general discussion. Besides, since they are not physically present in the village during most part of the day, their non-availability to their kinsmen adversely affect their attention towards other household members, including the elderlies. Daily commuters, thus, have, comparatively less social interaction within the village. Occupational mobility has resulted in disintegration of extended households that provided the elderlies psychological satisfaction, authority and status. Among the lower castes, increasing number of men and women are in government jobs. They, thus, have little time to spare for the elderly parents-in-laws.

Urbanization

Process of urbanization has greatly influenced the lifestyle, social values and general attitude of the Galibpurians. Ever increasing contacts of the village population with the urbanites, mainly due to occupational mobility, has enlarged the friendship circle, diversifying individuals' interests and affecting their interaction with the other household members, including the elderlies.

Urbanization, along with the spread of education, has reduced the degree of women and children participation in traditional occupations like agriculture which earlier often provided a common topic for discussion and on which the elderlies provided counselling with authority and pride. Increasing cost of up-bringing children, their education etc., has also affected distribution of income of the younger generation. Urbanization, thus, has contributed more to reduce the status of an elderly as adviser and spokesman of the village and as a guide to the household.

Communication

Through mass media like the radio and the television, a common man is much exposed to the outside world. He has variety of topics for discussion. However, since the television sets are generally kept in the living room where women and children watch television, male elderlies do not normally watch television programmes due to 'purdah' and relationship of avoidance; they largely confine to 'baithaks' (sitting room for males) for most of their time. Now, with the growth of individual 'baithak's, more among the Jats, degree of interpersonal communication among the elderlies has further reduced since they prefer to be visited in their own 'baithaks'.

Although 'pucca' roads and bus service have significantly improved the transportation particularly during the last two decades or so, for the elderlies Galibpur is almost their whole world as they do not go outside the village until it becomes absolutely necessary in matters such as medical assistance.

Increasing Tilt Towards Affinal Kins

Competition for material achievements among the patrilineal kinsmen has led a common villager in general, and the village Jat in particular, to jealousy and growing egoism. Consequently, there is increasing tilt towards affinal relations like 'Sausra' (wife's father), 'Sala' (wife's brother), 'Sadoo' (wife sister's husband), and 'Sali' (wife's sister) which is reflected in increasing agricultural and financial interdependence and exchange for visits. Affinal kins of an individual now more actively participate in important household functions like marriage etc. All these have resulted in loosening of paternal ties and threat to fraternal authority, leading ultimately to a somewhat indifferent attitude towards the elderlies.

Predominantly rural agrarian Indian society is gradually giving way to urbanization and industrialization. Traditional extended household system is giving way to simple household. In the context of this changing social milieu, position of the rural elderlies is now in a state of flux. Fortunately, the magnitude of the problems of the rural elderlies has not reached the extent it has in the urban societies.

The rural elderlies, by and large, still enjoy power, authority, respect and security mainly due to our traditional values, dependence on traditional occupations, residential immobility and strong kinship relationships. But, in this rapidly transforming Indian society, how long?

References

Kapadia, K.M. (1966): *Marriage and Family in India.* Bombay, Oxford University Press. 267.

Madan, T.N. (1965): *Family and Kinship: A Study of the Pandits of Rural Kashmir.* Bombay: Asian Publishing House. 137.

Mandelbaum, David G. (1972): *Society in India.* Bombay: Popular Prakashan. 79.

Orenstein, H. (1965): *Conflict and Cohesion in an Indian Village.* Princeton: Princeton University Press. 47–48.

CHAPTER 26

Elderly Women of Kachhi Basti

A Socio-Psychological Profile

K.L. Sharma

According to the 1991 Census, the proportion of female elderly is slightly higher than males and the patterns expected to follow in future also (Rajan et al., 1999). In the process of development women play most important role, although their role and contributions are generally underestimated by the society. The women are the essential source for the development of the society. It is therefore essential to look after them properly. It is generally seen that the health needs of children and male members are given priority over the needs of women, specially the aged women. They suffer due to the physical deformities and malnutrition. Due to the poverty, in spite of their poor health the aged women have to work. This situation is more worst in villages and for the women living in Kachhi Basties. The people living in Kachhi Basties are those who have mostly migrated from nearby villages or from the villages of other states. The aged women who have come from villages with their children, they generally do not like city life, their other family members are ignoring them.

In order to get a better deal for the elderly women, the increasing sexism and ageism, both, need to be countered in the system of family, religion, market and the state, through efforts for public awareness by voluntary organizations and academic institutions. A focus on women is necessary in a policy for ageing and in the legal provisions for housing, maintenance and protection from abuse.

IJG, 1999, Vol. 13, No. 1 and 2, pp. 40–57.

Some genuine studies have been conducted in India on the problems of elderly women (Bagchi, 1997; Dayabati Devi and Bagga, 1997; Prakash, 1991, 1993, 1996; Sen, 1996; Bambawale, 1996; Jamuna et al., 1993, 1994, 1996). Although these studies have covered rural aged women and elderly widows but have not given much emphasis on the problems of poor elderly women living in Kachhi Basties of big cities. Most of the elderly came here in search of livelihood with their husbands from their villages and thus these women have been uprooted from their native villages and living in unhygienic conditions and working all sorts of menial jobs. They are living in cities and are also aware of the good living conditions of cities but are unable to get those facilities for them. This situation creates a kind of psychological tension, frustration and increases level of aspiration in them.

The problems of aged women are not so much a product of the ageing process per se as they are a product of subordinate status of women through their life cycle. It is also recognized that the problems of ageing are increasingly women's problem. Older women are likely to be more in number and more ill than older men; and they are more likely to be poor, to be widowed/ divorced and, therefore, lonely, to be caregivers, to other relatives and to be institutionalized.

The present study was aimed to find out the socio-psychological problems of aged women living in Jawahar Nagar Kachhi Basti of Jaipur (Rajasthan).

Method

Sample

Jawahar Nagar Kachhi Basti is situated in the east of Jawahar Nagar, Jaipur. It is situated on seven Tibas (sand dunes). There are approximately thirty thousands people of different castes – skilled and non-skilled labourers and persons working in offices as peons and even clerical jobs lives in this Basti. One hundred and fifty aged women (age ranging from 60–85 years) were selected randomly for this study. These women belong to 28 castes. Out of these 150 women, 15 belong to Muslim religion, 10 to Sikh religion and remaining 125 belong to Hindu religion and non-belongs to Christian religion. The Hindu subjects were classified in the following categories: ST=33, SC=32, OBC=38, Upper castes (Brahmins, Rajputs, Agarwals, etc.)=22.

According to their marital status 90 women were widows and 60 women were non-widows or married.

The following table shows the years of their widowhood:

1–5 years	6–10 years	11–15 years	16–20 years	20 + years
8 (9%)	13 (15%)	14 (16%)	18 (20%)	37 (40%)

Out of these women, 10 women widowed approximately 40 years back. One woman widowed at the age of 7 years (child widow), she did not get remarried, and she does not have any child and looked after by her neighbours.

Out of these 90 widows, 41 (46%) still work and 49 (54%) do not work. Most of these non-working women are looked after by their children properly, but some women do not work due to their age (10 women were of old group, that is 80+) or due to their sickness. But these women worked throughout their life to bring up their children.

Out of 60 married women of the sample 22 (31%) are working and the remaining 38 (69%) are not working. Some of the women reported that they have stopped going out to work. They stay at home to look after grandchildren and to help in other activities of the family. The differences of working and non-working elderly women is significant within the group and between the groups. 69 per cent married women are not working while in widows this number is 54 per cent, perhaps the reason may be that their husbands can look after them or due to presence of their husbands, children are also looking after them properly.

The range of marriage age varied from 3 years to 20 years. The following table gives a view of the marriage age of this sample:

Age	3–6 Years	7–9 Years	10–14 Years	15–17 Years	18–20 Years
N=150	12	32	46	46	14

Seven woman (six married and one widow) did not have any issue, 11 women of the sample have one female child and 4 women have only one male child. The remaining 128 women have children from 2–9 as has been given in the following table:

No. of Children	9	8	7	6	5	4	3	2
No. of Subjects	7	9	17	16	33	21	14	11

Tools

An interview schedule was prepared to find out their socio-economic and psychological problems. The interview schedule consisted of questions related to personal information, information related to family, health, interpersonal relationships, leisure time activities, worries of old age, good points about old age and their interest in the participation in social activities.

Procedure

Each subject was interviewed individually. It was specially kept in mind that the subjects should be interviewed in the absence of their daughters-in-law and other members of family so that as far as possible right answers may be elicited from them. In some cases the interview was taken in two to three sittings, because most of these young olds (60–65) are still going out to work and also helping in their family jobs. It was really a very difficult task to collect the right information from these older women in the presence of their family members. Even in the absence of family members some of them were frightened to give right answers. Not only this, some of the women refused to give interview thinking that this survey is concerned with some political party.

Content analysis technique was used to analyse the data. On the basis of frequencies, percentages were calculated and rank order correlations were also computed.

Results and Discussion

Leisure time activities are the sources of coping with the physical and emotional stresses. These activities are the big sources of successful ageing. Although almost all the respondents of this study generally said that they do not have leisure time since they have to work and have to look after the family chores. About 54 per cent of the total numbers of widows (N=90) do not go to work anywhere where 46 per cent widows are working for their living. The percentage of non-working elderly married women was 69 per cent and working women was 31 per cent. When these elderly women (N=150) were asked what they do whenever they have free time? 59 per cent respondents said that they sleep in the day. Gossiping with friends and neighbours comes second. Care of children, smoking, social activities, watching TV or listening radio, bhajan-kirtan, sitting alone and doing nothing and care of body are the activities which are performed by these subjects in the order given above.

Participation in social activities help the individual to stay connected him with his relatives and friends and also help him to see his life as meaningful.

It is generally seen that religion plays an important part in the life of an individual, specially in old age, but in this sample religious activity such as bhajan-kirtan was given 6th preference out of 9 activities. In a study conducted by the author on leisure time activities of retired persons religious activities were given a very high ranking (Sharma, 1969).

It is also quite interesting to note that the preference for leisure time activities of elderly widows and married women significantly differed. For elderly widows the order of preferences is as follows: care of children, sleeping in the day, gossiping with neighbours, smoking, taking part in social activities, watching TV, bhajan-kirtan, and sitting alone.

For married women sleeping in the day is the first preference, gossiping with neighbours, bhajan-kirtan, social activities, care of grandchildren, watching TV and care of body are the preferred leisure time activities in the above mentioned order. It seems that widows give more time in child rearing. In a sense they contribute more time in household activities. For detailed comparison see Table 1.

Satisfiers of Life

Everybody wants some kind of satisfaction in life. Satisfaction in life motivates a person to work hard and provides him meaning in the life. Pleasure or pain as consequences of our acts are important determinants of behaviour. According to this view, we all do those things which give us pleasure and avoid pain. The positive reinforcers or satisfiers help in the individual's adjustment in his life. It is very difficult to give an objective definition of satisfiers. Satisfiers may vary according to physical, psychological and social situations. They also have an important relation with the needs of the person. For example, elderly widow women and non-widow (married) women apart from common satisfiers also had different set of satisfiers. It is evident from the data presented in the following tables (See Tables 2A, 2B and 2C).

Table 1

Leisure time activities of the aged women of Kachhi Basti

Leisure time activities	*Total*		*Widows*		*Married*	
	F	*N=150*	*F*	*N=90*	*F*	*N=60*
Care of children	73	49% (3)	56	62% (1)	17	27% (5)
Sleeping in the day	89	59% (1)	5	50% (2)	44	73% (1)
Gossiping with neighbours	80	53% (2)	48	53% (2)	32	53% (2)
Smoking	63	42% (4)	45	50% (2)	18	30% (4)
Social activities	37	25% (5)	23	25% (5)	14	23% (7)
Watching TV	25	17% (7)	9	10% (2)	16	26% (6)
Bhajan-Kirtan	27	18% (6)	7	8% (7)	20	33% (3)
Sitting alone	4	3% (8)	4	5% (8)	—	—
Care of body	2	1% (9)	—	—	2	3% (8)

In parentheses ranks have been given.
F represents frequencies of responses.

Table 2A

Common sources of satisfactions for all the subjects (N=150)

	Sources	*F*	*%*	*Ranks*
1.	Caring children	89	59	1
2.	Money	80	53	2
3.	Good food and clothes	75	50	3
4.	Good job of children	58	39	4
5.	Good health	53	35	5.5
6.	House	52	35	5.5
7.	Kirtan Bhajan	38	25	7
8.	Comfortable life	36	24	8
9.	Peace in the family	34	23	9
10.	Grandchildren	17	11	10
11.	Mental peace	10	7	11

Table 2B

Source of satisfaction in old age (married aged women, N=60)

	Sources	*F*	*%*	*Ranks*
1.	Well settled children (stable and good job)	40	67	01
2.	Completely happy life	36	60	02
3.	Enough money	30	50	3.5
4.	Good health	30	50	3.5
5.	Good food and clothes	25	42	05
6.	Comfortable living	24	40	06
7.	Time for Kirthan Bhajan	20	33	7.5
8.	Peace in family	20	33	7.5
9.	Caring children	18	30	09
10.	Good and caring husband	17	28	10
11.	Good house	16	27	11
12.	Respect by younger people	11	18	12.5
13.	Grandsons and daughters	11	18	12.5
14.	Responsible daughters-in-law	09	15	14.5
15.	Personal agricultural land	09	15	14.5
16.	Free from debts	06	10	16
17.	Satisfaction in life (or mental peace)	04	06	17

Table 2C

Source of satisfaction in old age (Widows N=90)

	Sources	*F*	*%*	*Ranks*
1.	Caring children	71	78	1
2.	Food and clothes	50	55	2.5
3.	Money	50	55	2.5
4.	Good food	46	50	4
5.	Good house	36	40	5
6.	Good health	23	25	6
7.	Good job (to children)	18	20	7
8.	Kirtan Bhajan	14	15	9
9.	Peace in the family	14	15	9
10.	All facilities	14	15	9
11.	Good neighbours	10	10	11.5
12.	Husband should be alive	09	10	11.5
13.	Complete rest	06	5	14.5
14.	Social prestige	06	5	14.5
15.	Playing with grandchildren	06	5	14.5
16.	Mental peace	06	5	14.5

If we look Table 2A, then we find that in the old age most important satisfier is the care of children. The subjects of this study have given it highest ranking. For older persons there must be someone who can look after their needs. Money, good food and proper clothings, good jobs for their children, personal good health, participation in religious activities (kirtan-bhajan), comfortable life, grandchildren and peace of mind are the main satisfiers of these subjects. But if we compare the satisfiers of married women and widows than we find some differences.

For example, married women gave the names of 6 more satisfiers which are quite different from the elderly widows of this sample. The names of the satisfiers which were indicated by married women are: complete happy life, good and caring husband, respect by younger people, responsible daughters-in-law, personal agricultural land and freedom from debts (see Table 2B).

The widow respondents of this study mentioned different satisfiers which are quite different from the responses given by married women. These subjects think that all types of facilities can give satisfaction to the individual. Their next preferences are: good neighbours, presence of husband, complete rest and social prestige (See Table 2C).

This difference indicates towards the personal experiences of these subjects. Satisfiers play an important role in the development and adjustment in the life of an individual.

Difficulties Faced in Old Age

The physical abilities, psychological capacities decrease with age and habits and personality traits become more rigid. These biological and psychological changes play an important role in determining the adjustment in old age and create difficulties to them in their social adjustment. About 43 per cent subjects reported that they have problems related to eyesights, for 41 per cent women physical weakness is common cause of difficulty. Personal health 35 per cent, housing problem 23 per cent, and unability to earn 15 per cent, were also reported by these subjects as the cause of difficulties (See Table 3A). All these difficulties are mainly related to physical health, living conditions and financial problems.

Table 3A

Common difficulties felt in old age (N=50)

Difficulties	*F*	*%*	*Ranks*
1. Eyesight	64	43	1
2. Physical weakness	62	41	2
3. Personal health	52	35	3
4. Housing problems	35	23	4
5. Unable to earn	23	15	5

Apart from these difficulties married women reported some more causes such as: difficulty in performing domestic activities (50%), children do not care/ignore (28%) and loneliness (18%). For detailed comparison see Table 3B given below:

Table 3B

Difficulties in old age (Married women N=60)

	Difficulties	*F*	*%*	*Ranks*
1.	Physical weakness	35	59	1
2.	Difficulty in performing domestic activities	30	50	2.5
3.	Weak eyesight	30	50	2.5
4.	Housing problem	18	30	4
5.	Children ignore/do not care	17	28	5
6.	Sickness (personal)	16	27	6
7.	Loneliness	11	18	7
8.	Difficulty in earning	9	15	8

In Table 3C those factors have been given which are the main sources of difficulties given by the widows of this study. These respondents have given some more sources which are different from as given by married women. These are dependency (26%), nobody looks after (20%), lack of proper source of earning (20%), debt (15%), maltreatment by children (10%), no proper clothing (7%) and 4 per cent respondents reported that they do not have any difficulty (See Table 3C).

Table 3C

Difficulties in old age (Widows N=90)

	Difficulties	*F*	*%*	*Ranks*
1.	Weak eyesight	46	50	1
2.	Personal health	36	40	2
3.	Physical weakness	27	30	3
4.	Dependency	23	26	4
5.	Nobody looks after	19	20	5.5
6.	Lack of proper source of earning	18	20	5.5
7.	Housing problem	17	18	7
8.	Debt	14	15	8.5
9.	Can't earn	14	15	8.5
10.	Maltreatment by children	9	10	10
11.	No proper clothes	7	7	11
12.	No difficulty	4	5	12

The elderly persons are more worried about their future due to lack of money, poor health, children's negative attitude and so on. The common worries reported by these subjects may be classified in two categories: personal (which include health, financial position, living conditions etc.) and social (this category includes family relations, problems of the family members who are financially dependent on them and other problems of family).

The common worries mentioned by these respondents are: who will look after (50%), money (28%), marriage of children (27%) what will happen in the future (26%) and sickness in the family (see Table 4A).

Table 4A

Common worried in old age (N=150)

	Worries	*F*	*%*	*Ranks*
1.	Who will look after me	74	50	1
2.	Lack of money (poverty)	42	28	2
3.	Marriage of children	41	27	3
4.	What will happen in the future	39	25	4
5.	Sickness in the family	16	11	5

The married women of this sample expressed some more worries apart from the worries expressed generally by these respondents. Children's job (40%), husband's alcoholism (20%), debt (15%) and sickness of the husband (10%). For detailed comparison see Table 4B.

Table 4B

Worries of old age (Married Women N=60)

	Worries	*F*	*%*	*Ranks*
1.	Who will look after illness	24	40	1.5
2.	Children's job	24	40	1.5
3.	Shortage of money	21	35	3
4.	What will happen in the future	20	33	4
5.	Marriage of children	18	30	5
6.	Husband's alcoholism	15	20	6
7.	Debt	9	15	7
8.	Sickness of husband	6	10	8

Some worries of the widows of the sample are different from the worries expressed by the married elderly women. Personal sickness (15%), other family problems (13%), sickness in the family (10%) and loneliness (4%). For other comparisons see Table 4C given below:

Table 4C

Worries of old age (Widows N=90)

	Worries	*F*	*%*	*Ranks*
1.	Who will look after	50	55	1
2.	Marriage of children	23	25	2
3.	Poverty (money)	21	23	3
4.	What will happen in the future	19	20	4.5
5.	Children's job	18	20	4.5
6.	Personal sickness	14	15	6
7.	Other family problems	12	13	7
8.	Sickness in the family	10	10	8
9.	Loneliness	4	4	9

Interpersonal Relationship

About 37 per cent of the total number of respondents (N=150) said, that they have very good relation with their family members. Almost 43 per cent reported that the relation is satisfactory and 20 per cent reported that the relations are not good. There is a significant difference between these categories of responses.

Whereas 33 per cent widows and 43 per cent married women were of the view that they are satisfied with their family members. 22 per cent widows and 17 per cent married women reported that they do not have good relation with their family members. Between the groups and within the groups differences may be explained by various factors. Death of spouse in old age significantly influence the later life of the individual. Caring children are also important factor which positively influence the life of the older people. Most of the widows of the sample are those whose husbands died quite early and they had to work hard for their own survival and the survival of their children, 46 per cent widows are still working for their livelihood, therefore in a sense they are not burden on their family.

If we combine the percentage of satisfactory and not good (66%) in the case of widows then this number is very high in comparison to 33 per cent women who responded that they have good relation with other family members. For detail comparison see Table 5 given below:

Table 5

Relationship with family

		Very good	*Satisfactory*	*Not Good*
Total	N=150	(56) 37%	(64) 43%	(30) 20%
Widow	N=90	(30) 33%	(40) 44%	(20) 22%
Married	N=60	(26) 43%	(24) 40%	(10) 17%

In response to the question whether your husband, son daughter-in-law, daughter and others take your advice or not? 29 per cent (26) widows replied that their sons take advice in all the matters, while 26 per cent (23) subjects of this study reported that they take advice some times, 41 per cent (37) women reported that they never take their advice. 16 per cent (14) women did not answer this question. Out of these 16 per cent (14) women one widow did not have any issue, 4 per cent (4) women have only one married daughter, remaining 10 per cent (9) respondents did not answer most probable they did not want to say against their sons and daughters-in-law.

About 29 per cent (26) women said that their son take advice in all the matters but only 18 per cent (16) respondents said that their daughters-in-law take advice in all the matters. 36 per cent (32) daughters-in-law take advice only in domestic matters, 19 per cent (17) reported that they are consulted only in the matters of marriage of children and relatives, 14 per cent (13) women are consulted in the matters related to jobs or work, regarding money matters only 9 per cent (8) women are consulted, 13 per cent (12) women reported that they are not consulted in the external matters. About 26 per cent (23) women said that their daughters-in-law do not consult them in any matter, 18 per cent (17) women reported that younger sons consult but elder sons do not consult them in any matter, 6 per cent (6) respondents said that their grandsons consult them in all the matters. Only 8 per cent (7) women said that other persons such as sisters-in-law, relatives, neighbours also take their help in problem solving. It is interesting to note that their daughter also take their advice in family matters and in their work or jobs.

When the same question was asked to married elderly women 36 (60%) said that their husbands always take their advice in all the matters, [8% (5) respondents said whatever they say is followed in the family, in other words their orders are followed in the family], 22 per cent (13) replied that they are consulted only in some matters or some time, while 35 per cent (21) they are not consulted by their husbands in any matters.

About 22 per cent (13) are consulted by their sons in all the matters, 30 per cent (18) are consulted some times and 30 per cent (18) said that they are not consulted by their sons, 18 per cent did not answer (some of these respondents did not have any son or daughter and some have only one daughter). While 20 per cent (23) said that they are consulted only at the time of marriages, 54 per cent (32) in domestic works, 65 per cent (39) reported that they are not taken in confidence in the matters related to job (kam-dhandha) and money matters.

Although it was reported by married elderly women that 54 per cent (32) husbands look after them in their sickness but when they were asked do you have words with your husbands? Only 17 per cent (10) reported that they do not fight with each other.

In response to the question does your husband beat you? About 73 per cent (44) of these subjects reported that their husbands do not beat them, 17 per cent (10) answered some times and only 10 per cent (6) reported that they are beaten by their husband generally.

In response to the causes of fight 42 per cent (17) women reported that cause of fight is husband's bad habits such as drinking alcohol, investing money in lotteries, not going for work regularly and snatching the earnings of their wives. 35 per cent (21) reported that husbands do not take advice in any matter. 17 per cent (10) reported that their husbands do not give money for essential things, 12 per cent (7) reported that husband force them to go for work, husband does not take interest in domestic work 23 per cent (14), children (grand son and grand daughters) are also cause of fight 12 per cent (7), 20 per cent (12) reported that some time the causes of fight are very small such as speaking loudly, when I fall sick, if he (husband) is disturbed and angry on some other issues, does not like my work etc. Sons and their wives are also important factor in creating disturbance in the family 27 per cent (16), marriages of the children 8 per cent (5) and debt 10 per cent (6) are also causes of fight.

Nearly 13 per cent (12) elderly widows reported that there is always fight in the family, 69 per cent (62) said that fight is not regular and it may occur sometimes and 18 per cent (16) women reported that we never fight.

As regard to the causes of fight, these women reported that poverty is the main cause 32 per cent (29), sons and daughter-in-laws think that they are burden on them because now they are unable to earn their living due old age and sickness. 8 per cent (7) women said that they cannot help financially to their daughters and this becomes the cause of fight. 12 per cent (10) women reported that they do not have good relations with their sons-in-law, daughters-in-law do not want that they should live with them 8 per cent (7), distribution of property is also one of the causes 4 per cent (4). Some of the women reported that they live with their grandsons, some are looked after by their daughters although they do not want it due to social customs. Children are also cause of fight (6%). Only 12 per cent women did not reply to this question.

Health Status

Out of 60 married elderly women 22 (37%) subjects are still working, and 38 (63%) are not working anywhere. Some women reported that they used to go out to work but now they have stopped to work because they have lot of domestic work to perform. Some of the non-working women showed interest in doing some light work.

About 23 per cent (23) respondents answered that their health is good, 53 per cent (32) reported difficulty in walking and doing some work, they get fatigued early. 25 per cent (16) respondents had problems related to eyesight, gastric trouble 10 per cent (6), allergy 5 per cent (3), pain in ribs 6 per cent (4), difficulties in summers and mental retardedness 11 per cent (7) were also reported as sickness by these respondents.

Out of 90 widows 16 per cent (14) reported that their health is good, 44 per cent (48) said that their health is not very good, just so-so and 40 per cent (38%) informed that their health is not good.

The chronic diseases they reported were weakness (difficulty in walking) 2 per cent (61), poor eyesight 52 per cent (51), blood pressure, TB, asthma, arthritis, gastric trouble, deformities in hand and leg.

Table 6

Who looks after you in your sickness

	Total N=150	*Widow N=90*	*Married N=60*
1. Husband	(33)22%	—	(33)54%
2. Son	(87)58%	(54)64%	(33)54%
3. Daughter	(31)21%	(19)21%	(12)20%
4. Daughter-in-law	(40)27%	(25)28%	(15)25%
5. Grandson	(21)14%	(18)20%	(3)5%
6. Relatives	(20)13%	(15)16%	(5)8%
7. Neighbours	(30)20%	(27)30%	(3)5%
8. Others/ God	(3)2%	—	(3)5%

Table 7

What do you think are the causes of your sickness it? (N=150)

1. Age (75) 50 per cent
2. Physical deformity (11) 7 per cent
3. Family problems (52) 35 per cent [Family problems according to widows (35) 39%, for married (17) 28%].
4. Unhygienic environment (15) 10 per cent
5. Accident and Injury (14) 9 per cent
6. Other causes (20) 13 per cent

Deprivations or Aspirations of Life

The married women were asked about their deprivations. 26 per cent (44) respondents said that they feel that they should get good food and proper clothings. The other deprivations they reported were: Shortage of income/money 47 per cent (28), do not have facilities like electricity, pipeline, TV etc., 27 per cent (16), did not have money for proper care and education for the children 11 per cent (7), hospital 2 per cent (2), water facilities 6 per cent (4), pakka (good) house 10 per cent (6), do not have land and property 6 per cent (4), debt 10 per cent (8), money for daughter's marriage 8 per cent (5), lack of cleanliness 6 per cent (4), children's marriage 6 per cent (4) do not have rest 8 per cent (5), money for medical treatment 11 per cent (7), no fixed source of income 6 per cent (4), inflation/mahngai 13 per cent (8), 20 per cent (12) women responded that they are happy with the situation and do not have any ambitions in life.

The deprivations or aspirations reported by elderly widows were: Proper food and clothes 47 per cent (42), poverty or insufficient money 49 per cent (44), less income and more expenditure 17 per cent (15), regular income of sons and grandsons 36 per cent (33), absence of husband 53 per cent (48), proper facilities for medicines and care 20 per cent (18), proper care and respect 10 per cent (8), basic amenities 16 per cent (14), nobody to look after 14 per cent (12). Three women reported that they are living with their daughters and other relatives, 6 per cent (5) do not have son or son does not live with them (6).

Sources of Happiness and Unhappiness

Every human being wants happiness in life. Happiness or pleasure is the end or summum bonum of life. Sources of happiness or objects of happiness vary from person to person. Sociocultural factors also play an important role in determining happiness and unhappiness. Although the meaning of words 'happiness' and 'pleasure' have different connotations. The word pleasure is generally used for bodily comforts and happiness is used for mental happiness. But here we are using these words synonymously. Happiness or unhappiness is purely subjective and depends on number of factors (Sharma, 1971).

When these subjects were asked a direct question whether they are happy or not? Out of 90 elderly widows 41 (46%) replied in 'yes' and 49 (54%) replied in 'no'. It means 45 per cent of these women are satisfied with their present situation and 54 per cent are not satisfied. Out of 60 married women 46 (75%) replied that the they are satisfied and 14 (25%) reported that they are not happy with the situation. If we compare these findings then we find that, within the group, difference between widows is not very significant but in the case of married women this difference is quite significant. If we compare these findings in between the groups then we find that this difference is most significant.

The reasons are quite obvious that either some of these widows did not show their unhappiness due to the fear of their family members or they have adjusted with the situation. If we look into the factors leading to happiness and unhappiness in widows and married elderly women then we also find a significant differences in their responses.

The causes of unhappiness reported by the widows were death of the husband 48 per cent (43), death of children 19 per cent (17), death of other family members 15 per cent (14), destruction of the hut 5 per cent (5), nobody helped in the crisis 7 per cent (6), did hard work and struggle to survival 16 per cent (15), children are not caring 19 per cent (17), personal sickness 10 per cent (8), no financial support and still earning, 13 per cent (12), had to leave the native village 4 per cent (4), lost agricultural land 2 per cent (2), husband was alcoholic 5 per cent (5), fight in the family 57 per cent (51), do not have own house 15 per cent (14), son is alcoholic 6 per cent (6), too many children 3 per cent (3), son does not have any issue 2 per cent (2), do not have our own child 1 per cent (1), do not have male child 4 per cent (4), other family problems 8 per cent (7), whole life lived as unhappy 5 per cent (5), debt 8 per cent (7) and 8 per cent (7) women did not give any reason for their unhappiness.

These respondents reported 17 factors for their satisfaction. These factors were: caring son and daughter-in-law 17 per cent (15), get food both the times 17 per cent (15), one son is looking after 10 per cent (8), daughter-in-law is good and caring 12 per cent (11), children's job is satisfactory 4 per cent (4), daughter and son-in-law are very good and caring 6 per cent (6), grandsons care 10 per cent (8), finished the responsibility of the marriages of daughters 5 per cent (5), get respect in the family 4 per cent (4), own house 8 per cent (7), members of the family are happy 3 per cent (3), satisfaction 6 per cent (6) and 5 per cent (5) respondents did not give any response.

Married elderly women gave the following reasons for the unhappiness: children do not care 13 per cent (8), various problems in the family 27 per cent (10), do not have any child 10 per cent (6), do not have son 10 per cent (7), the behaviour of the sons and daughters-in-law is not good 10 per cent (6), house was destroyed in the rainy season or flood 10 per cent (6), death of son 7 per cent (4), lack of basic amenities such as fan, TV, cooking gas 10 per cent (7), personal sickness 7 per cent (4), do not have good relations with the husband 3 per cent (5), sickness of the husband 8 per cent (5), separation of son and daughter-in-law from the family 10 per cent (7), lack of money for necessities 10 per cent (6), lost land in the village 5 per cent (3), marriage of the children 8 per cent (5), husband have to work hard to survive 7 per cent (4), husband is alcoholic 5 per cent (3).

The reasons given for satisfaction by these respondents were: get food for both the times 25 per cent (15), support of the husband 20 per cent (12), son's job is satisfactory 7 per cent (4), family is happy 10 per cent (6), caring son and daughter-in-law 20 per cent (12), son's help 8 per cent (5), God's grace 13 per cent (8), living with husband 3 per cent (2), have our own house 17 per cent (10), playing with grandsons and granddaughters 7 per cent (4), finished the responsibility of marriages of the daughters 7 per cent (4), daughter-in-law is caring 7 per cent (4).

References

Bagchi, K. (Ed.) (1997): *Elderly Females in India: Their Status and Suffering.* New Delhi: Society for Gerontological Research and Help Age.

Bambawale, Usha (1996): *Abuse of the Aged in Aging: Indian Perspective and Global Scenario.* (Ed.) Vinod Kumar, IIMS, New Delhi.

Dayabati Devi and Bagga, A. (1997): "Health Status of Older Women in Manipur". *Aging and Society.* 7 (1 and 2): 27–42.

Jamuna, D. and Ramamurti, P.V. (1994): "Self-others Perception of Issues and Problems of Aged Women in Andhra Pradesh". *Indian Journal of Gerontology.* 8 (1 and 2): 29–36.

Jamuna, D. and Reddy, L.K. (1993): "Impact of Age and Length of Widowhood on the Self-concept of Elderly Widows". *Indian Journal of Gerontology.* 7 (3 and 4): 91–95.

——. (1996): "Psychological Aspects of Elder Widows" in *Aging: Indian Perspective and Global Scenario.* (Ed.). Vinod Kumar, All India Institute of Medical Sciences, New Delhi.

Prakash, Indira J. (1991): "Psychological Profile of Aging Indian Women". In Indira J. Prakash (Ed.) *Quality Aging: Collected Papers.* Varanasi.

——. (1993): "Gender Aging: Psychological Issues". *Indian Journal of Gerontology.* 7 (1 and 2): 24–29.

——. (1996): "Coping with Ageing: Psychosocial of Older Indian Women in Aging". *Indian Perspective and Global Scenario* (Ed.). Vinod Kumar, All India Institute of Medical Sciences, New Delhi.

Rajan, S. Irudaya (1999): *India's Elderly: Burden or Challenge*. Sage Publications, New Delhi.

Sen, Tulika (1996): "A Health and Socio-economic Profile of the Aged Bengali Women" in *Aging: Indian Perspective and Global Scenario* (Ed.) Vinod Kumar. All India Institute of Medical Sciences, New Delhi.

Sharma, K.L. (1969): "Leisure Time Activities of Retired Persons". *Indian Journal of Gerontology*. 1(1).

——. (1971): "A Survey of the Happiness and Unhappiness in Old Age". *Indian Journal of Gerontology*. 3 (3 and 4): 76–77.

CHAPTER 27

Scenario of Segregated Seniors

A Case Study of the Inmates of Old Age Homes

Saraswati Mishra

Never before have the problems of the aged people been such central concern to the field of welfare (Friedlander and Apte, 1982). Due to increased importance of achieved properties, the resourceless old people are forced to lead miserable life in the modern society (D'souza, 1971). Since the aged themselves are unable and their families are not prepared to solve their problems, the society has to come forward for their rescue. In this regard only, we find 'Old Age Home', to keep them away from the families in order to satisfy their needs.

In Indian society, the idea of institutionalization of the aged people have been borrowed from the Western societies whose values and norms are quite different. In West, the children get separated from the parents in quite an early age. In such societies children are not expected to look after their parents in old age and even parents prefer to live independently. But even in such societies, the gradual abandoning of homes for the aged people is being considered (Townsend, 1963; Friedlander and Apte, 1982).

On the contrary, children in India live with their parents for quite a considerable period of time and the social values and norms do not permit the sons to leave their old parents to struggle themselves in later years of life. As it is the typical characteristics of pre-industrial societies (Simmons, 1960). In India metaphorically the sons are

IJG, 1993, Vol. 7, No. 3 and 4, pp. 104–110.

expected to serve their parents as hands, feet, ears and eyes. Even now these values are existing (Bose, 1982). But gradually increasing materialistic and individualistic values in the Indian society have led to a situation where new generation is not prepared to sacrifice much for the sake of older generation, specially in the case of financially constrained situation.

A number of studies of western societies (e.g., Donahue et al., 1960), Eastern society (Lee and Ishii-Kuntz, 1987) and our own study (Mishra, 1987) have demonstrated that the aged people want to remain socially integrated, not segregated. It suggests that in India probably no one would like to stay willingly in 'old age homes' and this is one of the reasons that the programme of 'old age homes' has not been very successful. The fulfilment of socio-psychological needs such as love, care, emotional security, new experiences, sense of belonging, identity and status, interaction and activeness, being useful and significant person in own world of near and dear ones etc., cannot be fulfilled while living in old age homes. These needs become quite important in later years of life (Chowdhary, 1981).

Therefore, the institutionalization of the aged people should not be encouraged beyond a point (Chowdhary, 1981) and their living with family members should be encouraged by society. D'souza (1976) has stated, apart from old people's point of view, institutionalization of aged is a very costly affair for the country like India. But at the same time old people are to be kept satisfied and happy.

In this context the present empirical study of the institutionalized aged people was conducted to evaluate the importance of family and our society for the well-being of the aged people. The main objective of this study has been to find out the extent to which the institutionalization of the aged people should be encouraged in India.

Method

Sample

Since the number of inmates of the three old age homes located in Delhi was small i.e., 46 only, all of them have been included as sample for the present study. These participants were in the group of 61–70 years, spouseless, having low level of education and poor health conditions.

Procedure

The superintendents of old age homes were contacted in order to obtain preliminary information of homes. The inmates were interviewed individually for the purpose of studying their various kinds of problems of past and present life. Among the inmates most of them were aged females. Besides the interview, a measure of life satisfaction was also used.

This measure consisted of ten statements, having five point response categories, ranging from strongly agree (1) to strongly disagree (5) was individually administered.

Results and Discussion

After the collection of information, it was coded and tabulated. Due to the small number of inmates and scattered frequency distribution in the tables, the application of any statistical devices to find out the significance of differences or the association between two variables was not possible.

Earlier Living Arrangements of the Inmates of Old Age Homes and Reasons of their Conflicts with Family Members

Most of the respondents of the present study were spouseless and all those, living with others, did not enjoy good relationship with other family members. Table 1 presents the information about their living arrangements and the reasons of conflicts with their family members. More than one-fifth of them i.e., 21.74 per cent, were living alone and almost half of them i.e., 47.82 per cent living with their married children, with or without spouse, which is worth noting. While only 4.35 per cent of the inmates were living with their spouse and unmarried children, 26.09 per cent of them accommodated themselves with their relatives, somehow. As far as the reasons of bad relationship with family members is concerned, financial crisis has emerged as the main cause of conflicts. In the case of bad health also, financial requirement for the treatment of ailments, plays an important role. Almost 65.48 per cent of the aged did not get required health care by other members of household. Since they could not look after themselves, they were maltreated as burden and any financial help from the children was denied to them.

Table 1

Distribution of the inmates of old age home according to earlier living arrangements and reasons for bad family relationship and conflicts

Living arrangements	*Reasons for bad relationship and conflicts*					*Total*
	Financial	*Health*	*Financial and health*	*Difference of opinion*	*Not applicable*	
Living alone	—	—	—	—	10	10 (21.74)
Living with spouse and unmarried children	—	2	—	—	—	2 (4.35)
Living with spouse and married children	—	3	—	—	—	3 (6.52)
Living with married children	7	3	6	3	—	19 (41.30)
Living with relatives	2	3	5	2	—	12 (26.09)
Total	9 (19.57)	11 (23.91)	11 (23.91)	5 (10.87)	10 (21.74)	46

Relationship with the Separated Children: Financial Help and Mutual Visits

Almost all of those, having grown-up children living separately, did not have smooth relationship with them. Table 2 shows the facts that they never used to get any financial help from their financially independent children but they used to meet them through mutual visits, atleast once in a year which is worth noting.

Specific Reasons to Leave Own Home and the Possibility of Its Avoidance

When the inmates of 'Old Age Homes' were asked to specify the reason behind their decision of shifting there, 45.65 per cent and 15.22 per cent of them reported that, they left their respective homes due to frequent conflicts with family members and lack of their proper care by the younger generation respectively. Isolation and loneliness, and lack of own house for living, were their prominent reasons behind their shifting. When these probed into the possibility of its avoidance with some conditions, it was found that most of them were of the opinion that, with sufficient financial assistance and free medical aid at door step from outside, they could have continued with their earlier living arrangements. In the case of 70 per cent of inmates, their family members were not in position to support and serve them, mainly due to financial constraints. And when they took the decision of shifting to the institution, the children neither objected nor showed any symptoms of sadness at the time of parting but they felt relieved.

Present Life Satisfaction and the Main Reason Behind Dissatisfaction

About various needs satisfaction of inmates, the present data demonstrates that, regarding the basic, financial and medical needs, the present level of satisfaction is higher than the pre-institutionalized period of their life, but, regarding the social and psychological needs, the state is totally opposite, that is, the present life, satisfaction level is lower than the earlier one (Mishra, 1987). On the whole, no inmate was highly satisfied, whereas 67.39 per cent of them belonged to the category of low satisfaction. Majority of them were dissatisfied due to the segregation from their own known world. They felt that they were thrown away from the world of near and dear ones mercilessly. This

Table 2

Distribution of the inmates of old age home according to financial help from separated children and frequency of mutual visits

Financial help from	*Frequency of Mutual Visits*				
	Once in more than a year	*Once in a year*	*More than once in a year*	*Not applicable*	*Total*
Not applicable	—	—	—	32 (69.57)	32 (69.57)
No	5	7	2	—	14 (30.43)
Yes	—	—	—	—	00
Total	5 (10.87)	7 (15.21)	2 (4.35)	32 (69.57)	46 (100.00)

finding very clearly demonstrates the fact that the aged derive full satisfaction while living among their family members only.

Table 3 very clearly demonstrates the fact that the aged people want to remain integrated in the society but the society segregates them which is quite frustrating for them. They are not enjoying the life while living in the old age homes.

Possibility of Rehabilitation

About 56.25 per cent of the inmates expressed their willingness to go back to their respective places under the changed circumstances, characterized by the provision of various services and facilities by government or voluntary agencies. 43.38 per cent of those living with someone, expressed that they will be accepted back by their family members in the changed situation. Quite a few of them said that although their children had love and concern for parents and wanted to keep them at home but they were helpless due to financial crisis. They could not satisfy their own basic needs properly, then how could they fulfil the requirements of parents.

The Table 4 shows very clearly that under the changed situation characterized by the provision of various facilities and services, majority of the inmates of old age homes would like to go back to their respective places and a considerable number of them think that they will be accepted by the household members.

Expectations

In the last, the inmates of old age homes were asked to suggest some measures through which government or society should help the aged people regarding their financial, health, residential, entertainment and household aspects of their life. Almost all of them expressed their views that a house to live, sufficient old age pension, and free medical aid at doorsteps as well as in the hospitals, should be provided by the government to the needy aged people. Some of them also expressed their opinion in favour of the 'old age homes' for the totally helpless aged. The poverty stricken residents of these institutions could not think much about the provision of other services. But still some of the educated inmates suggested that the domicilliary supportive services should be provided to the physically weak aged living in the family or alone. Thus, most of them expressed that the aged should be kept integrated in the main stream of population.

Table 3

The degree of satisfaction of the inmates with their present life and the reason of dissatisfaction

Degree of present life satisfaction	*Main reason of Dissatisfaction*				
	Improper care in the institution	*Physical ailments*	*Segregation from the own world*	*No response*	*Total*
Low	5	7	19	—	31(67.39)
Medium	—	6	7	—	13(28.26)
High	—	—	—	—	—
No Response	—	—	—	2	2(4.35)
Total	5(10.87)	13(28.26)	26(56.52)	2(4.35)	46(100.00)

Table 4

Distribution of the inmates according to the possibility of rehabilitation under the changed situation characterized by the provision of various facilities and services

Under the changed situation acceptance by the household members	*Willingness to go back under changed situation*				
	Yes	*Undecided*	*No*	*No response*	*Total*
Yes	11	—	9	—	20(43.48)
Undecided	—	7	2	—	9(19.36)
No	5	—	—	—	5(10.87)
No Response	—	—	—	2	2(54.35)
Not applicable	10	—	—	—	10(21.74)
Total	26	7	11	2	46(100.00)

In this way we can conclude that normally people do not want to stay in the 'old age homes' but the circumstances force them to do so. While staying there, they do not remain very happy and satisfied and given a chance i.e., various facilities and services, they would still like to go back and live among their near and dear ones and according to their perception, they will be accepted back by the family members under the changed circumstances.

These findings suggest that only for the totally helpless aged people institutionalization should be encouraged in India. Regarding other resourceless aged people every effort should be made to encourage their living with their family members by sharing the family's burden of looking after its aged members by the society.

References

Bose, Ashish (1982): "Aspects of Aging in India". *Social Action*. January March: 1–19.

Chowdhary, Paul D. (1981): *A Hand Book of Social Welfare*. Atma Ram and Sons, Delhi.

D'souza, V.S. (1976): "An Emerging Social Problem". *Science Today*. II, October 25–27.

D'souza, V.S. (1971): "Changes in Social Structure and Changing Roles of Older People in India". *Sociology and Social Research*. 55, 297–304.

Donahue, Wilma, Orbach Harold, L. and Otto Pollack (1960): "The Emerging Social Pattern", 330–406 in *Hand Book of Social Gerontology:* Chicago: The University of Chicago Press.

Friedlander, Walter A. and Apte Robert Z. (1982): *Introduction to Social Welfare*. Prentice Hall of India, Delhi

Lee, Gary R. and Ishii-Kuntz, Masako (1987): "Social Interaction, Loneliness and Emotional Well-being among the Elderly". *Research on Aging*. 9, 4: 450–482.

Mishra, Saraswati (1987): *The Problems and Social Adjustment in Old Age*. Gyan Publishers, Delhi

Simmons, Leo W. (1960): "Aging in Pre-industrial Society" in T. Clark (Ed.) *Hand Book of Social Gerontology*. Chicago: The University of Chicago Press.

Townsend, Peter (1963): "The Argument for Gradually Abandoning Communal Homes for the Aged". *International Social Science Journal*. XV: 427–437.

Section F
Successful Ageing

One of the most commonly used terms to describe a good old age is 'successful aging', often attributed to R. J. Havighurst (1961). Interest in successful ageing has remained high through the successive decades, and peaked again with Rowe and Kahn's article in *Science* (1987) in which they recommended that research on successful ageing should focus on people with better than average physiological and psychosocial characteristics in late life, or 'successful agers' as opposed to average or 'usual agers'. In the early 1990s, a major set of studies on predictors of successful ageing was commissioned by the MacArthur Foundation and conducted under Rowe's leadership (Berkman et al., 1993; Seeman et al., 1994).

What do gerontologists mean by successful ageing? Not surprisingly, given the ambiguity of the term 'success' itself, there is no single well-accepted definition or model of successful ageing. Havighurst (1961) defined it as "adding life to the years" and "getting satisfaction from life". Rowe and Kahn (1987) defined it in terms of multiple physiological and psychosocial variables. The MacArthur studies looked at outcomes pertaining to physical performance and other indicators of functional status. Ryff (1982), a psychologist, defined successful ageing as positive or ideal functioning related to developmental work over the life course. Fisher (1992) interviewed 19 senior centre participants, age 62–85 and found that they tended to define successful ageing in terms of strategies for coping. Gibson (1995) stated that successful ageing "refers to reaching one's potential and arriving at a level of physical, social, and psychological well-being in old age that is pleasing to both self and others". In the *Encyclopedia of Ageing*, Palmore (1995) says that a comprehensive definition of successful ageing "would combine survival (longevity), health (lack of disability), and life satisfaction (happiness)". Additionally, some gerontologists have discussed similar issues using different terms such as 'adjustment' or 'adaptation' to ageing.

The shifting meanings of successful ageing have paralleled changes in prevailing theories of social and psychological aspects of ageing, because ideas of what constitutes successful ageing are implicitly contained in each theory. One of the first theories of ageing, Cumming and Henry's *Disengagement Theory* (1961), proposed that in the normal course of ageing, people gradually withdrew or disengaged from social roles as a natural response to lessened capabilities and diminished interest, and to societal disincentives for participation. In this model, the successfully ageing person willingly retires from work or family life and contentedly takes to a rocking chair, or pursues other solitary, passive activities while preparing for death. Although the theory seems dated today, it made sense in an era characterized by shorter life expectancy, earlier onset of disability, physically demanding work roles, mandatory retirement and few organized activities for older adults. To social scientists in the 1960s, what was typical or common among older people may have shaped the perception of what was optimal or possible.

A second major theory of aging, referred to as *Activity Theory*, proposed that people age most successfully when they participate in a full round of daily activities, that is, keep busy (Lemon, Bengtson and Peterson, 1972). This theory seemed to explain the surge of volunteerism and senior activism in the 1960s and 1970s and may have been partly responsible for public policies which underwrote the development of senior centres and other recreational facilities in that period. Today, the theory has been discarded by gerontologists who view it as too narrow in its implied advocacy of one particular lifestyle. Empirical research has demonstrated the heterogeneity of older people, including many people who prefer less structured lives or do not have the health or means to pursue a full schedule of activities. Nevertheless, activity is widely touted by older adults themselves as the key to successful ageing, so much so that gerontologists have dubbed this philosophy "the busy ethic" (Ekerdt, 1986).

A third theory of ageing which has been viewed with much favour in recent years is called *Continuity Theory* (Atchley, 1972). This theory proposes that the people who age most successfully are those who carry forward the habits, preferences, lifestyles and relationships from midlife into late life. This theory has gained considerable support from the results of major longitudinal research studies which have shown that variables measured in midlife are strong predictors of outcomes in later life, and that many psychological and social characteristics are stable across the life span. For most people, late life does not represent a radical break with the past; changes often occur gradually and sometimes imperceptibly.

Concurrent with these developments in social gerontology, theorists and researchers in the biomedical arena have also been proposing and testing models of successful ageing. Until the 1980s, many researchers defined successful ageing in terms of length of life. More recently, considerable attention has been given to investigating ways to delay the onset of disability, thereby lengthening the number of years of 'active life expectancy', that is, the number of years of life spent without significant disease or disability (Fries and Crapo, 1981). Biomedical researchers now have started to realize that *quality* of life is as important as *quantity* of life, or is at least a necessary part of successful ageing.

An informal review of the gerontological literature suggests that two new models of successful ageing are coming into their own in gerontology in the 1990s. One approach emphasizes the strengths and growth potential of ageing individuals (Sullivan and Fisher, 1994). Presented as an alternative to the 'loss-deficit' model of ageing, this approach uses such concepts as control or self-efficacy (Bandura, 1982), mindfulness, possible selves (Markus and Nurius, 1986), life enrichment and empowerment (Myers, 1990) to describe a lifestyle and stage of life characterized by self-actualization.

Austin in his paper"Ageing Well", (1991) has reminded the gerontological community not to forget those who cannot age well because of social factors over the life course (e.g., poverty, rural residence, poor nutrition, substandard housing, limited educational opportunities, abuse or catastrophic losses) that reduce life chances and limit access to an 'ageing well lifestyle'.

Diverging from works of the 1980s that emphasize 'maximizing independence' or 'enhancing autonomy' in the frail elderly, Lustbader (1994) described the possibilities for finding satisfaction and meaning even in a state of dependency, including moments of vivid aliveness, true intimacy between family members, and spiritual revival. A recent book on enhancing the spiritual well-being of people with Alzheimer's disease (Gwyther, 1995) also addresses some of the same issues in a severely impaired population.

As the older population becomes increasingly diverse, the concept of successful ageing may become even more difficult to define without expanding the number of models. Successful ageing is measured with indicators of subjective well-being such as life satisfaction, happiness, morale, contentment, perceived quality of life or other related measures of negativity such as depression, anxiety, etc. New efforts in the measurement of quality of life (Guyatt and Cook, 1994) and personal goals (Bearon et al., 1994), and innovative qualitative studies on older adult perceptions of life satisfaction and successful ageing (Fisher, 1992) suggest that there may be new and fruitful avenues for capturing and comparing individualized outcomes and developing a more multicoloured view of successful ageing.

Successful ageing in an art of coping with growing older. Coping is about having a sense of being in control of one's life, coupled with a feeling that life is meaningful. Ineffective coping behaviour is often the result of a person's feeling powerless, alienated and obsolete. These older persons who are able to learn new coping mechanisms have belief that life has meaning and adopt a flexible, spontaneous and creative response to rapidly changing world. A range of realistic developmental aspects for advancing creativity (to bring something new into being), which contributes to optimal ageing and effective coping mechanisms for ageing to be successful. In other words, the transformation of the self by engaging in novel enterprises and creative activities promotes active ageing, which in turn promotes active ageing. Thus, the creative living may alleviate later life stress by providing a sense of order and meaning in life.

Summary of Papers

This section contains six papers. Harinder Kaur Paintal in her paper "Factors Related to Successful Ageing in Medical Men", is of the view that although health is an important condition but engagement in leisure and recreational activities seems to be associated with successful ageing. Those who are not well adjusted after 65 years seem to have rather poor health. Further, reduced sense of economic security is not exclusively associated with poor adjustment. Ageing per se seems to affect sense of economic security even among those who are well adjusted. Reality orientation and engagement seems to aid successful ageing.

N.K. Chadha in his paper "Self Concept and Life-Satisfaction among Aged" studied three groups of elderly persons: A—non-institutionalized (staying with family members), B—non-institutionalized (living with spouse) and C—institutionalized. A significant difference between the subjects of group A and group B was found on ideal self, significant difference was found with regard to life satisfaction. Group B differed from group C on ideal self, self-concept discrepancy and life satisfaction. Group A and C were also compared and a significant difference was also noticed.

N.K. Chadha and John Van Willigen in their paper "The Life Scale: The Development of a Measure of Successful Ageing" describes the process of development of a measure of *successful aging* called the *Life Scale.* The life scale was developed for use with Hindi speaking older people. The scale consists of 27 items, both positively and negatively stated, presented in Likert-scale question frame.

World Health Organisation, in 1996, issued guidelines for promoting physical activity among older persons called the Heidelberg Guidelines. These guidelines were developed primarily to promote physical activity in the later half of the life course. Indira Jai Prakash and M. Sreenivas have emphasized in their study "Physical Activity Among the Elderly: An Exploratory Study" conducted on fifty seven retired persons that the physically active lifestyle not only enhances the chances of disease free life in later years, but also increases the sense of psychological well-being.

K.L. Sharma tried to find out the modes of leisure time activities of retired persons. Leisure time activities are influenced by the factors like educational level, income, cast, marital status and health. The retired persons cannot cope with various kinds of problems so they derive satisfaction from different kinds of leisure activities. The varied form of recreations are the forms of self expressions of the retired persons.

The socio-economic and psycho-physiological phenomena associated with old age arouse anxiety in individuals and thus create a special need for reassurance and security in life which have throughout the ages come from religious belief. K.L. Sharma and U.C. Jain in their paper "Religiosity and Fear of Death in Young and Retired Persons" studied 125 persons of different age groups (students=63 and retired persons=62) and found invert relationship between religiosity and fear of death and also age differences in fear of death and religiosity.

References

Atchley, R.C. (1972): *The Social Forces in Later Life: An Introduction to Social Gerontology*. Belmont, CA: Wadsworth.

Austin, C.D. (1991): "Aging Well: What Are the Odds?". *Generations*. 15(1): 73–75.

Bandura, A. (1982): "Self-efficacy: Mechanisms in Human Agency". *American Psychologist*. 37(2), 122–147.

Bearon, L.B., Crowley, G.M., Chandler, J., Studenski, S. and Robbins, M. (1994): Personal Functional Goals: A New Approach to Assessing Patient-relevant Outcomes. Paper presented at the annual scientific meeting of the Gerontological Society of America, Atlanta, Georgia.

Berkman, L. et al. (1993): "High, Usual and Impaired Functioning in Community-dwelling Older Men and Women: Findings from the MacArthur Foundation Research Network on Successful Aging". *Journal of Clinical Epidemiology*. 46(10): 1129–1140.

Cumming, E. and Henry, W.E. (1961): *Growing Old: The Process of Disengagement*. New York: Basic Books Inc.

Ekerdt, D.J. (1986): "The Busy Ethic: Moral Continuity between Work and Retirement". *The Gerontologist*. 26(3): 239–244.

Fisher, B.J. (1992): "Successful Aging and Life Satisfaction: A Pilot Study for Conceptual Clarification". *Journal of Aging Studies*. 6(2): 191–202.

Fries, J.F. and Crapo, L.M. (1981): *Vitality and Aging*. San Francisco: W.H. Freeman.

Gibson, R.C. (1995): "Promoting Successful and Productive Aging in Minority Populations". 279–288 in L.A. Bond, S.J. Cutler and A. Grams (Eds.) *Promoting Successful and Productive Aging*. Thousand Oaks, CA: Sage.

Guyatt, G.H. and Cook, D.J. (1994): "Health Status, Quality of Life and the Individual". *Journal of the American Medical Association*. 272(8): 630–631.

Gwyther, L.P. (1995): *You Are One of Us: Successful Clergy/church Connections to Alzheimer's Families*. Durham, NC: Duke University Medical Center.

Havighurst, R.J. (1961): "Successful Aging". *The Gerontologist*. 1(1): 8–13.

Lemon, B.W., Bengtson, V.L. and Petersen, J.A. (1972): "An Exploration of the Activity Theory of Aging: Activity Types and Life Expectation among In-movers to a Retirement Community". *Journal of Gerontology*. 27(4): 511–23.

Lustbader, W. (1994): *Counting on Kindness: The Dilemmas of Dependency*. New York: Free Press.

Markus, H. and Nurius, P. (1986): "Possible Selves". *American Psychologist*. 41: 954–969.

Myers, J.E. (1990): Empowerment for Later Life. Ann Arbor, MI: The University of Michigan, ERIC Counseling and Personnel Services Clearinghouse.

Palmore, E.B. (1995): "Successful Aging". 914–915 in G.L. Maddox. (Ed.) *Encyclopedia of Aging: A Comprehensive Resource in Gerontology and Geriatrics*. 2nd edition. New York: Springer.

Rowe, J.W. and Kahn, R.L. (1987): "Human Aging: Usual and Successful". *Science*. 237: 143–149.

Ryff, C.D. (1982): Successful Aging: A Developmental Approach. *The Gerontologist*, 22, 209–214.

Seeman, T.E. et al. (1994): "Predicting Changes in Physical Performance in a High-functioning Elderly Cohort: MacArthur Studies of Successful Aging. *Journals of Gerontology: Medical Sciences*. 49(3): M97–M108.

Sullivan, W.P., and Fisher, B.J. (1994): "Intervening for Success: Strengths-based Case Management and Successful Aging". *Journal of Gerontological Social Work*. 22(): 61–74.

CHAPTER 28

Factors Related to Successful Ageing in Medical Men

Harinder Kaur Paintal

It is well known that profession is an important relevant variable in the studies of adjustment to ageing (Donahue 1956). Profession which pose a serious retirement crisis would have different effect on the ageing person than professions which do not pose such problems (Havighurst and Shanas 1953). Many of the reported studies in ageing and adjustment in old age have dealt with old people who were recipients of old age assistance or are institutionalized, (Morgan, 1937; Landis, 1942 and Shans, 1950) or from the general population (Caven, Burgess, Havighurst and Goldhamer, 1949; Tuckman and Lorge 1954; Kuntner, Fanshel, Togo and Langner, 1956; Havighurst, 1957; Ramamurthy, 1969). Some studies have considered retired professors (McOre, 1951), retired Y.M.C.A. Secretaries (Britton and Britton, 1951); retired school teachers (Britton, 1953), industrial workers (Richard, Livson and Peterson, 1962) and manual workers (Heyman and Jeffers, 1964). Not many studies on ageing have been carried out on other professional groups such as medical men, engineers and owners of private business which are relatively free from retirement problems. This study deals with successful ageing in senior medical men. The purpose was to find out what characterizes successful ageing and further, to delineate factors which characteristically discriminate better adjusted elderly men from poorly adjusted ones in each of the three age groups 45 to 54, 55 to 64 and 65 to 74 years.

IJG, 1991, Vol. 5, No. 3 and 4, pp. 85–91.

Successful ageing is operationally defined as a feeling of happiness and satisfaction with one's life, present status and activities. The successfully ageing persons feel useful to others, satisfied with health, family, work and finances. They show zest, positive self-concept, happy and optimistic mood-tone (Havighurst, 1953).

Methodology

Sample

A complete list of Hindu, male registered medical men (licentiates, graduates and postgraduates) between the age of 45 to 74 years, residing in Bangalore city, India was drawn from two main available sources. One was the latest Mysore medical register and the other was the complete list of the members of the Indian Medical Association, Bangalore branch. Thus, a list of 185 names fulfilling the above mentioned conditions with complete addresses was prepared. Out of these, 61 could not be contacted due to paucity of time. Among the 124 men who were individually contacted, 30 turned out to be either younger or older than the age range, were out of town, had changed their residential quarters or were dead. Some of them completely refused in spite of several polite visits. These were not further contacted. The rest of the 94 subjects were individually contacted and interviewed either at their residence, clinic or office. Interview time ranged from 4 to 6 hours which was spread over 3 to 4 interview-sessions.

Tools

"Your Activities and Attitudes Inventory" (Burgess, Caven, Havighurst and Goldhamer, 1949) and Life Satisfaction Index-A (Neugarten, Havighurst and Tobin, 1961) which were slightly modified to suit the local condition, were used in this study.

Measurement of Successful Ageing

Measures of successful ageing were obtained by two instruments: LSI-A (Life Satisfaction Index-A) and "Chicago Attitudes Inventory". Eight out of the 20 original items of LSI-A and 21 out of 56 items of the "Chicago Attitude Inventory" were found to be highly discriminative on the basis of item analysis. These were the two criteria to measure successful adjustment to ageing. Those who consistently scored lower than – 1 on both the criteria, formed the poorly adjusted group. Those who consistently scored above Q3 on both the criteria tests formed the well adjusted group. Thus, 31 and 39 subjects respectively constituted poorly and well adjusted groups. The inconsistent scores numbering 24 were not further considered. Further, to study the relationship of health, recreational and social activities, economic security and religion to ageing, the entire sample was sub-divided into 3 age levels: 45–54, 55–64 and 65–74 years. The distribution of the subjects according to age and adjustment is given in Table 1.

Table 1

Distribution of the low and high scorers in the three age-groups

Grade of Scores	*45–54 yrs*	*55–64 yrs*	*65–74 yrs*	*Total*
Low	06	09	16	31
High	16	14	09	39
Total	22	23	25	70

The sum of the scores on five areas constituted the activity score of each individual. Thus, there were 30 means of low and high scores in the three age groups in the five activity areas.

Results

The results of the analysis of variance is given in Table 3. The significant 't' values are given in Table 4.

Comparison of Poorly and Well Adjusted Groups

Health

In the 45–54 age group poorly and well adjusted subjects are not discriminated on the factor of health.

In the 55–64 age group, the mean scores of poorly and well adjusted subjects are respectively, 5.3±3.09 and 8.0±2.04 which is significantly different at 0.05 level.

In the 65–74 age group the means of the poorly and well adjusted subjects are respectively 4.0±2.68 and 8.2±2.05 differentiating at 0.01 level.

Table 2

Mean scores and standard deviations of the low and high scores in the age groups on five activity variables

Age group	*Health*		*Intimate contacts*		*Leisure and recreation*		*Economic security*		*Religion*	
	M	*SD*	*M*	*SD*	*M*	*SD*	*M*	*SD*	*M*	*SD*
Low Scores										
45-54	7.5	1.89	5.8	1.72	5.5	2.59	9.2	2.04	2.8	1.33
55-65	5.2	3.09	5.3	0.86	5.8	1.1	5.8	3.6	4.1	2.37
65-74	4.0	2.68	5.5	1.55	5.2	1.7	4.4	2.85	4.2	2.08
High Scores										
45-54	8.4	1.82	6.1	1.26	5.8	2.53	10.0	0.0	3.6	1.46
55-64	8.0	2.04	6.1	1.77	5.8	1.68	7.9	2.27	4.6	2.56
65-74	8.2	2.05	5.4	1.23	6.6	1.42	5.2	3.23	3.4	3.47

Table 3

Analysis of variance

Source of variation	*Degree of freedom d.f.*	*Sum of squares s.s.*	*Mean sum of squares M.S.S.*	*F with df in(Bracket)*	
Adjustment groups	1	7.3	7.3	14.04	(1.8)**
Age groups	2	7.9	3.95	7.60	(2.8)*
Activities	4	41.3	10.32	19.85	(4.8)**
Interaction:					
Adjustment X age	2	0.6	0.3	1.73	(8.2)NS
Adjustment X activities	4	6.1	1.52	2.92	(4.8)NS
Age X activities	8	20.6	2.57	4.94	(8.8)*
Error	8	4.2	0.52		
Total	29	88.0			

Note: **Significant at 0.05 and 0.01, *Significant at 0.05 only, N.S.=Not Significant.

Table 4

't' test results with significant 't' values

Between	*For Groups*	*Health*	*Intimate contacts*	*Leisure and recreation*	*Economic security*	*Religion*
Low Scores and	45.54	N.S.	N.S.	N.S.	N.S.	N.S.
High Scores	55.64	2.72*	N.S.	N.S.	N.S.	N.S.
65-74	4.30**	N.S.	2.31*	N.S.	N.S.	N.S.
45-54 and	L	N.S.	N.S.	N.S.	N.S.	N.S.
55-64 years	H	N.S.	N.S.	N.S.	4.11*	N.S.
55-64 and	L	N.S.	N.S.	N.S.	N.S.	
65-74 years	H	N.S.	N.S.	N.S.	2.39*	N.S.
45-54 and	L	3.04**	N.S.	N.S.	3.90**	N.S.
65-74 years	H	N.S.	N.S.	N.S.	6.32**	N.S.

Note: ** Significant at 0.05 and 0.01, * Significant at 0.05 only, N.S.=Not Significant.

Leisure and Recreation

Subjects in 45–54 and 55–64 age groups do not show significant differences. However, in the 65–74 age group the differences between the poorly and well adjusted subjects are significant at 0.05 level, the means being 5.2±1.7 and 6.6±1.42, respectively.

Comparison of Three Age Groups

Between 45–54 and 55–64 Age Group

Among the well adjusted subjects only, ageing seem to have a significant effect (at 0.01 level) on one's sense of economic security, the mean scores being 10.0±0 and 7.9±2.27 respectively for the above mentioned age groups.

Between 55–64 and 65–74 Age Groups

As above, ageing has significant effect (at 0.05 level) on one's sense of economic security among the well adjusted subjects only, the means for the two groups being respectively 8.5±1.89 and 4.0±2.68.

Between 45–64 and 65–74 Age Groups

Here, health and economic security are significantly differentiated on account of ageing. Among the poorly adjusted subjects the means on health activity are 7.5±1.89 and 4.0±2.68 for the two age groups as mentioned above. This mean difference is significant at the 0.01 level. There is no significant difference in the mean health score among the well adjusted subjects in the two age groups.

Sense of economic security seems to be significantly affected (at 0.01 level) due to ageing in both the poorly and well adjusted subjects. Among the poorly adjusted subjects the means are 9.2±2.04 and 4.4±2.85 and among the well adjusted subjects, the means are 10.±0 and 5.2±3.23 respectively for 45–54 and 65–74 age groups.

Discussion

In medical men, the factors of health, leisure, recreation and sense of economic security seems to be significantly related to one's sense of well-being and satisfaction as one ages from middle years to old age i.e., from 45 years onwards.

Health depends upon presence or absence of various physical and psychological problems and handicaps and to the extent one is bed-ridden. Such factors may not greatly effect the mobility in middle years when the individual preoccupied in various role-enactments. However, after the age of retirement i.e., 55 years in India (Upreti, 1969) these factors which determine health, achieve greater significance. It should be noted that health seems to deteriorate much more among the men who are coincidently dissatisfied and unhappy as they age from 45 years onwards. In other words, health of the unhappy, dissatisfied, and poorly adjusted men seems to be definitely adversely effected by ageing. Havigurst and Alberchť (1953) had reported that poor health was related to poor adjustment in elderly people. The present author suggests that poor adjustment in middle years can hasten deterioration in health which is due to ageing processes. This hypothesis is being suggested on the basis of present study in the context of several other studies which have reported that those men who were poorly adjusted in the present (at the time of testing) were also poorly adjusted in the past. (Caven, 1952; Havigurst, 1957; Ramamurthy, 1969). Thus, if we assume that those adults who are unhappy and dissatisfied in the present, if continue to be so in future, which is quite probable according to these studies, then the ageing process will relatively hasten the deterioration of their physical health. The state of psychological feeling of well-being, satisfaction and high morale seems to reduce the insults of ageing and conversely unhappy and dissatisfied mental state seems to aggravate and hasten the ageing processes. It is probably more correct to say that the healthy mind has a healthy body. It is well known that many of the mesomorphic, athletic-built healthy men are moral degenerates and are criminally disposed (Crotes and Ghati, 1972). On the other hand, men with happy and contended disposition seem to live fairly successfully despite many bodily ills and against odds. The emphasis is on the mental health which is likely to safe guard the physical health.

The present study further suggests that after the age of 64 especially, engagement in a number of leisure, recreational and organizational activities such as reading, writing, working on a number of hobbies, attending movies, playing games and cards, shopping, attending clubs and other social and professional organizations and having plans for future seems to be related to successful and satisfactory ageing, provided health is fairly good, as has been found in the present study where better adjusted men in 65–74 years age group were in relatively better health. In old age when earlier professional activities and responsibilities shrink or cease to have significance. It is the engagement in other solitary and group activities, which seem to be related to satisfaction.

Further, ageing seems to effects one's sense of economic security in the well-adjusted men. If we assume that the well-adjusted men are more realistic than the dissatisfied men, then we can safely suggest that the well-adjusted men have the capacity to perceive realistically and accept unhesitatingly the fact, that ageing has an adverse effect on their sense of economic security which declines with ageing. The absence of this relationship in the poorly adjusted men between 45 and 64 years may point out to their inability to accept painful realities, if we assume that maladjusted persons have unrealistic approach to life. Beyond 65 years irrespective of adjustment level, individuals are likely to feel reduced sense of economic security. In conclusion, ageing seems to have adverse effect on the health of specially those individuals who are dissatisfied, unhappy and not in tune with themselves. Ageing also reduces ones sense of economic security which is generally perceived by reality-oriented well-adjusted individuals. Finally, it is the engagement in various social and recreational activities which seems to be related to the feeling of well-being in old age.

References

Britton, J.H. (1953): "The Personal Adjustment of Retired School Teachers". *J. Gerentol.* 3: 333–338.

Britton, J.O. and Britton, J.H. (1951): "Factors Related to Adjustment of Retired Y.M.C.A. Secretaries". *J. Gerentol.* 1: 34–38.

Burgess, E.W., Caven, R.S., Havighurst, R.J. and Goldhamer, H. (1949): *Examiner's Manual for Your Activities and Attitudes.* Chicago: Science Research Associates.

Caven, R.C. (1952): "Personal Adjustment in Old Age". In A.I. Lansing (Ed.) *Cowedry's Problems of Aging* (3rd ed.), Baltimore: Williams and Wilkins Co.

Cortes, J.P. and Ghatti, F.M. (1972): *Delinquency and Crime: A Biopsycho-social Approach.* New York: Seminar Press.

Donahue, W. (1956): "Psychologic Research Needs in Gerontology". *J. Gerontol.* 11: 196–203.

Havighrust, R.J. and Albrecht, R. (1953): *Older People.* New York: Longmans Green.

Havighurst, R.J. (1953): "Successful Aging". *The Gerontologist.* 1: 8–13.

Havighurst, R.J. (1957): "The Social Competence of Middle-aged People". *Genet Psychol. Monogr.* 56: 297–375.

Heyman, D.K. and Jeffers, F.C. (1964): "Study of the Relative Influences of Race and Socio-economic Status Upon the Activities and Attitudes of a Southern Aged Population". *J. Gerontol.* 19: 225–229.

Kunter, B., Fanshel, D., Togo, A.M. and Langner, T.S. (1956): *Five Hundred Over Sixty: A Community Survey on Ageing.* New York: Russel Sage Foundation.

Landis, J.T. (1942): "Social Psychological Factors in Aging". *Social Forces* 20: 468–470.

Moore, E.G. (1951): "Professors in Retirement". *J. Gerontol.* 3: 243–252.

Morgan, C.M. (1983): "The Attitude and Adjustment of Recipients of Old Age Assistance in Upsate and Metropolitan". New York. Arch. Psychol., 30 131, 1937 (Cited by Gravatt, "A.E., Family Relations in Old Age: A Review", *J. Gerontol.* 8: 197–201.

Neugarten, B., Havigurst, R.J. and Tobin, S.S. (1961): "The Measurement of Life Satisfaction". *J. Gerontol.* 16: 134–143.

Ramamurthy, P.V. (1969): A Study of Some Factors Related to Adjustment of Some Urban Aged Men. Unpublished Doctoral Thesis, S.V. University, Tirupati, India.

Richard, S., Livson, F. and Peterson, P.G., (1962): *Ageing and Personality.* New York: Wiley.

Shanas, E. (1950): "The Personal Adjustment of Recipients of Old Age Assistance". *J. Gerontol.* 3: 249–253.

Tuckman, J. and Lorge, I. (1954): "Classification of the Self as Young, Middle Aged or Old". *Geriatrics* 9: 534–536.

Upreti, H.C. (1969): "Approaches to the Study of Old Age". *Indian J. Gerontol.* 1: 38–44.

CHAPTER 29

Self-Concept and Life Satisfaction among Aged

N.K. Chadha

It is obvious that some individuals are physically old at 40 and some young at 60 as measured by their physical abilities and activity. And that at 75 year one individual is young and spry, while another is old and decrepit. Individuals have different rates of ageing that do not correspond to the years they have lived.

The rapid development of the medical science during the last two or three decades, the falling birthrate, the mass application of immunization against infectious-diseases, great reduction of premature deaths from infectious diseases, improvements in nutrition and living standards have brought about remarkable changes in the age structure of the Indian population. (Surpal, 1990). In India, average life expectancy at birth was about 22.9 years in 1900, 32.1 in 1950 and 54.4 in 1980; now, it stands at 57 or 58 years. This clearly indicates that an average extension of life about 35 years in the last 90 years, and is likely to rise further in future. It has been reported that while the total population of Asia is projected to increase by 52 per cent by the year 2000, the number in the 60+ age group is expected to rise by 102 per cent. In this age group there were more than 48 million Indians (6.5% of the total population) in 1986, and the number is likely to exceed 76 million (7.6% of the total population) in 2000. The important point to note over here is that these demographic trends are likely to have serious medical,

IJG, 1991, Vol. 5, No. 1 and 2, pp. 47–54.

psychological and socio-economic implications in our future development and the country's socio-political system.

'Old-age', is characterized by a sense of hopelessness towards the world. A sense of loss shadowed by loneliness, lack of care, respect for self and others. Of course the feeling of insecurity persists coupled with high expectations which are often childlike. Conflicts arise when the sick, tired mind and body cannot cope with psychological, emotional and physical stress/es.

Studies of vision, hearing, muscular strength, reaction time, complex psychomotor performance, job performance, and accidents have shown great individual differences at every age among those who are old as well as among those who are young. As a result, it is impossible to classify anyone as 'typically old' or any trait as 'typically that of an oldster'.

The reason different people age differently is that they have different hereditary endowments, different socio-economic and educational background, and different pattern of living. This is true within the same sex group but even more so when members of the two sexes are compared, because ageing takes place at different rates for the two sexes. As Badar and Hoffman (1966) have explained, "Older people are a very diverse group, more so than their younger counterparts, because of differences in social, cultural, and economic experiences extending over a long period of time, and these differences tend to increase with age."

As differences increase with age, they predispose the individual to react differently to the same situation. For example, men react very differently to the same situation. For example, men react very differently to retirement from work. To some, it is a blessing, while to others, it is regarded as a cursed. Why they react differently to the same situation? Havighurst has explained that from middle age onward, the person confronts changes in the social environment and in his physical body which requires adjustments on his part; society does things to him, and his body changes negatively, but different personalities react differently to the same set of social pressures and the same set of bodily changes.

Whether ageing should be taken as a psycho-social problem is a question to be considered. Is it a state of affair which needs correction? Yes, but the correction is required in the lack of preparation for the sudden appearance of large number of older people and the lack of ability of social institutions to cater to the needs of increasing aged population. According to Sati (1988) lack of facilities and interventions can be dealt by active action planning at the psycho-social level on individual and community basis.

United Nations defines a 'young society' where the population of 60+ is 4 per cent or less; a 'mature society' if it is between 4 per cent and 7 per cent, and an 'ageing society' if it is above 7 per cent. The changes in the age structure of Indian population in the coming decade is going to be striking, and its impact alarming. From a 'mature society' it is going to be an 'ageing' one (Surpal, 1990).

A common problem of the elderly is learning a new role. Becoming old means facing a time of transition; most elderly people are giving up a comfortable role for one that is essentially devalued in society. In essence, becoming old is being demoted, a personal condition that is unsettling and threatening. Thus, it is a stage of life that increases the likelihood of psychological problems of low self-esteem and depression. These problems can be tempered by the adequacy of the individual's actual social support. Friends, co-workers, family and neighbours can ease the burden. But, if one is cut off from work (retirement), from children (who live far away, a high probability in our mobile society) and from a spouse (widowhood), the chances of personal trauma increase manifold.

In the present time, the aged have become an isolated unit, the caring traditions of the youth have changed due to rapid industrialization and modernization of the Indian society. The major factor being the breaking up of the joint family system. The nuclear family system which has replaced the joint system is more practical and economical.

Gangrade (1988) in a sociological survey of one hundred and ninety parent-youth pairs found the 98 per cent of the youth felt obligated towards their parents in providing financial support. However, 89 per cent of them preferred 'nuclear families', thanks to the family planning propaganda.

The residential institutions are few in number in India and usually have discriminatory religious leanings for memberships due to control by Church and Hindu Samaj. The sociocultural dimensions hence take into account the effect of changing familial patterns and economic factors on the status of the aged.

Chadha (1989) conducted a study to see the impact of institutionalization on the psychological well-being and depression among the aged. Older men and women were employed to measure psychological well-being and depression. The result indicates that older person in non-institutionalized setting were better on psychological well-being and also their depression level was low as compared to institutionalized setting older persons. Family support was found to be the important factor in this study for better psychological health.

Aggarwal and Chadha (1990) conducted a study of 109 older men and women. The sample was further divided with respect to married and widow/widower and three psychological measures taken were hopelessness, alienation and life satisfaction. The result indicates that female were high on hopelessness and less satisfied with life as compared to males. Also married older people were found to be low on hopelessness and high on life satisfaction as compared to their widow/widower counterparts.

In an other study (Chadha and Aggarwal, 1990) on 'Social Support and Aging' conducted in New Delhi, found that (1) the size of the social support network is more for the married as compared to the widow counterparts, (2) friendship support is one of the most important factors associated with positive changes among both males and females, and (3) two-third of the network consisted of family members.

Methodology

Objectives

The main objectives of the present research are the following:

1. To see the differences, if any, between non-institutionalized (staying with family members), non-institutionalized (staying with spouse only) and institutionalized older people on self-concept and life satisfaction.
2. To see the difference, if any, between male older people and female older people on self-concept and life satisfaction.

The Sample

Three group of samples were selected in the present research. These are shown as below:

The institutionalized sample was taken from two old age homes in Delhi. The non-institutionalized sample was also selected from

Delhi. The basic characteristics of the three group of samples are presented in Table 1.

The Measuring Instruments

1. *Chadha Self-Concept Scale* was used to measure perceived-self and ideal-self. The scale also provided the discrepancy between the perceived-self of the person and the ideal-self of the person.
2. *Chadha and Van Willigen (1990) Life Scale* was used to measure the life satisfaction of the older person. This scale was prepared as a part of the joint research project on 'Social Aging In India' by the present author and Prof. John Van Willigen (University of Kentucky, USA). This scale gives global life satisfaction.

Results and Interpretations

The data obtained was subjected to t-test only to study the objectives of the research. Firstly, the three groups were compared and the results are presented in Table 2.

The Table 2 clearly revealed that group A (non-institutionalized: staying with other family members) differs significantly from group B (non-institutionalized: staying with spouse only) found with regard to life satisfaction. Further group B differs from group C on ideal-self, self-concept discrepancy and life satisfaction. Finally group A and group C differ significantly with regard to ideal-self, perceived-self, self-concept discrepancy and life satisfaction.

To understand the sex differences on these variables, the males and females of the two groups A and B were compared. There were no females in group C and therefore at the time of sex comparison group C was not taken into consideration. The result of male and female comparison are presented in Table 3.

Table 3 shows that males and females differ significantly at 0.01 level in regard to ideal-self, self-concept discrepancy and life satisfaction. On viewing the mean scores it was observed that males scored higher than females on ideal-self, self-concept discrepancy and satisfaction.

To see the sex comparison between males and females with group A and group B, the separate sex comparisons were made and the results are presented in Tables 4 and 5.

Tables 4 and 5 revealed that males and females differ significantly with regard to self-concept discrepancy and life satisfaction.

Table 1

Summary of the Sample taken in the Study

	Group A (N=70) (Non-institutionalized staying with other family members)		*Group B (N=60) (Non-institutionalized staying with spouse only)*		*Group C (N=60) (Institutionalized)*
	Male (N=35)	*Female (N=35)*	*Male (N=30)*	*Female (N=30)*	*Male (N=60)*
Age Range	20-84 years	61-79 years	61-80 years	63-78 years	65-81 years
Mean	65.4 years	65.2 years	66.7 years	64.3 years	65.1 years
SD	18.7	17.4	15.6	19.8	18.7
Socio-economic status	Middle	Middle	Middle	Middle	Middle
Number of sons	2-4	2-4	1-3	1-3	1-4
Number of daughters	1-3	1-4	1-3	2-3	2-3

Table 2

Comparison between group A (non-institutionalized: Staying with family member), group B (Non-institutionalized: Staying with the spouse only), and group C (institutionalized) on self-concept and life satisfaction

Variables	*Group A (N=70)*		*Group B(N=60)*		*Group C(N=60)*		*t-values*		
	Mean	*SD*	*Mean*	*SD*	*Mean*	*SD*	*Gr. A vs Gr.B*	*Gr. B vs Gr. C*	*Gr C vs Gr. A*
Ideal-self	130.6	20.8	154.4	21.4	168.2	15.9	29.60**	4.01**	11.67**
Perceived-self	121.4	18.6	136.4	22.6	132.2	17.4	6.49**	1.14	3.42**
Discrepancy (Ideal-self Perceived-self)	9.2	11.6	18.0	14.2	36.0	15.1	3.91**	6.72**	11.21**
Life satisfaction	168.4	22.6	140.6	24.6	121.3	14.8	1.62	5.08**	14.27**

**$P<0.01$.

Table 3

Comparison between males and females on self-concept and life satisfaction

Variable	Male (N=65)		Female (N=65)		t-value
	Mean	SD	Mean	SD	
Ideal-self	149.1	23.1	136.0	19.1	3.52**
Perceived-self	126.2	18.5	131.7	22.7	1.53
Discrepancy (Ideal-self perceived-self)	22.9	13.3	4.3	11.50	8.53**
Life Satisfaction	165.2	23.2	143.9	22.6	5.30**

**P<0.01.

Table 4

Comparison between males and females belonging to Group A (non-institutionalized: staying with other family members) on self-concept and life satisfaction

Variable	Male (N=65)		Female (N=65)		t-value
	Mean	SD	Mean	SD	
Ideal-self	140.2	22.9	121.0	18.7	3.80**
Perceived-self	120.6	15.3	122.2	21.9	0.35
Discrepancy (Ideal-self perceived-self)	19.6	10.4	1.2	9.6	7.70
Life satisfaction	179.2	24.7	157.6	20.5	3.98

**P<0.01.

Table 5

Comparison between males and females belonging to Group B (non-institutionalized: staying with the spouse only) on self-concept and life satisfaction

Variable	Male (N=65)		Female (N=65)		t-value
	Mean	SD	Mean	SD	
Ideal-self	157.9	23.3	150.9	19.5	1.26
Perceived-self	131.7	21.7	141.1	23.5	1.61
Discrepancy (Ideal-self perceived-self)	26.2	16.2	9.8	13.3	4.28**
Life satisfaction	115.1	21.7	130.1	24.6	3.51**

**P<0.01.

Discussion

With regard to self-concept, the result indicates that there is more discrepancy on perceived- and ideal-self among older people from institutionalized group as compared to the two other non-institutionalized groups. In other words one could say that in the present case there is low self-concept in the institutionalized elderly subjects. The implied adverse impact of institutionalization is upheld for institutionalization may be seen as representing major discontinuity in the life of an aged individual (Rosen, 1967). When the elderly person enters a home for the aged, he has usually suffered various substantial role losses such as retirement, widowhood, loss of membership in formal and informal organs. All these changes represent modification in his lifestyles and may be expected to result in concomitant changes in self-concept is due to institutionalization itself or other factors associated with it.

Erikson (1963) states that a person constantly goes through crisis. Admission to a home for the aged is the first step towards a new life, and the person who takes it is subject to negative forces that impede the adjustment. He/she enters with a well established self-image which is the reflection of a number of values, attitudes and rules of conduct. Suddenly everything which he/she so long identified with themselves disappears. The residents must give up his own ways of scheduling his day and accept unfamiliar standardized surrounding and fixed programmes. As Kahana (1971) says that element of choice is severely limited in the institutional situation. In addition, elderly individual finds himself in a position of dependences, particularly because the admission is often the result of functionary losses and weakness and of the need for concrete and emotional assistance.. This process of becoming dependent causes uncertainty, foreboding and feeling of guilt, hence self-esteem and self-image are damaged.

Literature is not much consistent regarding the impact of institutionalization on self-concept. A number of studies have cast doubt on pervasiveness of decline in self-concept with institutional living (Braginsky et al., 1966, 1967 and 1969).

On sex comparison, female indicates less discrepancy between ideal and perceived self-concept as compared to males. This shows that females have more balanced self-concept than the males. This could be due to the fact that female generally do not aspire very high in life in Indian culture. It is the male who work outside the home and earn bread and butter for the family. Thus, discrepancy between ideal and perceived-self is low among female elderly.

The findings also state that the non-institutionalized groups have better life satisfaction as compared to the institutionalized group. These findings are also consistent with the author's own observations in the field for last four years and it did come during the interview that non-institutionalized elderly have immersed themselves more intensely in whatever roles remain in their repertories. This way was also reported by the non-institutionalized elders. One respondent replied "Old age has its own pleasures, though these are different from the pleasures of youth, but these are not less pleasures than youth. In spite of the problems here and there, one can enjoy life keeping oneself busy. If not with anything else, then with grandchildren one would not find old age boring." Thus, activity might be suspected as the reason of their high life satisfaction. Havighurst, Neugarten and Tobin's Activity Theory (1963) proposes that high morale, robust mental health and life satisfaction are best maintained during old age by means of active engagement in many social roles and interpersonal relationship as during early and middle adulthood. On the other hand institutionalized elderly have disengaged themselves from the active life.

Palmore and Luikart (1972) found a positive relationship between higher level of life satisfaction in the aged population and activity. Chandrika and Anantharaman (1982) also found that non-institutionalized older people were better in adjustment than the other two groups namely institutionalized and geriatric patients. Vijayshree (1989) also reported life satisfaction score of non-institutionalized (family-based) elderly significantly higher than institutionalized and non-institutionalized non-family-based elderly.

Based upon the above results it can be inferred that serious action planning is required especially for the institutionalized aged who need care and counseling. This planning should be at the community and social level.

References

Agarwal, V. and Chadha, N.K. (1990): "Social Network and Aging". *Spectra of Anthropological,* Vol. 12.

Badar, I.M. and Hoffman, A.M. (1966): "Research in Aging". *Journal Home Economics.* 3: 117–125.

Braginskhy, B, Grosse, M. and Ring, K. (1966): "Controlling Outcomes Through Impression Management: An Experimental Study of Manipulative Tactics of Mental Patients". *J. Consul. Psy.* 30: 295–300.

Braginsky, B., Braginsky, D. and Ring, K. (1969): *The Mental Hospital as a Last Resort*. New York: Holt, Rinehart and Winston.

Braginsky, B., Holzberg, L. Finison, L. and Ring L. (1967): "Correlates of the Mental Patients Acquisition of Hospital Information". *Journal of Person*. 38: 323–342.

Chadha, N.K. (1990): "Aging and Related Problems: A Synoptic Review". In P.C. Joshi and A. Mahajan (Eds.), *Studies in Medical Anthropology*. New Delhi: Reliance Pub. House.

Chadha, N.K. (1989): Impact of Institutionalization on the Psychological Well-being and Depression among the Aged. Paper presented at the UGC National Symposium "Stress, Anxiety and Depression in Modern Life". Patiala University, Patiala (3–4 November).

Chadha, N.K. and Aggarwal, V. (1991): Hopelessness, Alienation and Life Satisfaction Among Aged. Paper presented at the 78th session of Indian Science Congress Association, 3–8th January at Indore.

Chadha, N.K. and Van Willigen, J. (1990): Scale for Measuring Life Satisfaction. Unpublished scale.

Chandrika, P. and Anantharaman (1982): R.N. "Life Changes and Adjustment in Old Age". *J. Psy. Res.* 26 (3): 137–141.

Erikson, E.H. (1963): *Childhood and Society*. New York: W.W. Norton & Co.

Gangrade, K.D. (1988): "Social Networks and the Aged in India". In *The Aging in India: Problems and Potentialities* (Eds.) A.B. Bose and K.D. Grade, New Delhi: Abhinav Publication.

Havighurst, R.J. (1965): "Body-Self and Society". *Social Soc. Res.* 49: 261–267.

Havighurst, R.T., Neugartan, B.L. and Tobin, S.S. (1963): Disengagement and Patterns of Aging. Paper presented at the Meeting of the International Association of Gerontology, Copenhagen.

Kahana, E. (1971): "Emerging Issues in Institutional Services for Aging". *The Gerontologist*. 11(1): 57–58.

Palmore, E. and Luikart, S. (1972): "Successful Aging". Dalton and Lakmann (Eds.) *Transmission of Aging*. Academic Press: 157–159.

Rosen, J. (1967): *Social Integration of the Aged*. Glencoe: Free Press.

Sati, P.N. (1988): *Retired and Aging People*. New Delhi: Mittal Publications.

Surpal, B.B. (1990): "Increasing Population of Aged in India: Current Situation and Future Needs". *Geriatic India*. 2–3.

Van Willigen, J. and Chadha, N.K. (1990): "Techniques of Data Collection in Social Network". *Indian Journal of Social Work*. 2 (4): 615–621.

Vijayshree, J.B. (1989): Life Satisfaction and its Psychological Correlates amongst the Aged. Unpublished Master's Degree Dissertation, University of Delhi, Delhi.

CHAPTER 30

The Life Scale: The Development of a Measure of Successful Ageing

N.K. Chadha and John Van Willigen

Two concepts that have been examined a great deal in psychology are those of life satisfaction and morale. An operational definition about life satisfaction is forwarded that it refers to the "psychological well being" of the aged individual. Life satisfaction, often refers to the attitudes that individuals have about their past, present and future. Morale is generally considered to be the emotional component of life satisfaction. Very often the two terms are defined in such a way that they are interchangeable. The use of life satisfaction and other related measures have along been a part of social gerontological research. Some early examples of these measures are found in the work of Adams (1971), Neugarten, Havighurst and Tobin (1961), Cumming and Henry (1961), Lawton (1975). Some have equated high life satisfaction, with successful ageing (Havighurst, 1963; Sinha, 1971; Jamuna, 1994). These types of measurement have been applied in Indian settings (Sinha, 1971; Mishra, 1987; Ramamurti and Jamuna, 1993; Rathore, 1992; Jamuna, 1994, and others).

In their classic formulation Neugarten Havighurst and Tobin (1961) state that zest, resolution and fortitude; congruence between

IJG, 1995, Vol. 9, No. 3 and 4, pp. 83–90.

desired and achieved goals, positive self-concept; and mood tone constitute the psychological concepts of life satisfaction.

There are basically two approaches to life satisfaction (Neugarten et al., 1961). The first one focuses upon the overt behaviour of the individual and uses social criteria of success or competence. The second approach is the individual's own interpretation and evaluation of his present and past life, his satisfaction or his happiness. The former approach is based on variables like level and range of activities and extent of social participation. The latter approach studies variables like life satisfaction levels and self-concepts of the individuals. Our approach to measurement of life satisfaction takes the second approach.

Item Construction

Initially various scales were studied including the Philadelphia Geriatric Centre Morale Scale (PGC) (Lawton, 1975), Life Satisfaction Scale (Neugarten Havighurst, and Tobin, 1961) and the Memorial University of Newfoundland Scale of Happiness (MUNSH) (Kozma and Stones, 1980). Their applicability in the Indian cultural setting was assessed and it was found that none of these scales could be applied in totality on the Indian aged population. Taking the help of these scales and the opinion of the aged people regarding their life satisfaction index, items were generated. Those items that were from the already mentioned existing scales were modified to make the meaning clear to the respondents. New items were written. With this process, we generated 33 items to be answered, based on the widely used Likert-type seven-point response categories starting from strongly agree to strongly disagree. These items were in English.

Expert Opinion

At this point the 33 item scale was given to fifteen experts trained in psychology, gerontology, linguistics and working with older persons for further review. The task of these experts was to read every item and give the opinion regarding the meaning and content of these items for measuring life satisfaction. The experts were also free to modify the language of the item, if they feel it is needed. Those items were retained where the agreement among experts was 75 per cent on a particular item to be retained for the measure. With this process, no item was dropped.

Translation

Although English language psychological scales are widely used in India, we thought essential to translate into Hindi. A practical reason among all the potential semantic problems is that most Indian elderly people cannot understand English. Two way translation was done, first the English version of the scale was given to three professionals to translate the items into Hindi. These persons were teachers in various colleges in University of Delhi and had all been involved in teaching Hindi at the undergraduate level for the last 15 years. After obtaining the translation from this expert panel, it was given to another expert to combine versions into a single translation. The reconciled Hindi translation was then given to three more experts to translate it back into English. These experts were also from various colleges of University of Delhi, where they had been teaching English for the last 15 years to undergraduates. These English translations were combined to get the final English translation. The obtained English translation was compared with the original English instrument to ensure the similarity between the original and the new English version which came from the Hindi translation. There were no significant differences between these translations. This helped us assure the accuracy of the Hindi version of the Life Scale. The Hindi version is provided in Appendix A.

Item Analysis

Some of the items were negatively worded to remove the effect of one directional response tendency on the part of the respondent. All the 33 items were administered to 60 elderly people for the purpose of item analysis. After their responses were scored, it was possible to place them in two groups based on whether their individual scores were above or below the median life satisfaction score. The "higher life satisfaction score" and "lower life satisfaction score" groups were compared item by item to find the discriminating power of each item of the scale. This was based on the Chi-Square Test. The results are shown in Table 1.

Table 1
Discriminating index for item selection

Item No.	*Chi-Square value*	*Significance level*	*Remarks*
1.	18.35	0.01	Accepted
2.	4.61	NS	Rejected
3.	19.07	0.01	Accepted
4.	22.06	0.01	Accepted
5.	17.64	0.01	Accepted
6.	12.90	0.05	Accepted
7.	13.56	0.05	Accepted
8.	17.43	0.01	Accepted
9.	20.12	0.01	Accepted
10.	13.12	0.05	Accepted
11.	19.02	0.01	Accepted
12.	7.91	NS	Rejected
13.	14.95	0.05	Accepted
14.	2.46	NS	Rejected
15.	4.78	NS	Rejected
16.	16.23	0.05	Accepted
17.	14.35	0.05	Accepted
18.	19.63	0.01	Accepted
19.	15.21	0.05	Accepted
20.	20.34	0.01	Accepted
21.	22.87	0.01	Accepted
22.	19.34	0.01	Accepted
23.	18.60	0.01	Accepted
24.	18.51	0.01	Accepted
25.	12.90	0.05	Accepted
26.	13.24	0.05	Accepted
27.	18.36	0.01	Accepted
28.	19.21	0.01	Accepted
29.	14.20	0.05	Accepted
30.	13.59	0.05	Accepted
31.	16.98	0.05	Accepted
32.	18.37	0.01	Accepted
33.	3.78	NS	Rejected

Based on the discrimination index five items were rejected and thus we were left with 28 items.

Scoring: Positively worded item were scored from 7 to 1 for the response categories of strongly agree to strongly disagree. For the response of strongly agreed score will be 7; for a response of agree, score will be 6; for slightly agree, score will be 5 and so on. On the other hand for the negatively worded items, the score would be from 1 to 7 for the response categories of strongly agree to strongly disagree. For instance, for negatively worded items, if the respondent have a response of strongly agree the resulting score would be 1; for agree, a score of 2; for slightly agree, a score of 3 and so on. The positive and negative items are given below:

Reliability: The concept of reliability occupies central place in educational and psychological measurement. There are three important characteristics of a sound measuring instrument: reliability, validity and usability. Reliability is a primary requisite of any measuring instrument. The term reliability owes its origin to Spearman (1971), operationally it is self correlation. Reliability refers to internal consistency and temporal stability of the measurement. Consistency is meant to what extent the test is internally consistent when administered once. Logically, Guilford (1956) explained reliability on the basis of variance. Total variance of set of measurements are defined as the mean of the square of deviations from mean of the total variance of a set of scores or measurements is equal to the true variance plus error variance of the scores. Reliability is the proportion of this true variance in total variance. To quote Guilford (1956: 436). "The reliability of any set of measurements is logically defined as the proportion of their variance, that is, true variance".

For the present scale, split half reliability was established to find the internal consistency of the measuring instruments of life satisfaction. For this purpose, the 28 item scale was administered to another 30 respondents of the age of 60 to 78 years (mean age 66.7). The split-half reliability using the Spreman-Brown formula was 0.85 (Chadha, 1996). The reliability index was found to be significant at 0.01 of significance which clearly shows the internal consistency of the scale.

Another method employed to determine the reliability of the scale was the Cronback Alpha (Chadha, 1996) for the total scale as well for each item of the scale. This was done with the responses

Table 2

Item total relationship and Cronback alpha for each item

Item No.		*Mean*	*SD Correlation*	*Item Total Alpha*	*Cronback*
1.	My health is better as compared to most people of my age	4.70	2.36	0.66	0.951
2.	I have got more opportunities in life than most people I know	4.27	1.77	0.58	0.952
3.	I am sure that some interesting and pleasant thing will happen to me in future	4.06	1.83	0.74	0.951
4.	I feel old and somewhat tried	3.78	2.28	0.73	0.950
5.	I am least effected by the feel of my age	4.34	2.18	0.47	0.953
6.	I would not change my past life even if I could	4.50	1.57	0.45	0.953
7.	Compared to other people of my age I make a good appearance	4.63	2.25	0.65	0.951
8.	I always make plans before things in my life	4.47	1.90	0.52	0.952
9.	I plan my leisure time	4.18	1.88	0.51	0.953
10.	I enjoy my life	4.96	2.07	0.85	0.949
11.	This is a dull time of my life	4.27	2.31	0.61	0.952
12.	I am satisfied with my family life	5.48	1.95	0.65	0.951
13.	My religious/ spiritual life is well planned	5.61	1.60	0.35	0.954

Cont'd...

Cont'd...

14. Little things bother me more this year	4.23	2.07	0.66	0.951
15. I sometimes worry so much that I can't sleep	3.70	2.33	0.63	0.952
16. I get made more than I used to	4.59	2.10	0.62	0.952
17. Life is hard for me most of the time	4.22	2.08	0.64	0.951
18. I get upset easily	4.01	2.12	0.63	0.951
19. As you get older you are less useful	4.04	2.22	0.53	0.952
20. The things which I do are generally boring	4.83	2.02	0.74	0.950
21. The things I do are as interesting to me as they everywhere	4.54	2.08	0.79	0.950
22. If I review my previous life I find myself satisfied	4.57	2.39	0.64	0.951
23. As I get older things are becoming better and better	3.95	2.05	0.73	0.950
24. I generally feel lonely	4.56	2.46	0.67	0.951
25. I sometimes feel that life is not worth living	4.80	2.08	0.77	0.950
26. Most of the time I find life is hard for me	4.53	2.10	0.75	0.950
27. I am satisfied with my life today	5.16	2.09	0.71	0.951

The Cronback Alpha for the total scale was 0.95.

obtained from the sample of the study reported in this volume. The obtained results were:

Further item analysis was done with the data from the sample. The Cronback Alpha for one item indicated that it was somewhat inconsistent with the other items in the scale and had a skewed response. It was found that most of the respondents gave that standards and values in India are going down. This items produced a large number of strongly disagree responses by the respondents. Also the alpha value obtained was very low and did not reach the level of significance. This item was then removed from the scale. All results from the scale published in this monograph are based on the version of the Life Scale with 27 items.

The high value of Cronback alpha and also the significant correlations of each item with the total test scores ensure the high degree of reliability of the scale to measure the life satisfaction of the elderly population.

Scoring key

Positive Items	1	2	3	4	5	6	7	8
	9	10	12	13	21	22	23	27
Negative Items	4	11	14	15	16	17	18	19
	20	24	25	26				

References

Adams, D.L. (1971): "Correlates of Satisfaction Among the Elderly". *Gerontologist* 11: 64–68.

Chadha, N.K. (1995): *Problems of Older in Delhi.* India Council of Social Sciences Research Sponsored Project.

Chhabra, Vandana (1995): Psycho-social Well-being of Pre-retired, Retired and Post-retired Elderlies: A Cross-sectional Study. Unpublished Master's Dissertation, Department of Psychology, University of Delhi.

Cumming, E. and W.E. Henry, (1961): *Growing Old: The Process of Disengagement*. New York: Basic Books.

Guilford, J.P. (1956): *Fundamental Statistics in Psychology and Education.* New York: McGraw-Hill.

Havighurst, Robert, J. (1963): *Successful Aging: In Processes of Aging*. R. Williams, C. Tibbits and W. Donohue (Eds.) New York: Atherton.

Jamuna, D. (1994): "The Psychological and Social Correlates of Successful Aging among Elderly Indian Women". *Indian Journal of Gerontology*. 8: 18–23.

Kozma, Albert and M.J. Stones (1980): "The Measurement of Happiness: Development of the Memorial University of Newfoundland Scale of Happiness (MUNSH)". *Journal of Gerontology*. 35(6): 906–912.

Lawton, M. (1975): "Powell, The Philadelphia Geriatric Center Morale Scale: A Revision". *Journal of Gerontology*. 30 (1): 85–89.

Mathur, D. (1994): "Role Strain in Mother-in-law Relationship in Later Life". Unpublished M.Phil. Dissertation, University of Delhi, Delhi.

Mishra, Saraswati (1987): *Social Adjustment of Old Age*. Delhi: B.R. Publishing.

Neugarten, B.L., Havighurst, R.J. and Tobin, S.S. (1961): "The Measurement of Life Satisfaction". *Journal of Gerontology*. 16: 134–143.

Ramamurti, P.V. and Jamuna, D. (1993): "Some Predictors of Satisfaction with Present Life in an Indian Sample". *Indian Journal of Gerontology*. 7 (3 and 4): 96–103.

Rathore, Saroj. (1992): "Subjective Well-being in Old Age". *Indian Journal of Gerontology*. 6(1 and 2): 37–43.

Sinha, S.N. (1971): "Socio-psychological Aspects of Mental Illness in the Aged". *Indian Journal of Gerontology*. 3 (1 and 2): 36–38.

Spearman, C. (1971): "Demonstration of the Formula for True-Measurement of Correlation". *American Journal of Psychology*. 18: 161–169.

Appendix A

Hindi Translation of the Life Scale

निम्नलिखित वाक्य आपके अपने जीवन कार्यों एवं दूसरों से मिलने वाले संतोष को मापने हेतु लिखे गये हैं। यह स्केल अभी प्रायोगिक स्थिति में है। आपके द्वारा दिए गए उत्तर यह निर्णय करने में मदद देंगे कि लिखा गया प्रश्न प्रभावपूर्ण है अथवा नहीं। अतः यह और भी महत्त्वपूर्ण है कि आपके उत्तर 'सत्य' एवं 'ठीक' हो। कोई उत्तर 'सही' या 'गलत' नहीं हैं। आपके उत्तर पूर्णतया गुप्त रखे जायेंगे। कृपया सभी प्रश्नों का उत्तर दें तथा मन में आने वाले प्रथम विचार के अनुरूप ही जवाब दें।

प्रत्येक वाक्य का जवाब देते समय निम्नलिखित पैमाने का प्रयोग करें।

पूर्ण असहमति	असहमति	थोड़ी असहमति	अनिर्णीत
1	2	3	4
थोड़ी सहमति	सहमति	पूर्ण सहमति	
5	6	7	

1. हमउम्र लोगों की तुलना में मेरा स्वास्थ्य बेहतर है।
2. अपनी जान पहचान के लोगों की अपेक्षा मुझे अधिक अवसर मिले हैं।
3. मुझे विश्वास है कि आने वाला समय मेरे लिये ज्यादा आनन्दकर एवं खुशी का होगा।
4. मैं खुद को बूढ़ा और कुछ सीमा/हद तक थका हुआ महसूस करता हूँ।
5. बढ़ती उम्र के अहसास का मुझ पर बिल्कुल कोई असर नहीं है।
6. यदि मैं अपने पिछले जीवन को बदलने में समर्थ होता तब भी मैं उसे नहीं बदलता।
7. अपनी उम्र के अन्य लोगों की तुलना में मैं देखने में अच्छा लगता हूँ।
8. मैं अपने जीवन में हमेशा पूर्व योजना बनाता हूँ।
9. मैं अपने अवकाश काल की योजना बनाता हूँ।
10. मैं अपना जीवन मजे/मौज में बिताता हूँ।
11. यह मेरे जीवन का अरोचक समय है।
12. मैं अपने पारिवारिक जीवन से सन्तुष्ट हूँ।
13. मेरा धार्मिक/आध्यात्मिक जीवन योजनाबद्ध है।
14. छोटी–छोटी बातें भी इस साल मुझे अधिक परेशान करती हैं।
15. मैं कभी–कभी इतना चिंतित हो जाता हूँ कि सो भी नहीं पाता।
16. पहले की अपेक्षा मैं अपना मानसिक संतुलन जल्दी खो बैठता हूँ।
17. मेरे लिए जीवन अधिकतर कठिन रहा है।
18. मैं जल्दी ही परेशान हो जाता हूँ।
19. जैसे–जैसे आप बूढ़े होते हैं आप कम उपयोगी होते जाते हैं।
20. जो मैं करता हूँ वह अक्सर उबाऊ होता है।
21. जो काम मैं कर रहा हूँ वह पहले की तरह रोचक है।
22. अपनी पिछली जिन्दगी की तुलना में मैं अपने आपको सन्तुष्ट पाता हूँ।
23. जैसे–तैसे उम्र बढ़ती जा रही है, स्थितियाँ बेहतर होती जा रही हैं।
24. मैं अक्सर अकेलेपन का अहसास करता हूँ।
25. कभी–कभी मुझे जीवन जीने योग्य नहीं लगता।
26. अक्सर मुझे जीवन मुश्किल लगता है।
27. फिलहाल मैं अपने जीवन से सन्तुष्ट हूँ।

CHAPTER 31

Physical Activity Among the Elderly

An Exploratory Study

Indira Jai Prakash and M. Sreenivas

World Health Organization, in 1996, issued guidelines for promoting physical activity among older persons called the "Heidelberge Guidelines". These guidelines are developed primarily to promote physical activity in the latter half of the life course. The contention is that regular physical, psychological and social hazards accompany with advancing age. Within these guidelines, physical activity is operationally defined as all movements of everyday life, including work, activities of daily living, recreation, exercise, and sporting activities. Regular physical activity is likely to have both immediate and long term effects, at physical, social and psychological levels.

There is sufficient accumulated evidence that a regular regimen of activity is indeed beneficial to ward off many disabilities that manifest themselves in old age. Physical activity and fitness programmes are found to reduce several health risks and enhance well-being (Bouchard et al., 1990; McAuley et al., 1991; Camacho et al., 1991). Jett et al. (1996) report that several studies throughout the past 15 years have demonstrated the positive benefits enhancing levels of physical activity in older persons. Older male exercisers achieved significant differences relative to controls in perceived anger, tension and overall social functioning and significant improvements in perceived vigour. In their study on fitness education with older women, Gilett White and Caserta (1996) found sedentary, obsess older women at increased risk for cardiovascular and cerebrovascular

IJG, 1997, Vol. 11, No. 1 and 2, pp. 21–27.

diseases. Long-term participation in exercise by obese older women played a major role in their physical independence and physical health by improving underlying fitness parameters such as aerobic power, body composition, muscular strength and endurance, flexibility, resisting and systolic and diastolic blood pressure.

In spite of the belief in goodness of exercise, sports and activity, participation rates of people in exercise and fitness programmes is considerably low even in health-conscious North American countries (McAuley, 1993). Exercise behaviour is complex and a host of determinants may be directly or indirectly related to degree of participation in exercise. Commonly identified general categories of determinants are: (1) Personal factors which may include demographic characteristics, activity history and biomedical status; (2) Environmental factors typically identified as barriers to activity participation; (3) Programmatic influences that include aspects of activity participation such as discomfort, dissatisfaction with programme elements; and (4) cognitive factors such as locus of control, motivation, attitudes and beliefs (McAuley, 1993). Exercise behaviour is considered to be related to participants' intrinsic motivation, their beliefs in their own abilities and their physiological condition.

Cultural differences may play an important part in defining what activities people are interested in. In the eleven country study by Heikkinen et al. (1983), there were great differences among older people's physical exercise habits in different localities. A study of four European countries showed difference between the sexes, urban and rural areas, and countries (Heikkinen, Karhu and Jokela, 1989). In India, such descriptive studies, which give information about activity profile of people's participation in sports, exercise and activity programmes are very few. An earlier study restricted to ageing Indian women revealed that women rarely engaged in physical fitness programmes as a method to counteract age related physical difficulties (Prakash, 1995). This exploratory study was taken up to describe the activity pattern of urban, retired men from Bangalore city. The information presented in this paper is a part of a larger study on physical activity of retired persons and older sports persons.

Method

Sample

Sixty men who had been in active service for at least 15 years and had retired from service, constituted the sample. The sampling was purposive and men above the retirement age of 58 years (in government service) and 60 years (in some educational institutions) were selected for this study. The sample was from Bangalore city (India). Three interviews could not be completed for various reasons, and thus the final sample had only 57 men. Mean age of the sample was 64.41 years and Standard Deviation was 5.71 years. 48 of the men were currently married.

Data Collection

A semi, structured interview schedule was developed specially for this study. This schedule is modeled after an exhaustive protocol used at the Institute for Gerontology, Heidelberg for the longitudinal study on active ageing (ILSE Longitudinal Study). The schedule is basically a guide to the interviewer to elicit exhaustive data regarding the type of physical activities the subject engages in past history of sports or exercise behaviour, present level of activity, reasons for engaging or not engaging in regular physical activity and also demographic details. Each interview took anywhere between 2 and 3 hours to complete. In this paper, information regarding physical activity of this sample has been discussed.

Results and Discussion

The interview data of fifty-seven retired men were analysed to find out the profit of their physical activity. In the following tables, some information about their work history and financial status are given.

Majority of the subjects had left the workforce after reaching the age of superannuation. Seven of the men had used the voluntary retirement scheme offered by their organizations to retire. Three had left the job due to family problems and four on their own as they had other plans and four of them did not mention any specific reason for retiring. 46 per cent of the men were getting regular pension, 28 per cent depended on their savings, 7 per cent each depended on children or on property, while 12 per cent mentioned 'other sources' as the source of their income in post-retirement years.

Interview schedule elicited subject's perceptions of their current financial position and also how retirement has affected their lifestyles. The Table 2 gives more details.

Since nearly half of the subjects received some sort of pension or had saved their provident fund/gratuity amounts, they had enough to live on in post-retirement years, though only 28 per cent found their lifestyle totally unaffected by retirement.

Table 1
Reasons for leaving the job

Reasons for leaving the job	*(n)*
Reached retirement age	39
Voluntary retirement	7
Decided to retire	4
Family problems	3
Other	4

Table 2
Effect of retirement on lifestyle and post-retirement financial position

Effect of Retirement on lifestyle	*(n)*	*Present financial status*	*(n)*
Very much effected	5	Wealthy	0
Much effected	21	Comfortable	20
Somewhat effected	15	Enough to live	27
Little effected	13	Can't make ends meet	7
Very little effected	3	Poor	3

Table 3
Average amount of time spent in different activities in a day

	Range	*Average in Minutes*
Reading	0–4 hr	89
Listen to radio	0–2 hr	30.52
Watch television	0–5 hr	105.26
Engaged in hobby	0–2 hr	40
Physical activity	0–2 hr	16.28

Activity Profile of the Retired Men

Subjects had been asked to indicate the amount of time they spent in different activities, both passive and active. Table 3 gives the average number of minutes per day spent in different activities.

Time spent every day in reading, watching TV, listening to radio or engaging in hobbies was found out. Hobbies included gardening, handiwork and such leisure time pursuits, though some mentioned reading as a hobby. Subjects had been asked about how much of time they devoted to watching sports events on TV and listening to sports news on the radio. Most did not mention any specific habit of watching exclusively sports events or listening to sports news. In a week, an average of 113.68 minutes were spent on physical activity such as going for walks, exercising, playing games actively. This does not include climbing up and down stairs as part of everyday activity. This refers only to deliberately engaging in activity for the sake of getting exercise or as part of physical fitness regime. It has been found that in this group a meagre quarter hour a day is spent on an average towards maintaining physical fitness.

Subjects had been asked as to whether they took a vacation every year and if so, whether they were in the habit of taking a 'sports vacation' such as hiking, sking, golfing or mountaineering. Nearly 40 (70%) of the subjects said they took vacation which usually consisted of visiting children or relatives living elsewhere or attending family gatherings in other places. None ever took a sports holiday as such. However, not engaging in such activities did not seem to substantially affect their health and physical efficiency. When asked how their physical efficiency and health were at present 'compared to people of their own age', most felt satisfied with their physical status, as can be seen from Table 4.

Table 4

Physical efficiency and health status as compared to peers

Physical efficiency	*At present*	*Health at present*	
Rather bad	5 (8.77%)	Worse	2 (3.5%)
Average	39 (68.42%)	Average	40 (70.17%)
Better	13 (22.8%)	Better	15 (26.31%)

In general, this sample of subjects seemed to be in fairly good physical condition. There were a series of questions about whether subjects were satisfied with their general bodily conditions such as body weight, appetite, heart rate, respiration, digestion, sleep, rest after effort etc., which were rated from +3 (very satisfactory) to –3 (very unsatisfactory). Also changes that subjects might have noticed in their bodies in the last five years were rated as definitely worse (–2), worsened (–1), no change (0), better (+1) and definitely better (+3). Table 5 gives the frequencies for each category of response.

Table 5

General bodily condition and changes in last five years (n)

Gen. Bodily Condition		*Changes Noticed*	
Very satisfactory	4 (7.02%)	Definitely worsened	0
Satisfactory	41 (71.93%)	Worsened	17 (29.82%)
Rather satisfactory	9 (15.29%)	No change	35 (61.40%)
Rather unsatisfactory	1 (1.75%)	Better	5 (8.77%)
Unsatisfactory	—	Definitely better	—
Very unsatisfactory	2 (351%)		

It is worth noting that nearly 95 per cent of the subjects interviewed feel that their bodily functions are quite satisfactory when compared to their age peers. Similarly most of them feel that there has not been any significant change in their physical status in terms of the reflexes, reaction time, ability to adapt to changes in the environment and to tolerate fatigue in the last five years. This could be due to the relative 'youth' of this sample, as men in 60s are found to maintain their earlier health status till the 70s.

Earlier history of participation of the subjects in sports during adolescence, in the school, and in adulthood had been enquired into. Only 20 subjects (35%) said they had been regular sportsmen during school days, while nearly 46 per cent had taken part in sports irregularly and the rest had not involved themselves in such activities at all. Currently, except two men who occasionally coached youngsters or supervised sports event, none of the others were engaged in any sports activity or fitness programme. The reasons for not taking up such schedules were varied. Most often cited reason was 'having no time for sports', (approximately 39%), 'not having opportunity, facility for such activities' (21%), 'having no interest in sports' (12%), 'other hobbies occupy time'(8.7%), 'financial expenses involved for such programmes are too heavy' (5.2%) and the fact that one 'feels well without sports also' (1.7%). Five of the subjects did not give any reason and two subjects were occasionally participating in sports.

It is interesting that most of the subjects seem satisfied with their passive lifestyles. When asked whether they would like to take up some sports activity and if so under what conditions, 12 (21%) said they would do so if doctors ordered them to. Five of them felt they would be ready to join a club or organization if people of their own age group were members in such groups. Two of them wanted sports facilities to be nearby, and two would go if their acquaintances and friends also went. Rest of the subjects did not give any answer. Almost 28 per cent of those who answered the question believed that sports and exercise would contribute to sense of 'well-being'. Such activities were described as 'fun' by 21 per cent, while 2 subjects each found physical activity helpful in toughening up and increasing resistances, reduce and control weight and induce relaxation. Eighteen of the subjects did not give any specific answer.

Physical activity is an important component of healthy ageing and lack of such activity in all likelihood may cause much of the degenerative changes associated with ageing. Western studies show that over 40 per cent of individuals 65 and over report no regular physical activity and less than a tenth of the population routinely participate in regular vigorous activity. In this sample, the rate of participation in rigorous activity is abysmally low. Except for walking and working as a part of their daily living, most of the subjects were not involved in any deliberate fitness programme. Previous history of not being actively engaged in such activity may be a factor that prevents these people from taking up fitness regimes now. It has been documented that education, socio-economic status, exposure and experience in organized physical activity during youth, availability and access to facilities play a role in motivating people to take up physical activities. Though the men interviewed in this sample report satisfaction with their physical condition and health status, it does not obviate the need for fitness programmes in such samples. With increase in life expectancy, many Indian elderly are likely to live well into the seventh and eighth decades. In the absence of a healthy and active lifestyle, chances of acquiring disabilities increase considerably reducing the quality of life left to live. This sample consists mainly of fairly educated, middle class people who had held relatively steady jobs over a period of time. It is possible that their life lacks the need for vigorous activity (typical of lower working class) and at the same time the facilities to pursue organized fitness programmes (that may be more accessible to the rich). Though the sample is by no means large or representative and as such generalizations are not warranted, the findings do cause concern. It is clear that there is an urgent need to create awareness and disseminate information about healthy ageing and create environment conducive to promotion of physical activity, especially among the elderly. It is also clear that more research is needed to understand factors that promote a healthy lifestyle in our people and methods to motivate them to take up fitness programmes seriously. Activity and leisure profiles of different groups such as, elderly women, minority groups, rural elderly, poor elderly have to be examined. Most important of all is to investigate the cultural factors and belief system of our people that may be responsible for such a passive lifestyle. Because, though all the subjects interviewed in this study expressed the view that regular exercise is essential for healthy ageing and were aware of some of the programmes on the television about health and fitness, they did not seem to incorporate such ideas in their own lives. It is possible that social and cultural factors play a role in how the elderly structure their time and what type of activities they engage in.

References

Bouchard, C., Shephard, R.J., Stephans, T., Sutton J.R. and McPherson, B.D.: *Exercise, Fitness and Health: A Consensus of Current Knowledge.* Champaign, IL: Human Kinetics, 1990.

Camacho, T.C., Roberts R.E., Lazarus, N.B., Kaplan, G.A. and Cohen, R.D.: "Physical Activity and Depression. Evidence from the Alameda Country Study". *American Journal of Epidemiology.* 134: 220–231, 1991.

Gillett, P.A., White, A.T. and Caserta, M.S.: "Effect of Exercise and/or Fitness Education of Fitness in Older, Sedentary Obese Women". *Journal of Aging and Physical Activity.* 4 (1): 42–55, 1996.

Heikkinen, E., Karhur, I. and Jokela, J.: "Physical Exercise and Related Factors among Elderly People in Four European Localities". In Harris, R. Harris and Seds. *Physical Activity, Aging and Sports.* Vol I. Scientific and Medical Research. 157–177. Center for the Study of Aging, Albany. NY.

Heikkinen, E., Walter W.E. and Brzezinski, Z.J.: *The Elderly in Even Countries: A Socio Medical Survey.* Copenhagen. WHO Regional Office for Europe (Public Health in Europe 21) 1983.

Jett, A.M.: "A Home Based Exercise Program for Non-Disabled Older Adults". *Journal of the American Geriatric Society.* 44 (6): 644–649, 1996 (cited in Abstracts of Social Gerontology 40 (1): 91, 1997).

McAuley, E.: "Self-Efficacy, Physical and Aging". In R. Kelly (ed) *Activity and Aging: Staying Involved in Later Life.* 187–205. London. Sage. 1993.

McAuley, E.: "Efficacy, Attributional and Affective Responses to Exercise Participation". *Journal of Sport and Exercise Psychology.* 13: 282–393, 1991.

Prakash, Indira J.: "Psychosocial Situation of Older Women's Lives in India and Potential for Empowerment". In S. Formosa (ed.). *Age-Vault.* An Anthology of INIA. Malta. 1995.

World Health Organization: *The Heidelberg Guidelines for Promoting Physical Activity Among Older Persons.* Guidelines Series for Healthy Aging-1. Geneva. 1996.

CHAPTER 32

Leisure Time Activities of Retired Persons

K.L. Sharma

It is generally understood that retired persons derive satisfaction from different kinds of life activities as compared to younger persons or employed persons of the same age group. This is presumably so as a great majority of retired persons, no longer have to cope with the various problems and routine activities – and pleasure of earning a livelihood. For these reasons, we could expect them to avail themselves of the many added hours of leisure and to look for different opportunities of self-expression and varied forms of recreation.

As opposed to this view, a more recent study Kelly, (1955) has shown that a constriction of interests in activities takes place in old age. The existence of a relatively high percentage of inactivity among elderly persons also has been corroborated by other studies as well (Fried, 1949). Accordingly a good number of old people begin to fill their leisure time with rest and sleeping (Allard, 1939). The implication of findings of the studies reported above are that retired people continue to feel that they are wanted by the human community and consequently they engage is more truly meaningful activities for themselves. Pressey and Kuhlen (1957) note that the recreational habits of adults show "a marked decrease in the sex-social activities so prominent in the lives of the adolescents", but that "the date about

IJG, 1969, Vol. 1, No. 1, pp. 31–37.

the later years of life are not clear cut". On the other hand, Kuhlen (1951) revealed that increased leisure time in old age is associated with more leisure activities. The discrepancies in the findings on activities of late maturity appear to be related to the methodology of various investigations and other factors such as, physiological (health), economic, sociocultural, and psychological conditions of the individual.

Objective and Purpose

The purpose of this study was to find out the modes of leisure time activities of retired persons. The present study also aims to investigate, precisely, how leisure time activities are influenced by factors like educational level, income, caste, and marital status.

Method

Questionnaire method was employed on a random sample of 44 male retired persons. The sample was selected so as to include persons of various socio-economic status, educational levels, and marital status. Twenty leisure time activities were kept in the questionnaire against each of the leisure time activities, categories, 1, 2, 3, 4, and 5 were indicated so as to symbolize the degree of participation and preference obtained in terms of such ratings as, very common, common, sometimes, often, and very often. These ratings were scored by assigning values, e.g., 100, 80, 60, 40 and 20 respectively. The questionnaire was administered individually.

Rank order correlations were computed between income Rs 201–100; Rs 100–301; Rs 201–301; as a monthly pension; Caste – Kayashta and Brahmin; Agarwal and Rajputs; Education – up to intermediate and BA and above, Marital status – wife alive and widower. In each case an appropriate test of significance was applied in order to find out if there was any relationship between each of the variables and the responses of the subjects.

Results and Discussion

The main results are shown in Table 1 and 2.

Table 1

Rank order correlation for the variables (N=20)

Variables	?d2	*Rho**	*Level of significance*
Income			
1. Below Rs 100	147.20	0.890	0.01
2. Rs 100–200	171.34	0.871	0.01
3. Rs 201–300	170.25	0.872	0.01
Caste			
1. Kayastha and Brahmin	74.90	0.944	0.01
2. Agarwal and Rajputs	241.54	0.806	0.01
Education			
1. Upto intermediate and above	117.82	0.912	0.01
2. BA and above	—	—	—
Personal Factors			
Married and widower	436.63	0.672	0.01

From Table 2 the most relevant information is obtained regarding the main objectives of the present study. The purpose of the present study was to find out the modes of leisure time activities of retired persons. Looking at Table 2, we find that a pattern of modes of leisure time activities of retired persons becomes evident. In terms of ranking assigned to the modes of recreation it becomes clear that the following first ten activities have been given a order of preference mentioned below, so as to fill their leisure time in that order: (1) Reading newspaper, (2) Household activities, (3) Morning and evening walks, (4) Listening radio, (5) Sitting and gossiping with children – son or grandson, (6) Chatting and gossiping with friends, (7) Talking with wife, (8) Kirtan and Bhajan, (9) Inviting and entertaining friends at home and (10) day sleeping.

In agreement of our common observation the present findings show that reading newspaper, morning and evening walks, household activities, listening radio, occupy the first, second, third and fourth preferences respectively in the allotment of leisure time activities. On

Table 2

Means in descending order

S.No.	Models of Recreation	All Respondents	Caste				Social Status		Pension	Marital status		Education	
			Aggarwals	Kayastha	Rajputs	Brahmins	Below Rs 100 p.m.	Rs 101-200 pm	Rs 201 above pm	Wife alive widower	Married	Upto intermediate	BA and above
		N-44	N-10	N-18	N-7	N-9	N-16	N-17	N-11	N-8	N-36	O-26	O-18
1.	Reading newspapers	84.65	82..50	86.11	85.91	83.33	85.93	80.88	88.63	87.5	84.02	86.53	81.94
2.	Household activities	70.45	55.00	73.61	71.42	80.55	67.18	75.00	68.18	59.37	72.91	67.30	75.00
3.	Morning and evening walks	65.90	67.50	66.66	64.28	63.88	59.37	70.58	68.18	87.50	61.11	66.34	65.27
4.	Listening radio	59.65	45.00	72.22	46.42	61.11	46.88	64.70	70.45	43.75	63.19	54.80	66.66
5.	Sitting and gossiping with children, son/grandson	59.09	60.00	58.33	57.85	63.88	56.25	57.35	65.90	53.12	60.14	58.65	57.72
6.	Chatting and gossiping with friends	56.25	60.00	52.77	64.28	52.77	59.37	44.11	70.45	53.12	55.94	55.76	59.72

Cont'd...

Cont'd...

7.	Talking with wife	52.84	50.00	58.33	32.14	63.88	51.56	51.47	56.81	-	64.58	44.23	65.27
8.	Kirtan and Bhajan	46.02	30.00	55.55	42.85	47.22	51.56	48.52	34.09	62.50	42.36	53.84	34.72
9.	Inviting and entertaining friends at home	44.88	40.00	41.66	53.57	50.00	40.62	45.58	50.00	50.00	43.75	43.26	47.22
10.	Day sleeping	44.31	50.00	45.83	53.57	27.77	56.88	44.11	45.45	56.25	41.66	46.15	41.66
11.	Social work	43.18	25.00	41.66	53.57	58.33	43.75	54.41	25.00	40.62	49.30	48.07	36.11
12.	Job-seeking	18.75	20.00	25.00	10.70	11.11	20.31	16.17	20.45	06.25	21.50	12.50	27.27
13.	Going to cinema	17.61	17.50	15.27	32.14	11.11	12.50	13.23	31.81	21.82	16.66	11.53	26.38
14.	Visiting restau-rants	15.90	12.50	18.05	17.85	13.88	10.93	11.76	29.54	12.00	16.66	08.65	26.38
15.	Games and sports	10.22	10.00	15.27	07.14	02.77	07.82	11.76	11.36	18.75	08.33	07.69	13.88
16.	Smoking and use of charas and bhang	10.22	32.50	06.94	—	—	12.50	04.42	15.90	09.37	10.41	13.46	05.558
17.	Playing cards	09.65	05.00	06.94	25.00	08.33	07.82	02.94	22.72	09.37	09.72	07.69	12.50
18.	Political work	07.38	05.00	06.94	14.28	05.55	12.50	0.42	04.54	—	09.02	07.69	06.94
19.	Drinking parties	04.54	—	08.33	07.14	—	10.93	—	02.27	—	05.55	05.76	02.77
20.	Gambling	0.56	—	01.38	—	—	—	—	—	03.12	—	—	01.38

the other hand smoking and use of charas and bhang, playing cards, political work, drink parties and gambling get lesser scores and their positions in the Table 2 are 15.5, 15.5, 18, 19 and 20 respectively. The possible reason of this being may be that the people approached were educated and want to keep themselves abreast of the up-to-date information about the world around them. The degenerating effects of smoking and use of charas and bhang as well as drink parties and gambling are also in their mind and they know the value of morning and evening walks to keep them physically fit. Going to cinema and visiting restaurants got 13th and 14th ranking respectively which unequivocally show that as age advances interest towards these modes of recreation decrease. These commercialized modes of recreation are becoming the most popular medium of entertainment for the young people and hence are resorted to in a moderate degree by the subjects under study. Likewise it may be said that although there is a complete or partial cession of sex activity yet talking to wife occupies fairly significant position that is 7th, in the assignment of the leisure time activity. The possible reason of this attachment with wife may be that is old age wife remains with them for greater periods in comparison to the time when they were in jobs. That is the death of life partner (wife) at this stage of life is felt much.

The precise manner in which leisure time activities are influenced by such variables as educational level, income, caste and marital status were ascertained by calculating the rank order correlation, between each of the variable and leisure time activities. Rho values obtained have been presented in Table 1.

It becomes amply clear from Table 1 that all the variables taken up in the present study are significantly related to the leisure time activities beyond. 0.01 level of confidence. This is presumably because the process of ageing has a dominant influence on the total leisure time activities beyond a certain age level. Thus after elderly persons have crossed the age level 55+ barriers of income, caste, education and marital status cease to exert their restrictive influence on the allocation of time spending on the leisure time activities. On the basis of the present investigation it can be said that although there is preference hierarchy in the participation of leisure time activities (as the ranking made by the subjects indicate) yet variables like income, level of education, caste and marital status play rather insignificant part in the determination of preferences of activities to fill the leisure time. Hence these findings suggest more positive conclusion that ageing itself plays a vital role in the participation of various type of leisure time activities.

References

Allard, L. (1939): *A Study of the Leisure Activities of Certain Elementary School Teachers of Long Island.* (Teachers College Contributions to Education No. 799), New York: Teachers College, Columbia University.

Fried, E.G. (1949): "Attitudes of the Older Population Groups Towards Activity and Inactivity". *J. Gerontol.* 4: 141–151.

Kelley, E.L. (1955): "Consistency of the Adult Personality". *American Psychology.* 10: 659–681.

Kuhlen, R.G. (1951): Expansion and Constriction of Life Activities During the Adult Life-Span. An Unpublished Manuscript Read at the Second International Gerontological Congress. St. Louis.

Pressey, S.L. and Kuhlen, R.G. (1957): *Psychological Development through the Life-Span.* New York: Harper and Bros. 278–280.

CHAPTER 33

Religiosity and Fear of Death in Young and Retired Persons

K.L. Sharma and U.C. Jain

The socio-economic and psycho-physiological phenomena associated with old age arouse anxiety in individuals and thus create a special need for reassurance and security in life which have throughout the ages come from religious belief. Participation in religious activities given fairly high position as compared to other leisure time activities by retired persons (Sharma, 1969). There is an immense need of serious and intensive research regarding the adjustment value of religion in old age (Pollak, 1948). Studies (Brinton, 1950; Cavan et al., 1949; Schmidt, 1951; Moberg, 1956) indicate that certain religious activities are related to good personal adjustment in old age.

The subject of death has been of concern to man in every age and the field of religion and attitude towards death is a subject that only recently has been opened for scientific investigation and even then with some stigma. At present, there is paucity of substantial research dealing with religion and death. The findings of few studies are inconsistent due to the definition of religiosity (Allport, 1961) or vague due to nebulous delineation of fear of death (Alexander et al., 1959). Many studies dealing with religiosity and fear of death employed statistical analysis of data. Two of these studies (Feifel, 1961; Faunce and Fulton, 1958) have concluded that fear of death is greater among the religiously oriented persons. Contrary to these findings there are

IJG, 1969, Vol. 1, No. 4, pp. 110–114.

studies which have concluded that fearful attitude towards death in older population tend to be found in persons with little religious activity (Swenson, 1961), and those who have reported greater religious participation indicated less fear of death (Martin et al.,1965).

Thus, there is a need to measure the prevalence of religiosity at various age levels and to correlate it with fear of death. On the basis of the findings of Swenson (1961) and contrary to Freudian postulation (Freud, 1965), it was hypothesized that:

1. There is an invert relationship between religiosity and fear of death.
2. There would be age differences in religiosity and fear of death.

Method

The study was conducted on an unselected sample of 125 male subjects of two age groups: Younger group (Students, N=63), and Retired person (N=62).

Two scales were used to assess the degree of religiosity and fear of death. The Religious Attitude Inventory (Ansubel and Schout, 1957) consisted of 50 items related to various aspects of religion. The items were scored on a five point scale as is done in Likert-type scales. There are both positive and negative items in the scale. The total score in religiosity may range from 50 to 250 and the degree of the religiosity which is relative to the sample score was measured in terms of total scores achieved by the individual.

The second instrument, was Death Scale (Feldman and Hersen, 1967) having 10 items related to the various modes of death fear. Subject was required to answer each question under the six categories: very frequently, frequently, mostly, sometime, seldom, never. The order of scoring was from 6 to 0 respectively. The amount of fear of death was measured on the basis of total score secured by the individual.

The scales were administered individually. Mean and Standard Deviations of Religiosity and Fear of Death Scales computed for both the groups. 't' test was used to find out the mean difference for both the groups for both the scales. The Product Moment Correlation of coefficient (r) was computed to find out the relationship between high and low religiosity with religiosity for both the groups. The subjects scoring above the median score were classified in high group and the subjects scoring below the median were kept in low group.

Table 1

Showing the obtained 'r' values between religiosity and fear of death for retired persons

Variables correlated	*'r' values*	*Level of significance*
High Religiosity vs Fear of Death N=29	–0.07	ns
Low Religiosity vs Fear of Death N=30	–0.05	ns
High Fear of Death vs Religiosity N=28	–0.77	0.01
Low Fear of Death vs Religiosity N=30	–0.22	ns

Table 2

Showing the obtained values between religiosity and fear of death students

Variables Correlated	*'r' values*	*Level of significance*
High Religiosity vs Fear of Death N=31	–0.65	0.01
Low Religiosity vs Fear of Death N=31	–0.82	0.01
High Fear of Death vs Religiosity N=26	–0.98	0.01
Low Fear of Death vs Religiosity N=30	–0.05	ns

Table 3

Showing the difference in the amount of religiosity between students and retired persons

	Mean	*SD*	*df*	*'t'*	*Level of significance*
Students (N=63)	151.36	28.50			
			123	2.38	0.01
Retired persons (N=62)	165.00	42.50			

Table 4

Showing the difference in the amount of fear of death between students and retired persons

	Mean	*SD*	*df*	*'t'*	*Level of significance*
Students (N=63)	6.34	1.63			
			123	0.60	ns
Retired persons (N=62)	6.88	4.91			

Table 5

Showing the difference in the amount of religiosity between the two age groups of retired persons

	Mean	*SD*	*df*	't'	*Level of significance*
Age 55 to 60 yrs (N=25)	164.88	29.29			
			60	0.03	
61 and above (N=37)	165.08	25.99			

Table 6

Showing the difference in the amount of feat of death between the two age groups of retired persons

	Mean	*SD*	*df*	't'	*Level of significance*
Age 55 to 60 yrs (N=25)	5.32	4.25			
			60	3.74*	0.01
61 and above (N=37)	8.10	5.67			

* One tailed 't' test was computed.

Discussion

The study aimed at focusing attention on the relationship between two important dimensions of human experience viz. religiosity and fear of death. Freud (1957) attributed religion to man's basic insecurity particularly focalized in his perception of death. The present investigation does not support the hypothesized Freudian relationship between religion and death. The obtained 'r' values for high religiosity and high death score group ($r=-0.07$ and $r=-0.77$) given in Table 1 tend to support this contention. These findings are in agreement with those of Williams and Spurgeon (1968). A similar correlation trend ($r=-0.65$ and $r=-0.98$) in the younger group is evident in Table 2, which indicates that there are no age differences (as far as the correlation is concerned) between death and religiosity.

A positive correlation (Table 1 and 2) in the low religiosity and the low fear of death groups implies that the low death scores of with low religiosity scores and vice versa. This finding supports the

Alexander and Alderstein (1959) contention that the difference between religious and non-religious persons may be dichotomus one rather than a continuous one.

In the light of these findings the first hypothesis of this study is sustained to a considerable extent.

The second hypothesis is about the question of religiosity and fear of death at different age levels. Table 3 compares the amount of religiosity between students and retired persons. It reveals a difference which is significant at 0.01 level of confidence. The difference in regard to the amount of fear of death in these groups is not statistically significant (Table 4). In the context of psychoanalytic thought a distinction has been made between overt conscious anxiety and more covert repressed insecurities. The non-significant differences between students and retired persons on death scale may be interpreted in the above mentioned Freudian context.

The tendency for the older members of the sample to report less fear of death has also been found by Martin and Wrightsman (1965).

When the two age groups of the retired persons (55 to 60 years, 61 and above) are compared it is found that the difference in religiosity is not significant (Table 5) whereas the difference in the amount of fear of death is significant at 0.01 level (Table 6). The higher degree of fear of death in the members of the older age group might mean that the relationship between religiosity and fear of death changes somewhat as people get older.

References

Alexander, I.E. and Alderstein, A.M. (1959): "Death and Religion". In H. Feifel (Ed.) *The Meaning of Death*. New York: McGraw Hill, 271–283.

Allport, G.W. (1961): "Comment on Earlier Chapters". In R. May (Ed.) *Existential Psychology*. New York: Random House. 94–99.

Ausubel, D.P. and Schont, S.H. (1957): "Prediction of Group Opinion as a Function of Extremers of Predictor Attitudes". *J. Soc. Psychol.* 46: 19–29.

Brintton, J.H. (1950): A Study of the Adjustment of Retired School Teachers. Unpublished Doctoral Dissertation, University of Chicago quoted from (1956). *Journal Soc. Psychol.* Vol. 43: 261–267.

Cavan, R.S. et al. (1949): "Personal Adjustment in Old Age". *Science Research Association,* Chicago.

Faunce, W.A. and Fulton, R.L. (1958): "The Sociology and Death: A Neglected Area of Research". *Soc. Forces*. Vol. 3: 205–209.

Feifel, H. (1961): "Death Relevant Variable in Psychology". In R. May (Ed.) *Existential Psychology*. New York: Randam House. 61–74.

Feldman, M.J. and Michel Hersen (1967): "Attitudes Toward Death in Nightmare Subjects". *J. Soc. Psychol.* 72 No. 5.

Freud, S. (1957): *The Future of Illusion*, Garden City, N.J. Doubleday.

Freud, S. (1965): *The Psychopathology of Every Day Life*. New York: Norton.

Martin, D. and Wrightsman, L.S. (1965): "The Relation between Religious Behaviours and Concern about Death". *J. Soc. Psychol.* 65: 317–323.

Moberg, D.O. (1956): Religious Activities and Personal Adjustment in Old Age. *Journal Soc. Psychol.* 43: 261–267.

Pollak, O. (1948): "Social Adjustment in Old Age". New York: *Social Science Research Council Bulletin*. 59: 161.

Schmidt, J.F. (1951): "Patterns of Poor Adjustment in Old Age". *American Journal of Sociology*. Vol. 57: 33–42.

Sharma, K.L. (1969): "Leisure Time Activities of Retired Persons". *Indian Journal of Gerontology*. Vol. 1, No. 1: 32–37.

Swenson, W. (1961): "Attitude Toward Death in Aged Population". *Journal Geront.* 16: 56–66.

Williams, R.L. and Spurgeon, Cole (1968): "Religiosity, Generalized Anxiety and Apprehension Concerning Death". *Journal Soc. Psychol.* 75: 111–117.

Contributors

Vandana Aggarwal, Department of Psychology, Delhi University, Delhi.

Meena Arya, Department of Psychology, Aligarh Muslim University, Aligrah (U.P.).

S.M. Ashrafimam, Department of Psychology, Aligarh Muslim University, Aligrah (U.P.).

S. Azmal Basha, Department of Psychology, S.V. University, Tirupati (A.P.).

Prabha Bhandari, Department of Philosophy and Psychology, University of Rajasthan, Jaipur.

N.K. Chadha, Professor of Psychology, Delhi University, Delhi.

M. Easwaramoorthy, Former Professor of Psychology, Delhi University, Delhi.

R.K. Gunthey, Department of Psychology, J.N.V. University, Jodhpur (Rajasthan).

Anshika Gupta, Gurukul Kangri University, Hardwar (Uttaranchal).

Akbar Husain, Professor, Department of Psychology, Aligarh Muslim University, Aligrah (U.P.).

Shamshad Hussain, Former Professor of Psychology, Nalanda Open University, Patna (Bihar).

U.C. Jain, Former Professor of Psychology, Barkatullah University, Bhopal (M.P.).

D. Jamuna, Professor of Psychology, S.V. University, Tirupati, (A.P.).

Priya Kanwar, Women's College, Delhi University, Delhi.

Renu Malhotra, Department of Psychology, Delhi University, Delhi.

A.P. Mangla, Former Deputy Director, ICCSR, New Delhi.

Sarita Mathur, Department of Psychology, J.N.V. University, Jodhpur (Rajasthan).

Saraswati Mishra, Professor, Department of Sociology, Jabalpur University, Jabalpur (M.P.).

Priyadarshini Narain, Department of Psychology, Patna Women's College, Patna (Bihar).

Harinder Kaur Paintal, Former Professor of Psychology, Lucknow University, Lucknow (U.P.).

Audrey Pinto, School of Social Work, Mangalore (Karnataka).

Indira Jai Prakash, Former Professor of Psychology, Bangalore University, Bangalore.

C.K. Purohit, Department of Social and Preventive Medicine, S.M.S. Medical College, Jaipur.

Vidya Raghani, Department of Sociology, University of Rajasthan, Jaipur.

P.V. Ramamurti, Former Professor of Psychology, S.V. University, Tirupati, (A.P.).

Saroj Rathore, Department of Psychology, University of Rajasthan, Jaipur.

K.L. Sharma, Editor, *Indian Journal of Gerontology*.

Rameshwar Sharma, Former Professor, Social and Preventive Medicine, S.M.S. Medical College, Jaipur.

Richa Singh, Department of Psychology, Dayalbagh Deemed University, Agra (U.P.).

Narendra K. Singhi, Former Professor of Sociology, University of Rajasthan, Jaipur.

S.P. Sinha, Professor, Department of Psychology, Dayalbagh Deemed University, Agra (U.P.).

M. Sreenivas, Department of Psychology, Bangalore University, Bangalore.

A.L. Srivastava, Professor, Department of Sociology, Banaras Hindu University, Varanasi (U.P.).

S.K. Srivastava, Department of Psychology, Gurukul Kangri University, Hardwar (Uttaranchal).

S. Ushasree, Professor, Department of Psychology, S.V. University, Tirupati (A.P.).

John Van Willigen, Formerly, Visiting Professor, Department of Psychology, Delhi University, Delhi.